WIT'S END

WIT'S END

Days and Nights of the Algonquin Round Table

James R. Gaines

Harcourt Brace Jovanovich
New York and London

Printed in the United States of America

The author wishes to express his gratitude for permission to quote from the following sources:

The works of Heywood Broun, reprinted by permission of Patricia and Heywood Hale Broun. *The Twenties* by Edmund Wilson, edited with an Introduction by Leon Edel, copyright © 1975 by Elena Wilson, executrix of the estate of Edmund Wilson, Introduction © 1975 by Leon Edel, reprinted by permission of Farrar, Straus and Giroux, Inc. "The Command Is Forward," reprinted by permission of Joseph Hennessey, literary executor of the Alexander Woollcott estate. *The Vicious Circle* by Margaret Case Harriman, copyright 1951 by Margaret Case Harriman; and *Voices Offstage* by Marc Connelly, copyright © 1968 by Marc Connelly, reprinted by permission of Holt, Rinehart and Winston, Publishers. Material by Robert Benchley used by permission of International Creative Management, all rights reserved. Previously uncollected poems of Dorothy Parker, reprinted by permission of the National Association for the Advancement of Colored People. "The Enquiring Reporter," August 25, 1929, © 1925, 1953 The New Yorker Magazine, Inc., reprinted by permission of The New Yorker Magazine, Inc. *By a Stroke of Luck! An Autobiography* by Donald Ogden Stewart, © 1975 by Donald Ogden Stewart, reprinted by permission of Paddington Press, Ltd., the Two Continents Publishing Group. *Ross, The New Yorker and Me* by Jane Grant, © 1968 by Jane Grant, reprinted by permission of Reynal and Co. in association with William & Company, Inc. Unpublished letters and notes of Robert E. Sherwood, reprinted by permission of Mrs. Robert Emmet Sherwood. *The Diary of Our Own Samuel Pepys* by Franklin P. Adams, copyright © 1935 by Franklin P. Adams, © renewed 1963 by Anthony, Jonathan, Timothy and Persephone Adams, reprinted by permission of Simon & Schuster, a division of Gulf & Western Corporation. *Exile's Return* by Malcolm Cowley, copyright 1934, © renewed 1962 by Malcolm Cowley; "For a Sad Lady" and "Résumé," from *The Portable Dorothy Parker*, copyright 1926, 1954 by Dorothy Parker; "From the Diary of a New York Lady," from *The Portable Dorothy Parker*, copyright 1933, © renewed 1961 by Dorothy Parker; and *The Letters of Alexander Woollcott*, edited by Beatrice Kaufman and Joseph Hennessey, copyright 1944 by The Viking Press, Inc., © renewed 1972 by Joseph Hennessey; reprinted by permission of The Viking Press.

Library of Congress Cataloging in Publication Data
Gaines, James.
  Wit's end.
  Includes index.
  1. Authors, American 20th century Biography. 2. New York (City) Intellectual life. I. Title.
PS129.G34 820′.9 77-73050
ISBN 0-15-197521-3

First edition B C D E

Art Direction: Harris Lewine
Design: Stephanie Tevonian

For My Mother and Father

CONTENTS

Millions of words have been written about the Algonquin Round Table and its members, and it is a fair question why the world needs 65,000 more. The old turf, it is true, has been thoroughly looted of *bon mots*. But this is not a book about *that* Round Table. Rather, it is an attempt to look beyond and beneath the mosaic of their anecdotal legend, to find the measure of the group in its historical context and in its influence on the lives and works of the men and women who were members of it.

In trying to write this interpretive biographical essay about the group, I have chosen to focus on those people who, it seemed to me, played the most significant or most prominent roles in the group's social, cultural and literary experience. The Vicious Circle, after all, had grown quite large by the end of the Twenties, and weaving in all the dozens of people who had some part in it would, I believe, have necessitated sacrificing the whole in favor of the parts.

Interviewing contemporaries of the group proved sometimes difficult and frequently unavailing. A couple of the survivors demurred, claiming to be talked out on the subject, and one was saving up for a book of her own. Beyond that, some of the people who consented to be interviewed remembered only stories they had read, not events they had witnessed. "Don't be too surprised," Alice Guinzburg said. "There was so much drinking in those days!"

Most of the interviews, I hasten to add, were fruitful, and in addition to the spadework done by several of the group's biographers—notably Nathaniel Benchley, John Mason Brown (Sherwood), Samuel Hopkins Adams (Woollcott) and John Keats (Parker)—the reservoir of primary sources is abundant, including the work of the Round Table writers themselves, which is the underpinning of this book. The narrative is informed by the memoirs of, among others, Jane Grant, Donald Ogden Stewart, Marc Connelly, Howard Dietz, John Baragwanath, Edna Ferber, Ruth Gordon, Harpo Marx and Henry Wise Miller. Franklin P. Adams's two-volume compendium of columns, *The Diary of Our Own Samuel Pepys,* has been an invaluable guide to the day-to-day activities of the Algonquinites and to the gradual evolution of the group.

To all those people who spent hours being interviewed and reinterviewed, to all the libraries and research librarians who helped locate and arrange access

WIT'S END

to the correspondence of members of the group and to the people who were kind enough to delve into attics and basements for the photographs in this book, I here extend my thanks and acknowledgment:

Dr. Alvan Barach, Anita Loos, Alice Guinzburg, Howard Dietz, Lucinda Ballard, Marc Connelly, the late Frank Sullivan, George Oppenheimer, Marshall Best, Gov. Averell Harriman, Beatrice Ames, Nathaniel Benchley, Paul Hyde Bonner, Jr., Alice Longworth, Peggy Wood, Murdock Pemberton, Herbert Swope, Jr., Joseph Hennessey, the late Morris Ernst, Jeanne Ballot, Archibald MacLeish, Hawley Truax, James Thomas Flexner, Ferdinand Lundberg, Kathryn Abbe, Mrs. Fannie Brennan, Mrs. Richard Meyers, Richard Carver Wood, Honoria Murphy Donnelly, Mr. and Mrs. Robert Lovett, Albert Baragwanath; Mary Henderson of the Museum of the City of New York; Dr. Howard Gottlieb, Director of the Mugar Memorial Library at Boston University; Louis A. Rachow of the Walter Hampden Memorial Library at the Players; Susan Dalton of the Wisconsin University Center for Film and Theater Research; the Burke Library of Hamilton College; David Farmer of the Humanities Research Center, University of Texas; Paul Mills and the staff of the New York Public Library Theatre Collection at Lincoln Center; the staff of the New York Public Library Picture Collection; Charles Silver of the Museum of Modern Art; Donald Gallup of the Beinecke Rare Book and Manuscript Library at Yale University; David Crosson of the Library at the University of Wyoming; John C. Broderick of the Library of Congress Manuscript Division; Andrew Anspach of the Algonquin Hotel; and the staff of the Houghton Library at Harvard.

I would like especially to thank Joseph Mask and the pages and clerks who work the stacks of the New York Public Library at Fifth Avenue and Forty-second Street and who were unstintingly helpful. Nor can I fail to mention the moral support generously extended by my colleagues in the Frederick Lewis Allen Memorial Room, where this book was written and where, but for their bolstering when despair struck, it might have been abandoned. Leonard Ellis listened patiently all along and applied his scholarship and shrewd editorial eye to the manuscript, and Pamela Lloyd Shakespeare was its dedicated copy editor. I must also thank Paul Fussell for timely, encouraging words, Herman H. Schwartz for his special support, and Dan Okrent, my friend and my editor, for whose unfailing confidence and good advice I am deeply grateful.

For this book's physical beauty, the credit goes to Harris Lewine, an art director who worked beyond the call; to Stephanie Tevonian, who designed it; and to Laurie Platt Winfrey and Susan Storer Gombocz, whose initiative in finding the photographs was impressive.

Last and most, I thank Allison, who is younger than this project and whose wonderful interruptions of it kept her father human even in its painful last days, and Leslie, about whose loving support and unselfish sacrifices words fail. She made this book possible.

Brooklyn Heights, N.Y.
March 1977

The American writer, having struck out with his new note, becomes—how often!—progressively less and less himself. The blighted career, the arrested career, the diverted career, are, with us, the rule. The chronic state of our literature is that of a youthful promise which is never redeemed.... Let us call it local patriotism, the spirit of the times, the hunger of the public for this, that or the other: to some of these demands, these promptings from without, the "normal" American writer always allows himself to become a slave.

—Van Wyck Brooks, *1922*

Silly of me to blame it on dates, but so it happened to be. Dammit, it was the Twenties, and we had to be smarty.

—Dorothy Parker, *1958*

TO WAR AND BACK: A PROLOGUE

Few of the men and women destined for the Algonquin Round Table were much troubled by the advent of World War I. Most of them were busy making careers. Marc Connelly and George S. Kaufman were trying desperately to break into the commercial theater while supporting themselves as Broadway reporters. Connelly collected backstage gossip for the *Morning Telegraph,* whose preponderance of theater news earned it the nickname "the chorus girl's breakfast." Kaufman did the same, along with some second-string reviewing, for the *Tribune* and then the *Times.* Both men were delighted to get military deferments; Connelly had a mother in Pittsburgh to support and Kaufman, a new bride. Dorothy Rothschild Parker spent the war years writing captions for *Vogue* ("Brevity is the Soul of Lingerie, as the Petticoat said to the Chemise") and filling in as drama critic for *Vanity Fair.* She must have thought bitterly about the war when she thought of it at all; her husband, Edwin Pond Parker II, was in France only months after they were married, and she watched the war make him a bottle-a-day drinker and watched what love she had for him dissolve in the distance the war put between them. But until much later, consciousness of the war never entered her work except in the most superficial way: "Right *Dress!* For milady's motor jaunt."

There were two important exceptions—Robert Charles Benchley (Harvard '15) and Robert Emmet Sherwood (Harvard '18, had he stayed to graduate). Sherwood's attitude was the prevailing one on the Ivy League's war-hungry campuses and in the eastern seaboard's most exclusive private schools. Rather than wait for the draft, many of his social peers joined the Ambulance Corps. After he was rejected by his draft board as too light for his six-foot-seven frame, Sherwood bolted to Canada and joined the Black Watch regiment. Before he left, as president of the *Lampoon,* he wrote an editorial stating his belief (and Harvard's) that intervention made the United States "an honorable co-worker in the cause of civilization . . . waging glorious battle against an autocracy whose only doctrines are the doctrines of war and whose survival means unmitigated Hell on earth. . . . We have at least vindicated our national honor."

The young Robert Benchley was very much less sure of that. His family, like Sherwood's, were staunch Republicans (his grandfather had been lieutenant

WIT'S END

The fourth of five children, Robert Sherwood had been one of the worst students in the history of the Milton Academy, and one of the best liked. In June of 1914, he was denied a diploma (a certificate of attendance was enough to get him into Harvard the next fall), but he was elected to give the valedictory address. It was a work of youth and the prewar innocence, foreseeing a "marvelous" future based on "the ideals of sincerity, simplicity, and uprightness which make for better men." Thrown out for poor grades and re-admitted twice by Harvard, Sherwood excelled only in extracurriculars—Glee Club, intramural football, Hasty Pudding and *Lampoon*—until duty called him to leave school in 1917.

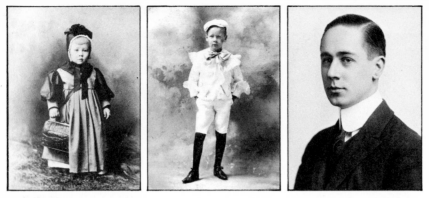

As the Benchleys' unexpected second son, Robert (left, at ages three, eight and twenty-one) was at first the family's odd-one-out. Later, he was excessively pampered by his mother, in part as her recompense for having said, on hearing of Edmund's death: "Why couldn't it have been Robert?"

governor of Massachusetts), but Benchley's only brother, Edmund, who was thirteen years older than he, had been killed in action during the Spanish-American War when Robert was only nine years old. Edmund's death drove Mrs. Benchley to hysterical antimilitarism, and Robert grew up in a household where toy guns, uniforms and even firecrackers were forbidden. As the war in Europe threatened increasingly to entangle his country, Robert clung to pacifism despite his classmates' opposite views. "If anyone is to lose, I hope that it is Germany and Austria," he allowed in his diary in the summer of 1914, but as late as 1917 the conflict was unresolved: "I am hovering," he wrote, "between a desire to see German Prussianism buried for the good of the future world's peace, and the feeling that if war is wrong it is wrong, and no pratings of honor can justify it." No answer ever came to him. He lost his job on the *Tribune's* Sunday magazine in May of that year. The chance to write subtitles for the Metro Film Corporation left him cold—"not being quite reconciled to mixing up in circles which must consist of the country's most frothy and inconsequential citizens." His marriage to a childhood sweetheart, Gertrude Darling, spared him from the draft, but in mid-1917 he finessed his scruples to take a job in Washington keeping the press as ignorant as possible about the work of the Aircraft Board.

The mood of American troops who joined the war that fall of 1917 was strangely jubilant; they put flowers in their bayonets and sang bouncy songs about the war in an exotic land most would otherwise never have seen—too young to have known the terrors of earlier wars except in glorious tale. The Americans who joined the war early as ambulance corpsmen, including such writers of the so-called Lost Generation as Hemingway, cummings and Dos Passos, would suffer many of the same psychic scars as the first combatants. But the war held for most American recruits the surface appeal of an elaborate, titillating prank—an appeal that proved remarkably sturdy, perhaps because barely nine months of fighting were left when American troops reached the shores of France and because so many of them would never see action. "We lived through the war with blinders on," Murdock Pemberton recalled in 1975. "How else could anyone survive?" Pemberton, a founder of the Round Table, spent the

Jennie's devotion to Edmund (above, with Robert, not long before his death) was equalled only by that of young Robert, who eagerly awaited the family's outings to West Point to see Edmund march in the color guard. His only reservation about going was the sunset gun, before whose report he would find some relatively soundproof place to hide. Edmund was killed on July 1, 1898.

FPA in 1909 was well enough known and respected to collaborate with O. Henry on a musical comedy called *Lo!*—and well enough off, despite its failure, to lend O. Henry money for his daughter's schooling. *Lo!* was FPA's last such effort.

war years in Washington working as a censor, but one of the most astonishing examples of that peculiar form of bunker psychology blossomed only a journalist's arm's length from the fighting—in the Paris office of the AEF's weekly newspaper, the *Stars and Stripes,* where Capt. Franklin P. Adams, Sgt. Alexander Woollcott and Pvt. Harold Ross first met, brought together "to give a voice to the Army," as one editorial put it, "and thereby boost the morale of the American Expeditionary Force."

None of them was committed to the war when they enlisted; they just fell into it. Woollcott, who was already the *Times*'s first-string drama critic, had lost both his mother and his first love in 1916 and enlisted in part to escape the pain of those losses. Ross, whose prospects for romance as a tramp reporter had tapped out at a half-dozen newspapers in as many cities and years, was simply looking for more. And Adams certainly had no fixed opinion about whether the U.S. should have got involved in the war. His column of contributed light verse and epigrams in the *Tribune* (and later the *World*) was widely read, but it rarely addressed issues more controversial than nettling errors of grammar. When Germany unleashed its submarines on neutral as well as belligerent nations, Adams saw only an opportunity for a light quip: "Britannia rules the waves, but Germany waives the rules."

Their attraction to one another was immediate—and very much like the mutual attraction that would keep the Round Table together for a dozen years. In FPA, who was Woollcott's senior by six years and already one of the best-known columnists in New York, Woollcott found the higher sanction (and the audience) he needed for his constant performance. One of Woollcott's cousins said of him years later that he also "had a social eye-to-business that made him more or less obsequious to anyone who would be or who might be of use to him, including those who were or would be impressive and with whom it would be good publicity to be associated." Ross had the same quality. He "deliberately gushed over officers," his first wife Jane Grant would write, "until even the most pompous of them couldn't help feeling uncomfortable." Ross also knew that FPA's friendship could be a valuable asset after the war; he was known for giving first Big Chances to several young writers—Dorothy Parker, Robert

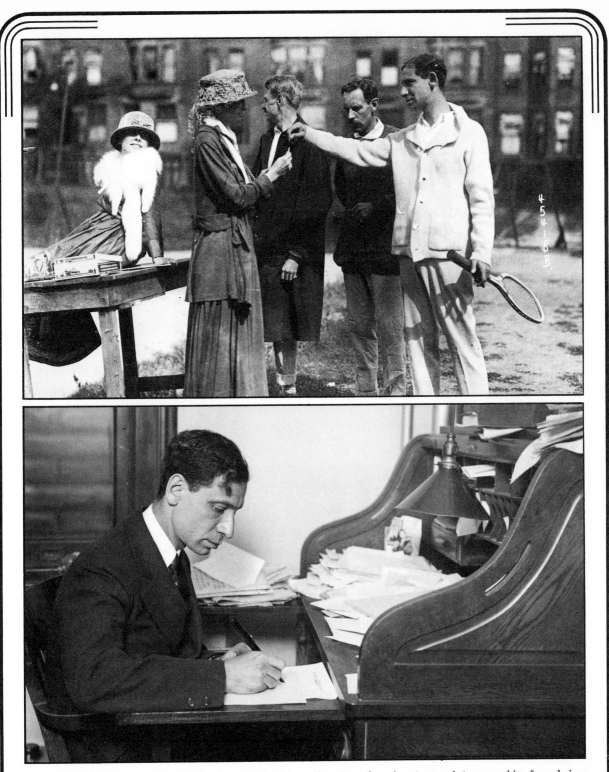

(Top) FPA drawing for serve on Morningside Heights in the fall of 1916 with, from left, Mrs. Grantland Rice, Mrs. Walter Turnbull, Fontaine Fox and Paul Gould. (Bottom) At work on the *Tribune*. Game playing had already impinged heavily on Adams's time at the office, though not enough to spare him from being tagged "the Comma Hunter of Park Row" after his habit of haunting the composing room to make sure that his "Conning Tower" column came out, typographically at least, just so.

Never were gourmands so amply fed in a war zone—or soldiers so lightheartedly entertained. Their happiest stories referred to the time FPA was actually asked to do calisthenics, and to the time Ross was stuck at the top of a carousel during Big Bertha's first assault on Paris.

Benchley, and George Kaufman among them—by running their poetry in his stateside column, helping to find them jobs and simply keeping their names at the tip of people's tongues. Among the rudest of men by every account, Adams was kindest to those people whose writing or acquaintance enhanced his column. He also suffered those who would pay him deference.

If Ross and Woollcott were as siblings in their relationship to FPA, it is difficult to imagine two siblings less alike. Ross, who had dropped out of high school in his sophomore year, harbored a fierce and abiding contempt for the "fancy pants" and "Eastern dudes" who had bothered to finish; Woollcott, an insufferably proud alumnus of Hamilton College, liked nothing better than posing as a dandy. Ross was starchy on sexual matters; Woollcott gloried in perversions, real and imagined. When Woollcott arrived at the *Stars and Stripes* office for the first time, Ross was indignant just at the sight of him. "Where'd you work before?" Ross asked suspiciously, and Woollcott drew himself up and fairly sang: "New York *Times*—dramatic critic." At that, Ross dissolved in laughter, and Woollcott went into a quiet rage. He knew he was no model of militarism; he was creased more than usual from his journey to Paris, and his thick glasses and spreading girth were not impressive features in a prospective war correspondent. But that was what he desperately wanted to be, and he was damned if he would be laughed at by the provincial Ross. "You know," Woollcott said evenly, "you remind me a great deal of my grandfather's coachman." Ross never could think of an answer for that, even years later, and perhaps that explains why they were drawn to one another. Woollcott had the sophisticate's fascination with an "authentic primitive," and Ross, "the born outsider" as Brendan Gill called him, had the outsider's irrepressible longing to be inside. However much Ross protested his distaste for city ways, he was happily astonished that people such as Adams and Woollcott would take an interest in him.

The three of them had terrific fun in Paris, even as they witnessed and reported on the worst of the war. In Woollcott's letters to Mrs. Alice Truax, the mother of a college friend who had taken him in after his mother's death, he wrote of nothing more enthusiastically than how well he was eating: "dinners

The soldiers for whom they wrote anticipated a good time no less than the *Stars and Stripes* writers themselves. The only regret among most of them when the fighting ended was that there hadn't been enough war to go around. Authentic World War I battle stories among Americans were few.

of partridge and rabbit, beef-steaks and perfect omelettes, patisserie worth going miles to eat and plenty of hot chocolate." Once FPA arrived, he added, "there were a good many parties . . . one at the Grand Guignol when the few seats occupied were largely occupied by Broadwayites so that it seemed like a first night once more." There was a weekly poker game in Montmartre, there were dinners with Elsie Janis, there were a few party-filled weeks with Heywood Broun and Ruth Hale, who were covering the war on their honeymoon. At reunions years later, memories of their good times were still potent.

But it was in their work, even more than in their endless hours of American-in-Paris play, that they displayed the blithe disconnectedness that would later characterize them, and their Algonquin mates, as a group. The *Stars and Stripes* was not exactly government propaganda. The paper was financially self-supporting (and profit making), and its writers were ready to resist firmly any suggestion that they distort a story. Their sympathies, moreover, genuinely lay with the privates who fought the worst of the war, and they attacked the wartime inhospitalities that officers tended to write off as "enlisted men's gripes."

Still, if it was not official propaganda, neither was it an honest reflection of the war. There were no unredeemed victims in its pages, only heroic cavaliers dying without regrets. Victory had no apparent price but glory, and death was always shrouded in soldierly virtue. Ignoring the mistakes or misjudgments of U.S. officials, ignoring the diplomatic and political issues behind the war, discounting its toll in lives and never questioning its ends, the *Stars and Stripes* stuck single-mindedly to the job of cheering up the men in the trenches and lavishing on their role all the romance and mission that hard-core propaganda possibly could have done. In a magazine article after the war, Woollcott boasted that the *Stars and Stripes* represented "the first successful use of a newspaper as a weapon in modern war" and that its success was due to the fact that its staff was "at all times thornily ready to resume peeling potatoes rather than write a line it considered faithless to the doughboy." But the fact that no censor was blue-penciling their stories on a regular basis proved nothing but that none was necessary.

The Stars and Stripes

The official publication of the American Expeditionary Forces; authorized by the Commander-in-Chief, A.E.F.

Published every Friday by and for the men of the A.E.F., all profits to accrue to subscribers' company funds.

Editorial: Guy T. Viskniskki, Capt., Inf., N.A. (Editor and General Manager); Franklin P. Adams., Capt., N.A.; Charles P. Cushing, 1st Lieut., U.S.M.C.R.; Alexander Woollcott, M.D.N.A.; Hudson Hawley, Pvt., M.G.Bn.; A. A. Wallgren, Pvt., U.S.M.C.; John T. Winterich, Pvt., A.S.; H. W. Ross, Pvt., Engrs., Ry.

Business: R. H. Waldo, Capt., Inf., U.S.R.; William K. Michael, 1st Lieut., Inf., U.S.R.; Adolph Ochs, 2nd Lieut., Cav., U.S.R.; Stuart Carroll, Q.M. Sgt., Q.M.C.; T.W. Palmer,Corp., Engrs., Ry.

Fifty centimes a copy. Subscription price to soldiers, 4 francs for three months. To civilians, 5 francs for three months. Local French money not accepted in payment of subscriptions.

Advertising rates on application.

Address all communications relating to text, art, subscriptions, advertising and all other matters, to THE STARS AND STRIPES, G 2, A.E.F., Rue des Italiens, Paris, France. Telephone, Gutenberg 12.95.

VERDUN BELLE, MARINE'S PAL, FINDS HER OWN

Trench Broken Mother-Dog Waits for Master on Battle's Rim

RETRIEVES OFFSPRING, TOO

Happy Family Reunion, Human and Canine, Is Held in Field Hospital

SEPARATED AFTER LONG HIKE

Young Soldier Started for Front With Seven Unweaned Puppies Added to His Pack

The Listening Post

LINES ON TAKING A NEW JOB

When I was a civilian in the typing days of peace,
I spilled a column daily, *sans* vacation or surcease.
I whittled many a mournful wheeze and many a halting rhyme
To cop the fleeting jitney and to snare the elusive dime.
I jested by the carload and I frolicked by the bale,
When I used to write a column on the
    New
        York
           Mail.

The years continued flitting, as the years are wont to do,
Until one New Year's Eve I went and shifted my H.Q.
I wrote a ton of trifles and a mass of metric junk
To give me daily ammunish for my Barrage of Bunk.
Oh, many a paragraph I pulled and many a sassy squib,
When I ran a daily column on the
    New
        York
           Trib.

Goodbye, O dull serenity! Ye days of peace, farewell!
I went—oho!—to fight the foe and hear the shot and shell.
Yet once again I find that I must hurl the merry josh,
Though I now command a column set against the beastly Boche.
But the grandest, proudest job I've ever had among the types
Is this job to run this column in
    THE
        STARS
           AND
              STRIPES.

Ross cared so much for anonymity even then that he eliminated the masthead (top, left) when he became the editor. Only columns, such as FPA's (bottom), were signed. Woollcott's byline never appeared in the paper, but it soon got around who was responsible for such poignant vignettes as "Verdun Belle" (top, right), which were unique in the paper. An enlisted fan wrote him a decade later, "God knows, you weren't fooled yourself, hut, man, you did a hell of a piece of work!"

"THE COMMAND IS 'FORWARD' "

It was late in the afternoon, and a tireless Yankee regiment that had already pursued the retreating Germans across more than ten miles of France was resting for a few moments in a roadside ditch, a battered old road that wound its shady way through the ancient forest of Fère. You would have seen them all luxuriating in their breathing spell, the young lieutenants lounging comfortably, the battalion commander sitting with his back propped against a tree.

His name was Leahy—Capt. Francis M. Leahy of Lawrence, Mass., one who had done his turn in the ranks and who used to tell of the days when he was orderly to Capt. Pershing out in the Philippines. He had just caught the signal from down the road that the regiment was to fall in and move on when, whining out of space, came a German shell.

It plowed up the earth and stretched on the ground several men who were just getting to their feet, wounding some of them. It hit the tree against which the captain was leaning and snapped it off like an asparagus stalk. A piece of the shell struck the captain in the back and tore its way through his chest.

"Goodbye, boys," he said, and his head sagged forward.

Then it was as if, somewhere in the universe, a Commander Invisible had called "Attention!" Captain Leahy raised his head. With clearing voice, he spoke the name of the officer to whom it would be his duty to turn over the battalion in the event of his being called away.

"Lieutenant Hansen," he said, "the command is 'Forward.' See the boys through."

Then he died.

"MOTHER'S LETTER" PLAN GIVES EVERY MAN IN A.E.F. SPECIAL OPPORTUNITY FOR OBSERVING MOTHER'S DAY

Every Bit of Army and Government Postal Machinery Will Help to Speed Your May 12th Message Home If You Follow the Rules

MAGIC WORDS WILL INSURE IT RIGHT OF WAY

Company Censors Will Work Overtime, Y.M.C.A. Will Provide Plenty of Paper, We Shall Remind You of Date, So Go to It

"MOTHER'S LETTER"

Aside from orphans, Ross's major campaigns in the *Stars and Stripes* were on behalf of Mother's Day and Father's Day. Such stories as the one at bottom, and his efforts as a tramp reporter, constitute Ross's complete published writings. Woollcott collected his own front-line reportage into a book whose title piece was "The Command is Forward" (top). It sold few copies to the readers of 1920.

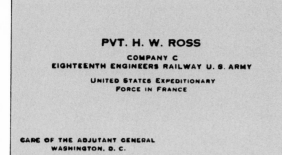

PVT. H. W. ROSS

COMPANY C
EIGHTEENTH ENGINEERS RAILWAY U. S. ARMY

UNITED STATES EXPEDITIONARY
FORCE IN FRANCE

CARE OF THE ADJUTANT GENERAL
WASHINGTON, D. C.

Surely one of the few soldiers with calling cards, Ross had gone AWOL to join the *Stars and Stripes* in Paris. He always managed to sabotage his chances of a promotion in rank, but his editorship of *Stars and Stripes* did entitle him to a limousine and chauffeur.

FPA was never very successful at glamorizing the war, in part because he had little sense of romance in him and in part because of his column, which he had been compiling for nearly twenty years when the war began. It traveled very badly indeed. Its focus had always been urban life and language, and he was neither inclined nor prepared to modify it (not to mention fill it all by himself, as he was virtually forced to do). The result for the soldiers in lice-infested trenches must have been mystifying: why, after all, would they want a detailed account of a croquet tournament in the Luxembourg gardens, or of the seven courses of ecstasy Adams had experienced in one of Paris's finer restaurants? It was clear from the start that his column would never work, but he was given a week's respite to rethink it. When he came back, it was if anything worse than before: either patriotic drivel ("the heavens are filled with service stars, but not until we win the war shall we be entitled to see the service stripe—the rainbow of hope") or just a bad wartime translation of the "Conning Tower" sensibility ("there ought to be some decoration for the regiment every one of whose members goes through one day without using the term 'camouflage'"). That column was his last.

Ross, on the other hand, thrived on the paper. He began as a utility writer, filling in on sports news for Capt. Grantland Rice's page, compiling opinions of the judge advocate, reporting on commendations and medals won by American soldiers, doing service stories ("What to Bring If You're Coming to France") and heart-warming features ("MP Is Reassigned His Home Town Job"). From the beginning, he took his job on the paper very seriously. Within a month of his arrival, he originated the paper's first and most successful campaign: "Take as Your Mascot a French War Orphan." For months, he wrote a story every week about the campaign's success, about children who had been adopted. The campaign moved American soldiers to contribute close to 2 million francs, with which the Red Cross was able to support more than 3,000 orphans.

Ross may have been seeking adventure when he decided to go to war, but what he actually drew from the experience were the satisfactions of a successful careerist. When jokes that soldiers sent to the *Stars and Stripes* began backing up because of the paper's eight-page limit, Ross saw his chance to start building

Ross day-dreamed in those days of emigrating to a South Seas island when the war was over, but he had also begun to think of publishing a "high-class tabloid" that would cover New York City the way the *Stars and Stripes* was covering the war.

the bankroll he would need after the war by putting them together in book form. Ross offered Pvt. John Winterich a fifty-fifty partnership if he would put the *Stars and Stripes* joke book together, but Winterich refused on the grounds that there was something altogether wrong about selling soldiers their own jokes. Undeterred, Ross convinced two members of the paper's circulation department to finance the pamphlet (*Yank Talk* was picked as a title), and he put it together himself with scissors and paste. Only a few days after publication, the Red Cross bought 50,000 copies, and that, together with a quick second offering— *More Yank Talk*—made Ross a $3,000 profit.

After the Armistice, during the demobilization, when the paper's editorial director was reassigned to Germany, Ross was elected by the staff to take his place. It was a sensible choice. His editorial acumen was a proven fact and more of an asset to the paper than his rambling, quasi-conversational writing style—and he was closer to the average enlisted man in temperament, background and sensibility than any of the college men on the paper. When the staff told him of its unanimous judgment that he should have the job, he made a show of reluctance, saying he thought Winterich, "the best copy man in the business," should get it. But when Winterich deferred, Ross accepted—on condition that "what I say goes. We'll hold weekly meetings and you can fire me if you don't like my way of running the paper. But while I'm in, I'm boss."

Ross never was fired, though Woollcott liked to complain that before each weekly meeting, Ross would contrive to send him on some faraway assignment. It was, still, a short and innocuous reign. With the armistice signed, the paper's only remaining task was to keep soldiers from going AWOL in giddy relief. Ross did manage to use his post to advantage. One day a representative of the Butterick Publishing Company stopped by the office to discuss plans for a stateside magazine called *Home Sector* that would replicate the *Stars and Stripes* for returned veterans. Ross was delighted by the part about his being its editor —at a salary of $12,000 a year—and within three days he signed individual contracts with Woollcott, Winterich and four other *Stars and Stripes* editorial hands. To seal the agreement, he gave each of them good-will payments in American dollars, a touch of entrepreneurial flair that made a lasting impression. But even without his *Yank Talk* profits and a job awaiting him in New York, Ross would have left the war immeasurably better off than he had come into it. He had found his future.

What Woollcott benefited from the war is far more complicated: a curious mix of male identity and sense of purpose that he would never again have to quite the same degree. From the beginning of the war, he was manifestly consumed by a need to prove himself a competent "regular" male—a need perhaps sharpened in him by the recent loss of his mother (his father had long since abandoned the family) and the marriage of Amelie Randall, whom he had said he loved and who left him for a successful surgeon in the year of his mother's death. Woollcott rarely showed suffering except to some specific end, but he gave himself to the war as one with nothing to lose. As a new recruit, he worked tirelessly at Base Hospital No. 8 in Savenay, a village of the Loire-Inférieure, tending patients in the venereal ward, measuring the dead for coffins, toiling over the company books and unloading freight cars. When exhaustion and depression overcame him, weakening his badly myopic eyes and maltreated stomach and forcing him into the hospital himself for recuperation, he refused to ask for a transfer. A soldier's duty, he told his physician, Dr. Edmund Devol, was to follow orders, not initiate them. Shortly thereafter, he was promoted to sergeant. He did not lobby for his transfer to the *Stars and Stripes*. He was drafted for the job.

Perhaps it was to compensate for what he perceived to be the sidelines role of a writer that he began to pour forth his sophomoric raptures about the American fighting man and everyone else connected to the Allied cause—from a village curé who would not abandon his humble church to advancing fire to his heroic "Verdun Belle," a mongrel who would not leave the side of a young corporal going into battle. For Woollcott, the war was not a matter of foreign policy, either inspired or misguided; it was not a defense of Western civilization from the Teuton hordes. Rather, it was a theater of proved manhood—one whose characters and motivations held his fascination and admiration as no Broadway production ever could. He had been happily laying wreaths on the war effort for six months before he found himself writing Mrs. Truax that he

WIT'S END

THE HOME SECTOR
A WEEKLY FOR THE NEW CIVILIAN
!OCTOBER 4, 1919

Volume I
Number 3

$5 Year
10 Cents a Copy

Published weekly by the Butterick Publishing Company, George W. Wilder, President; William A. Publow, Secretary; Charles D. Wilder, Treasurer; Butterick Building, Spring and Macdougal Streets, New York, N. Y.

CONTENTS

Conducted by the former editorial council of The Stars and Stripes, official newspaper of the American Expeditionary Forces. Editor, Harold W. Ross; Managing Editor, John T. Winterich. Editorial staff: Alexander Woollcott, Hudson Hawley (European correspondent, 30 Rue Louis le Grand, Paris), Abian A. Wallgren, C. Le Roy Baldridge, Philip A. Von Blon, J. W. Rixey Smith, Tyler H. Bliss, George Boas, R. J. Kirk, Edwin G. Burrows.

Copyright, 1919, by the Butterick Publishing Company. Application for entry as second class matter made at Postoffice, New York, N. Y.

TERMS OF SUBSCRIPTION: The price of THE HOME SECTOR is $5 a year, or 10 cents a copy in the United States, all possessions, Mexico, Canada and Cuba. Subscriptions should be sent by United States postal money order or bank draft, payable to THE HOME SECTOR.

The editors assume no risk for manuscripts and illustrations submitted to this magazine, but will use due care while they are in their possession.

THE HOME SECTOR

(Summarized from the announcement printed on the first page of the first issue)

THE HOME SECTOR is a weekly magazine designed to serve, inform, interest and entertain the new civilian.

It is dedicated and will be devoted to the four million, eight hundred thousand men who served the United States of America in the war against Germany: to the two million who went overseas—above all, to the seventy thousand of them who will never return; to the two million who were waiting on Armistice Day in the camps at home—"the last great reserve army of civilization"; to the men in blue who manned the fleet and the transports, holding open the longest line of communication that an army had ever dreamed of maintaining.

THE HOME SECTOR will be conducted by the former editorial council of "The Stars and Stripes," the official newspaper of the American Expeditionary Forces. A fortnight before peace was signed that newspaper published its final number, and so brought to an end the history of an institution which was born of the needs of the A. E. F.

But while "The Stars and Stripes" has been drawn down, folded up and put away, the journalistic principles which it embodied and the fun-loving, bunk-hating spirit which animated it can be and should be transplanted, and so the men whom chance and war brought together to edit the soldier's weekly are not now, in their red chevron days, parting company. They are keeping close formation to edit this new weekly, which will be the better if it can also enlist the aid of those wags and poets who, from dugouts and lousy billets and cold barracks, used to send in to "The Stars and Stripes" the things which they thought were funny and the thoughts they had which were beautiful. To be their voice in time of peace as surely as "The Stars and Stripes" was their voice in time of war—that is the ambition of THE HOME SECTOR.

THE HOME SECTOR
A WEEKLY FOR THE NEW CIVILIAN

CONDUCTED BY THE FORMER EDITORIAL COUNCIL OF

The Stars and Stripes

The first editorial of *Home Sector* began: "By the same bunch, for the same bunch, in the same spirit" —and so it was. A measure of its appeal is the fact that seven months after its premiere in the fall of 1919, it was bought by the American Legion—editorial backlog, circulation and staff—to build up the lamely run *American Legion Weekly,* which Ross edited until 1924.

(Left) Dorothy Parker and Edwin Pond Parker II (standing with his platoon, second from left) in 1917. After he was drafted—"fifteen minutes after our marriage," Parker would say later —she wrote to him every day. They weren't legally divorced until 1928, but they lived together for only two years after the war.

was "becoming week by week a passionate enthusiast on the subject of America, something I never was before." His conversion had not come until the summer of 1918, when American and French troops stopped the German drive on Paris at Château-Thierry. "I can think of nothing I would rather be than a private in the Marines," he wrote Mrs. Truax then. "You must think of me standing on a chair in the Champs Élysées, too choked to cheer as the bunch went by, some of whom I knew in camp, with the sun on their helmets and a grin on their faces . . . the hortensias showering all about them and a little American flag fluttering from every bayonet." The prose was pure Woollcott, as the doughboys had already come to know and love it. But now, almost as an afterthought, a belief in the American cause had joined his aesthetic pleasure in it, and his pieces, to the extent it was possible, became even more florid.

It was precisely Woollcott's unwillingness or inability to distinguish art from life in war, the strength of his private vision in the face of overwhelmingly contrary evidence, that enabled him to give the soldiers a one-sidedly romantic picture of themselves—and thereby win their approval. One *Stars and Stripes* reader wrote him ten years later that "if any other bird aspires to the title of Salesman Supreme, let me see him sell the idea to a lot of disillusioned, lousy, hungry, filthy, war-crazed men with that awful stench in their nostrils that war is glorious—and he's in your class." That Woollcott drew such approval from such men made the war "the peak of his career, in his own estimation," according to his biographer and lifelong friend, Samuel Hopkins Adams. And yet, rather like the butterfly collector who appreciates his specimens more in the display case than in flight, Woollcott's experience of the war was confined and special. He took insufferable pride in his role on the *Stars and Stripes* but found to his chagrin in later years that the war would come back to him only in impressions—the faint remembrance of a village scene or of a particularly fine wine. In all the magazine pieces he wrote about the war (except his rewrites of *Stars and Stripes* pieces for *Home Sector* and *American Legion Weekly*) he never returned to a scene of battle. In an article for *Everybody's* in 1931, he wrote: "When war made me a spellbound witness of some great occasions, some part of me—the incorrigible journalist I suppose—kept saying, 'This will be

Woollcott seriously opined that Irving Berlin (left, with Benny Kauff) had written the best war song since the Battle Hymn of the Republic in "Oh, How I Hate to Get Up in the Morning." He gushed equally over the antiwar spirit of *What Price Glory?,* which Lt. Col. Laurence Stallings (far left) would write with Maxwell Anderson in 1924.

something to remember. This will be something to remember.' Well, it seems I was wrong about that." The book in which that article was later reprinted is titled *While Rome Burns.*

The country they came home to in the spring of 1919 was dizzyingly changed and changing. Harding's successful appeal to "normalcy" in 1920 is some index of how abnormal the state of the union was then widely perceived to be. The world, Mark Sullivan wrote, was "chronically dazed," and the average American felt "a wish for settled ways, for conditions that remained the same long enough to become familiar and therefore dear . . . for a state of things in which it was possible to feel trust, to rely upon permanence." The homesickness then was for the last unclouded summer of 1914, as the yearning of the 1930s would be for the summer of 1929. But the years between, in which the Algonquin Round Table rose and began to fall, would change utterly the qualities of life to which Americans felt beckoned.

At first, for those who had been to war, came the difficult readjustment to civilian life. Woollcott went back to the *Times* in "a sort of fog of the soul" and remembered later in a letter to Thornton Wilder "how distasteful all my civilian friends seemed . . . like paper dolls." But the pervasive disillusion that came with the terms of peace seemed to touch Adams, Woollcott and Ross not at all. The latter two relished recapitulating their war in *Home Sector,* and if Adams's column is any indication, he forgot the war ever happened. If that was not enough to distance the group that gathered about them from their literary peers in exile and at home, the years that followed would open the gap still further.

For all the literary renascence of the American 1920s, the decade's loudest voice belonged to business. College professors on fixed salaries and the old rich with fortunes in bonds felt keenly the ravages of wartime inflation—as did those who had joined the rush of speculation on farmland in the war years only to face foreclosure as artificially high crop prices began to drop. But Salesmanship, Scientific Management and margin buying seemed to smooth that over in the larger public mind—and a new rich with inflation-proof land, stocks and

The lobby of the Algonquin looked little different during the war (above) from the way it would look in the following decade. The most pronounced change was in the Rose Room's portière, whose thick, dark drape would soon be replaced by a lighter, more colorful fabric. The furniture in the Rose Room would change not at all—except for the addition of a large round table.

goods began exerting both economic and cultural sway. At the same time publicity came of age; one could date its maturity from the wedding in May 1920 of Eddie Bernays, who coined the term "public relations" to describe his profession for wedding announcements. As the press agent's natural métier, the mass national culture born to the Twenties in radio, talkies and syndicated news understandably fixated on such overnight crazes as Mah Jong, flagpole sitting, marathon bicycle racing, sports spectaculars. The sudden acceleration in the pace of American life seemed to bring with it a false sense of exhilaration.

But far from being arbiters of their driven culture, the Round Table crowd would only mirror it, laughing all the way and little realizing that they too were becoming a craze: first as part of the nation's "smart set," when urban sophistication had become an attractive model in even the smallest cities; later as charter members of the first café society in America, a speakeasy-bred intermingling of intellect and wealth that enhanced the value of both. While Walter Lippmann, John Dos Passos, Joseph Wood Krutch and others tried to fill or reason their way out of the moral vacuum of the postwar period, while others illuminated it with art, the Algonquin group seemed just to relax and enjoy it. None of them identified strongly with the Lost Generation, except perhaps for Dorothy Parker, who would have identified with anything that was lost. Rather, they accepted the office of court jester to an anxious kingdom. If they were dancing in the dark, they seemed at times to say, what did that matter? They were dancing. But to many of their literary peers and betters who would never lunch at the Round Table—among them Eugene O'Neill, Edna St. Vincent Millay, Edmund Wilson, Sinclair Lewis, Stephen Vincent Benet, H. L. Mencken, as well as the writers who had committed themselves to exile—it seemed clear that the Round Table had surrendered to their Philistine culture. It would become just as clear, as their fortunes grew, that the terms of peace were seductively profitable.

A COINCIDENCE OF SELF-INTERESTS

The Algonquin Round Table would never have begun except for the work of an energetic press agent with a cause. The publicist was John Peter Toohey, and his cause was Eugene O'Neill, who was 30 years old in 1919 and had never had a play produced on Broadway. The Provincetown Players and even the nascent Theater Guild group had done several of O'Neill's one-act plays, and the critics had warmly approved of them, but a writer of tragedies without a track record uptown was a fearful prospect for a producer. Even if it was clearly just a matter of time before O'Neill would reach Broadway, that was by no means clear to him at the time, and Toohey's interest in O'Neill was a decided, if slightly discomfiting, boost to his morale.

Toohey was one of those remarkable men who have a talent for seeing the obvious before anyone else. In 1916 he had brought the work of another young playwright named George S. Kaufman to the attention of his boss, producer George C. Tyler, and months before Tyler showed an active interest in O'Neill, Toohey had begun trying to drum up public interest in him. Given the playwright's unease, that was not a simple task. When Toohey suggested sending a photographer to get some shots of the artist at work, O'Neill wrote back, "Come on, Mr. Toohey, that's a bit thick, isn't it? Have a heart. . . ." Undaunted, Toohey decided that pictures of the artist *not* at work would be even better. "To catch him penless, deskless, his chin unaccountably kept in place without the prop of a sensitive hand," he wrote, ". . . such a photo ought to establish his rep. as a 'sad bad glad mad' eccentric Nut, a defier of all our cherished traditions—and make him A-One copy." As it turned out, his efforts were in vain. Tyler produced O'Neill on Broadway, but not until years later. John Williams got credit for staging O'Neill's Broadway première, *Beyond the Horizon,* which won the Pulitzer Prize in 1920. But whether through blind luck or instinct or both, Toohey's crusade placed him at the birth of a phenomenon whose significance he could only have dimly predicted at the time—and one that gave him entree to sources and newspapermen that even O'Neill's reflected glory could never have afforded him.

In the early summer of 1919, Toohey made a call on O'Neill's behalf to Murdock Pemberton, the press agent of the Hippodrome. He told Pemberton that he wanted to talk to Alexander Woollcott of the *Times,* whom Pemberton

The Algonquin (above, as it looked in the 1920s) would have been called the Puritan had it not been for Frank Case, who worked at the hotel from its opening in 1902. In the years before the Round Table began, Case's love for and deference to writers and actors had already won the hotel such illustrious clients as Booth Tarkington, John Drew, the Barrymores, Elsie Janis and Douglas Fairbanks, Sr.

"The rudest man I ever knew," said several friends and clubmates of FPA, and Newman Levy, his friend and biographer, agreed: "He was wise to remain aloof and Olympian."

had known since childhood, because he had an item about O'Neill that Woollcott might want for his Sunday column, "Second Thoughts." Pemberton was happy to act as the go-between and arranged a lunch for the three of them the next day at the Algonquin, where the pastry cook, Sarah Victor, prepared an angel cake that could be counted upon to put the sweet-mad critic in a receptive frame of mind. Next day, they met as planned, and after ordering lunch, Toohey poured forth his story about O'Neill: how his father, after discovering Eugene had got a woman pregnant, got him senseless drunk and shipped him off on a merchant steamer so that he could not marry her. The story could well be true; if it is, the woman was his first wife, Kathleen, whom O'Neill had already secretly married before the ship left dock. But, as Pemberton remembered fifty-five years later, Woollcott would have none of it. In the first place, he said, the *Times* had *taste*. In the second, the story sounded dangerously libelous. With that, Woollcott summarily declared the subject dropped and launched into a long series of reminiscences of his recent days in Paris, each of which grandly began: "When I was in the theater of war . . ."

The two press agents knew it was the cross of the profession to bear Woollcott's self-promotion quietly, but it got them thinking about holding another lunch the following week for all of New York's theater journalists at which they could strike back. After lunch, the two of them walked back to Pemberton's office at the Hippodrome and set the typing pool to work on the invitation to a luncheon whose ostensible purpose was to welcome the dean of theater critics back from the war. The Hippodrome costume department ran up a green felt banner for the occasion that Pemberton designed to encompass several of Woollcott's menagerie of pet peeves: the columnist S. Jay Kaufman, who seemed to Woollcott a journalistic leech of the worst sort; deprecations of Woollcott's status as a warrior; misspellings of his name. Embossed in gold on the banner was the legend:

AWOL—COTT

S. Jay Kaufman Post No. 1

The typed agenda for the lunch listed a dozen speeches, each a wartime remi-

In 1920, Brock Pemberton would go on his own to produce *Enter Madam, Miss Lulu Bett, Six Characters* ... and many other plays. Most of his efforts deserved the fine notices they got from Round Table critics, but his having lunch with them nearly every day did nothing to diminish charges of logrolling.

niscence and each to be delivered by Woollcott, whose name Pemberton contrived to spell wrong a dozen different ways.

The scene thus set for the birth of the Algonquin group was entirely ridiculous—more fitting for a corporate roast or a back-slapping Elks get-together than for a gathering of distinguished journalists. As Pemberton began thumbtacking flags, some bunting, and his banner over a long table in the hotel's Pergola Room, the Algonquin's ever-decorous manager, Frank Case, must have been thinking to himself that his stylish inn, which even then counted some of the brightest theatrical and literary lights of the day among its patrons, would be rather diminished by such a puerile display. But he also knew that some of the most public people in New York would be there on that sunny spring afternoon, and what could be better for business?

Nearly all of New York's newspapers were represented at the Algonquin that day—and at that time there were twelve dailies in Manhattan alone and five more in Brooklyn. Pemberton had sent invitations to every theater critic and editor of note, and he recently remembered that about thirty-five people showed up. In that respect, the lunch was atypical; rarely more than ten people would eat at the Round Table later, and it was only a matter of a few weeks, Pemberton recalled, before Woollcott had winnowed out from his welcome-home rally those people who posed professional or stylistic competition—or who simply bored him.

The only two principals of the Round Table who were not present for the first gathering were Marc Connelly, whose reporting job on the *Morning Tele-graph* did not qualify him for Pemberton's list, and George S. Kaufman, Woollcott's assistant at the *Times,* who declined Woollcott's personal invitation. The rest were all invited either by Pemberton or by those Pemberton had invited. FPA, though not a critic, gave his opinion of most current plays in his popular daily column and was therefore prominent on every press agent's handout list. Dorothy Parker, then drama critic for *Vanity Fair,* brought Robert Benchley, who had recently been named managing editor. Murdock Pemberton brought his brother Brock, who had just left the *Times* drama desk to become Arthur Hopkins's assistant producer. Heywood Broun, who was then writing about both theater and sports for the *Tribune,* brought along his wife Ruth Hale. Woollcott

The happy triumvirate of *Vanity Fair*—Parker (top, left), Benchley (bottom, left) and Sherwood (bottom, right)—had first begun going to lunch together when the six-foot-seven Sherwood complained that some midgets then appearing at the Hippodrome had got into the habit of surrounding him on the street and shouting such questions as "How's the weather up there?" Broun (top, right) was a contributor to *Vanity Fair*, but in 1919 the only one of the three he knew was Benchley, who had worked with him on the *Tribune*.

Woollcott (above, in 1921) weighed what was for him a sylphlike 195 pounds when the Round Table began. By its end, he would be up to 255. The mustache would come and go many times in those years, but the three-piece suit would go more or less permanently in favor of capes and scarves.

himself invited Ross and his fiancée Jane Grant, who was a *Times* reporter. Benchley and Parker brought along the new man at *Vanity Fair,* Robert E. Sherwood.

Only a few fragments of memory have survived about that first lunch: one, that Ruth Hale dominated part of it by relating her decision to undergo Freudian analysis; another, that the press agent's send-up of Woollcott was misread. "It was maddening as hell," Pemberton remembered. "They all acted obeisant to 'the king of the drama critics,' which I guess is why they came in the first place. Woollcott's ego got the better of us, I suppose." There was some small consolation for them in one exchange between Woollcott and Arthur Samuels, then editor of *Harper's Bazaar.* Hearing Woollcott begin another of his when-I-was-in-the-theater-of-war stories, Samuels chimed in: "If you were ever in the theater of war, Aleck, it was in the last-row seat nearest the exit." This, of course, only goaded Woollcott into more war-story telling as self-defense.

It is no wonder that so few recollections have survived. No one could possibly have known that it would mark the beginning of a twelve-year convocation, even if they could have foreseen who among them would be selected for it. Those later elected were at the time both young and unprosperous. Except for Adams, who was 38, they were all in their twenties and early thirties. Parker, Benchley and Sherwood were on the verge of being fired from *Vanity Fair,* and their prestigious jobs paid so little they ordered eggs for the first year or so of the group's lunches. Kaufman and Connelly, working separately, had four flops to their credit and as little money as the *Vanity Fair* contingent. The columnists Adams, Broun and Woollcott were far from their peak celebrity or salary, and Ross's editorship of *Home Sector,* while well paying, hardly recommended him to anyone but wartime comrades. Herman Manckiewicz, who like so many others was their close associate everywhere but at the Round Table, dubbed them "the greatest collection of unsaleable wit in America."

It is the group's official version of the story (as told by Frank Case's daughter Margaret Case Harriman in *The Vicious Circle*) that John Toohey suggested, somewhat self-interestedly, as the first lunch was breaking up, "Why don't we do this every day?" and that the daily ritual began as simply as that.

The story is verified by Pemberton, but it leaves out, as legend often does, any principle of motivation. Certainly they met because they enjoyed one another's company enormously, but it is equally true that the luster of the group reflected flatteringly on each of its members. FPA, when he joined the group at night and on weekends, found himself in the admiring company of people he had helped to succeed in New York—Benchley, Parker, Connelly, and Kaufman most of all. Broun's simpler appetites for good food and good company could be satisfied at one sitting. Woollcott found in the group an audience more or less under his control. But there were good practical reasons for coming as well, particularly for the fledgling writers and for the Broadway ingenues who began coming on the arms of the press agents. It was a chance to join the company of people who were relatively successful and who could help them achieve the same goal. Toohey and Pemberton particularly benefited from combining business and pleasure over lunch; they could meet as peers and converse with precisely those people it was their job to cultivate—and then fill in other press agents and journalists on what was said, which would soon become the best item copy in town. No one came to the Round Table a "nobody"; they all held respectable positions in 1919 and after and were showing talent almost as prodigious as their ambition. Still, like most fervent self-believers, they also needed reassurance that they were indeed as good as they thought. That reassurance came almost as a perquisite of acceptance in the Algonquin group.

It is a measure of that need that the Round Table lasted as long as it did. If it was, as the legend goes, the greatest forum of presiding wits since the Mermaid Tavern, it was also a Bronx Zoo of contemporary neurotics, a group so dazzling in its assortment of idiosyncratic personalities that the wonder is simply that they spoke to each other at all, even in epigrams. There, from the beginning, was Broun with his hip flask at the ready to quell a battery of phobias, and Benchley with his abhorrence of alcohol and support for Prohibition. There was FPA with his infantile and self-destructive compulsion to compete badly at poker and physical games, and Kaufman with his card-sense and fear of physical contact. There were Parker and Woollcott, whose fragrant manners masked both terrible self-loathing and lethal wit. And in the midst of them all sat

Helen Hayes, who had learned to play the piano for *To the Ladies,* blew the opening line it occasioned at her first party among Round Tablers. "Anyone who wants my piano is willing to it," she said. Kaufman's reply was gentle: "That's very seldom of you, Helen."

Ross, with his resolute contempt for (and attraction to) "Eastern dudes." Each of them seemed to have found the perfect circumstances for coming undone—yet they kept coming back.

Reassurance of self-worth thus could not have been the draw for all of them. Sitting down to lunch with that group was a harrowing experience for anyone unequipped to deal with verbal abuse; the press agents and many of the actors and actresses who came on occasion knew that special terror. Woollcott seems to have relished having an audience of captive targets, and in determining who would be welcome and who would not, he made enemies gladly. "I disliked him intensely," Bennett Cerf wrote in his memoir. "The charm that he turned on for people he considered important was singularly lacking when he was dealing with people he considered his social inferiors. This is not my idea of the way a gentleman acts." Helen Hayes came to feel that she was admitted to the group's social gatherings only to provide proof of their superiority. At least, Woollcott allowed no ambiguity about who was in and who was out. As Ben Hecht wrote of Woollcott's coterie in the 1930s: "Fine actors, actresses, composers and writers were among them. But their fineness was a secondary matter. . . . Success was the only proof of artistry, or even intelligence. If you failed you were a fool and a second-rater."

If high promise was one's passport across the Round Table's closed border, barbed and often malevolent wit was the currency inside. Survival in this wit ritual required that one have, among other things, the ability to duck punches ("You could never play Lady Macbeth," Woollcott informed Peggy Wood over lunch one day) and then to respond in kind ("No, Aleck, but you could"). Marc Connelly's early baldness occasioned another famous example. "Your head feels just like my wife's behind," was the thrust. Connelly's parry: "So it does."

In the early days of the group, the verbal crossfire was not as vicious as it would later be, and the principals were especially careful with each other. Broun was never competitive or offensive with his wit, Benchley was always generous and good-humored, and Ross couldn't have got off a good line even if he could have thought of one. Even Kaufman was fairly gentle in those days. Dorothy Parker's earliest remembered contributions were at the expense of her then-

Woollcott had no small part in the marriage of John V. A. Weaver and Peggy Wood (top left and bottom, with Weaver on their honeymoon in Santa Maria, California, in 1924), and he introduced Weaver to the Round Table. The initiation was no snap. Ina Claire (top, right) was telling a story in those days about the time she threw Jed Harris to the ground. After Weaver's introduction to the group by Woollcott, someone suggested she demonstrate for him what she had done to Harris—and so she did. From the floor, Weaver said, "Listen, Mom, put on your glasses and let's fight fair." At that, Claire laughed and declared: "He's in, he's in. He'll do just fine."

Margalo Gillmore (left, in *He Who Gets Slapped*) came to the Round Table through Marc Connelly, who was her diligent and long-term suitor.

husband, Eddie, whose misadventures she described in glorious detail. But the rites of initiation were brutal even then. Margalo Gillmore brought a young actor to the Round Table one day and, hoping to ease him into Woollcott's favor, told the critic that the young man was a great admirer of his writings. "Oh," Woollcott said into his soup, "can he read?" (Moss Hart wrote about meeting Woollcott at a tea party Beatrice Kaufman gave in 1929. Woollcott was reading in a corner, and Hart's nervous opening line was, "You'll enjoy that book." Woollcott shot back, "How would *you* know?") Just as often, Woollcott would simply ignore the unwanted visitor until he got up to leave the table and then ask in a loud stage whisper, "Who brought *him*?" After a time, other members of the group began playing in his tragedy of bad manners with people he brought to the Round Table, which he thoroughly enjoyed.

That promising men and women would frequent a table whose centerpiece was Alexander Woollcott and risk abuse for that dubious pleasure betokens something more than Kaufman's later description of the Round Table as "a motley and nondescript bunch of people who wanted to eat lunch, and that's about all." In late 1919, simple reasons were perhaps enough: acceptance in such a promising company was flattering to some, professionally useful to others. But the group soon began to change. In 1920, Frank Case moved them from a long side table in the Pergola Room (now called the Oak Room) to a large round table in the center of the Rose Room. They stopped calling themselves "The Board" and then "The Luigi Board" (in honor of their waiter and the latest occult craze) in favor of "The Vicious Circle," and Case found he could safely stop bribing them with free stuffed celery, secure in the knowledge that they had built their own momentum and would be coming in every day at no one's urging but their own. By that time, the group had become more than a clique or coterie. It had begun to take shape as a public institution, one defined by the careers of its members and the cravings of a new public taste of which all of them, in various ways, were becoming premier retailers.

Perhaps success came too soon to "those amazing whelps," as *Vanity Fair*'s editor Frank Crowninshield called the three editors he hired during and just

(Top) Benchley and Parker in a set-up photograph with Crowninshield. (Bottom) Crowninshield at his desk. One result of the basic lack of regard for authority that Benchley and Parker displayed was that they lost their jobs—a fate that Benchley, with a family to support, could ill afford. They dashed off to lunch when it happened and laughed loud and long about it all, but when Condé Nast saw Parker later and invited her on an ocean voyage, she muttered as he left: "Oh *God,* make that ship sink!"

after the war. Still, Mr. Benchley, Mrs. Parker and Mr. Sherwood, as they always called each other, warranted the title. In 1920, Benchley, the managing editor, was twenty-nine; Parker was twenty-six; and Sherwood, who was called drama editor but actually did whatever editorial work needed doing, was twenty-four.

If ever there was a premium on youth, the immediate postwar years were the time: editors were hungry for new voices, new viewpoints, anything to keep their publications fresh and up to date and in the new, postwar atmosphere, the youngsters graduating from college came into the literary marketplace with hard-fought rebel victories behind them. As Malcolm Cowley wrote in *Exile's Return:*

> *Dreiser, Anderson, Robinson, Masters and Sandburg were all in their forties before they were able to devote most of their time to writing; Sinclair Lewis was thirty-five before he made his first success with* Main Street. *It was different with the new group of writers. Largely as a result of what the older group had accomplished, their public was ready for them, and they weren't forced to waste years working in a custom house, like Robinson, or writing advertising copy, like Anderson. At the age of twenty-four, Fitzgerald was earning eighteen thousand dollars a year with his stories and novels. Hemingway, Wilder, Dos Passos and Louis Bromfield were internationally known novelists before they were thirty. They had a chance which the older men lacked to develop their craftsmanship in book after book; from the very first they were professionals.*

In New York, one replacement for midnight oil and daylight drudge work was what Edmund Wilson called the "all-star literary vaudeville," in which one's social efforts counted toward one's working reputation much as performance on the golf course or at the country-club socials could help a corporate executive's rise to power. By the 1920s, the system of literary mentor-protégé relationships was highly developed, and it was through two of the city's most highly regarded journalists—FPA and Crowninshield—that most of the young Algonquinites came to enter the life of the literati.

Dorothy Parker was patronized first by Adams, perhaps in part because he paid his contributors nothing. She supported herself by playing piano for a dancing class in the evenings, and by day she set into verse her constant theme:

loves lost, fickle hearts and how romance always added up to a one-way proposition. Adams had printed several of them by the time Crowninshield finally bought one for twelve dollars in 1916 and gave her a starting job at *Vogue* for ten dollars a week. During the war, she was Crowninshield's date to parties at their publisher Condé Nast's home, she helped Crowninshield write a book called *High Society,* and she was allowed to fill in as drama critic of *Vanity Fair.* Eventually, she took over the job.

Sherwood's beginning was easier: his family knew Crowninshield, and Crowninshield knew young Sherwood from his work as editor of the *Harvard Lampoon.* He was also impressed with Sherwood's war record. Sherwood had been gassed and shot through both legs at the front, and he was canny enough to wear his uniform to an interview with Crowninshield in the fall of 1919. He came away with a three-month tryout as an editor at a salary of twenty-five dollars a week.

Benchley broke into literary circles as a "vaudevillian" from the start. His writing was first seen in New York in Frank Adams's "Conning Tower." Soon after, he was called upon to award the "coveted timepiece" that Adams gave his most prolific contributor each year. "I'm sending a young fellow named Bob Benchley to represent me," the absent Adams wrote to his "Contribution" dinner in 1916. "He's just out of Harvard and I think you'll like him." In the audience that night were Frank Crowninshield, Howard Dietz, Morrie Ryskind, Marc Connelly, Edna Millay, George Kaufman, Carolyn Wells and Deems Taylor, who was that year's winner. (Then editor of Western Electric's house organ, Taylor would soon be named music critic of FPA's paper, the New York *Tribune.*) Benchley's speech that night was a statistical biography of the watch, from its invention by John W. Watch to the present day. He had done such prankish after-dinner speeches before but never in the company of the people he hoped to join as peers, and his success that evening only redoubled Adams's confidence in him—confidence that translated into wartime jobs on the *Tribune* (both before and after the Aircraft Board) and then, indirectly, on *Vanity Fair.*

Donald Ogden Stewart, who moved to New York in 1920, made himself known in New York in a similar way. During his campaign to be published in

Deems Taylor (left) and Donald Ogden Stewart. What FPA was to Taylor, Crowninshield was to Stewart in the post "amazing whelps" days of *Vanity Fair*: a patron and entrée.

Vanity Fair, he wrote in his autobiography, "Crownie delightedly presented me one night to a club of writers, artists and musicians known as the Coffee House. The performance was a huge success, due partly to the fact that liquor could be obtained by club members, and I was launched into cultural circles as a public entertainer." Shortly thereafter, *Vanity Fair* published parodies he had written of Theodore Dreiser and James Branch Cabell. "The ability to create laughter," Stewart wrote, "seemed to present added possibilities for making 'contacts' both in the financial and the cultural fields." The fledglings of the Round Table played that game well—perhaps too well.

Even given the freedoms of the postwar period, *Vanity Fair* was not quite ready for the jubilant recklessness of the "amazing whelps." It was still, as Benchley put it, "a whited sepulcher," a magazine devoted to voguish European painters and writers and anything else of agreed-upon taste. It was said of Crowninshield that he would let his writers say anything as long as they said it in evening clothes. The magazine's sense of propriety extended even to the dress of employees, who were expected to look the part of cultural arbiters. Memoranda came down from the office manager forbidding editors from discussing salaries (Benchley, Parker and Sherwood began wearing placards bearing the information). When they were late, they were expected to fill out tardy slips explaining why (Benchley filled both sides of one with a story about how the Hippodrome elephants had got loose and how he, heroically, had tried to turn them back, which involved scampering after them as they trooped around the Plaza Hotel and down to the Hudson docks, making him—drat the luck!— eleven minutes late). At Christmas in 1919, neither Parker nor Sherwood got expected raises; Sherwood was told that Condé Nast's daughter's music teacher was being considered for his job. It is true that Mrs. Parker was actually fired for writing a scathing review of Billie Burke in the title role of *Caesar's Wife,* which drew down the wrath of her husband and producer, Florenz Ziegfeld, who was one of the magazine's best advertisers. It is true that in response Benchley and Sherwood threatened to resign over Crowninshield's blatant kowtowing to advertisers. But it is equally true that Crowninshield lost no time

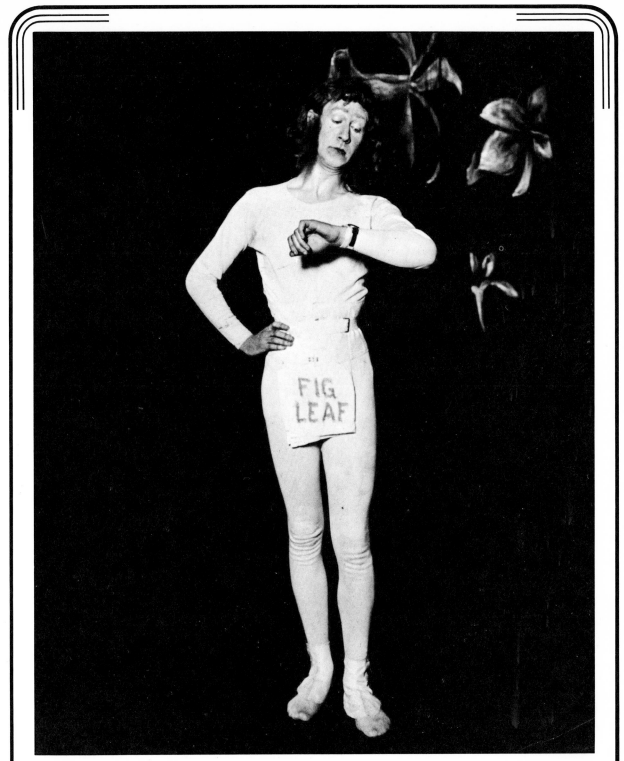

What Benchley is doing in this picture has been lost to history. The lean physique and lack of a mustache suggest it was taken in the early 1920s, but it is hard to believe it dates from Benchley's days as a practicing Prohibitionist, which ended with an Orange Blossom at Tony Soma's in 1922.

in telling them all he was sorry to see them go, giving them little chance to back down.

After that, Benchley and Parker took an office together above the Metropolitan Opera, where, they promised each other, they would write their best work and take out a joint cable address: Parkbench. Neither happened; their cable address is where they might as well have been. When Benchley went off on a trip with his wife, Gertrude, and their two sons, Parker wrote him disconsolately that things were so slow she was thinking of putting a new sign on the door that read, simply, "Men." That didn't happen either. Sherwood, however, had been busy. After helping to put together a Hasty Pudding show at Harvard that he had written several years earlier, he went to see Edward S. Martin, who had founded the *Harvard Lampoon* with Sherwood's father and was now editor of Charles Dana Gibson's humorous weekly magazine *Life*. After a few tryout pieces, Martin hired Sherwood as a regular contributor. By the summer of 1920, Benchley and Parker had been hired as well. The only trouble was that by then *Life* was a magazine whose time had come and gone.

Circulation was hearty enough, an all-time high in 1921 of almost 239,000, but magazines were changing fast, and even Crowninshield's prodigies were not to help this one keep pace. Still, on their way to being made coeditors of the magazine in 1924, Benchley and Sherwood did their best. Benchley did theater reviews and occasional pieces (such as "Family Life in America," about a sweet old grandmother talking to her deceased husband: "I certainly hope you're frying down there"), and Sherwood became the first critic of films for any national publication, writing a weekly column called "The Silent Drama," in addition to a fairly constant stream of other pieces. They were all prolific; even the deadline-phobic Parker managed to turn out a poem a week for the first two years. But they were severely constrained in what they wrote by space and expected tone and volume. Dorothy Parker's poems became predictable variations on her single theme: "And when in search of novelty, you stray,/ Oh, I can kiss you blithely as you go . . . / And what goes on, my love, while you're away/ You'll never know." With a regular deadline to make, experimentation and innovation gave way to the tried and known. Sherwood was particularly

seduced by *Life*'s lavish paycheck, which kept him from playwriting until 1927. Parker stated the problem directly in a long-forgotten poem she wrote for *Life* called "The Far-sighted Muse":

> *Everything's great, in this good old world;*
>   (This is the stuff they can always use.)
> *God's in His heaven, the hill's dew-pearled;*
>   (This will provide for the baby's shoes.)
> *Hunger and War do not mean a thing;*
>   *Everything's rosy where'er we roam;*
> *Hark, how the little birds gaily sing!*
>   (This is what fetches the bacon home.)

Kaufman was quite certain it was a fortune he wanted to make, which was perhaps his family's legacy to him of continual moves from boardinghouses to mansions and back. His motives in the theater were expressly commercial, and he proceeded to dig his fortune out of it.

There could never have been a better time. In 1920, the theater was "wide open as a virgin continent," Sherwood wrote later, "and as teeming with chances for adventure and fortune." Productions were cheap—$10,000 would usually suffice—and an audience of only a few hundred with top tickets priced between three and five dollars would keep even a fair play running for quite some time. The 1920s saw an unprecedented and still-unmatched boom in theater building and new productions; from 126 productions in the 1917 season, there were 208 in 1927 and 264 in 1928, a number which has never since been equaled or even approached. And there was a qualitative change to match the statistics: thousands of Americans had been left behind in the mud of Europe; Harding was elected on a platform of returning to normalcy; A. Mitchell Palmer was hunting for Bolsheviks and deporting innocents; Prohibition was proving to many Americans that scoff-laws had more fun. The world was topsy-turvy, no value was sacrosanct, and in the postwar years of Freud and flappers and hip flasks, American theater became more than the thoughtless entertainer it had been before; it began to judge and reflect, and in that role found its maturity. For

Connelly (left) and Kaufman talked over plots and characters for months in 1917 and 1918, until Kaufman one day asked Connelly: "Do you think we'll ever actually *write* anything?"

George Kaufman and his collaborators, the most significant fact was simply that the war had made the world safe for, and needful of, satire.

Kaufman owed almost everything to FPA's intercession on his behalf. As a Columbia Ribbon salesman in Passaic, New Jersey (his lust for security had already got the best of him), Kaufman saw his first poem published in FPA's column in the *Evening Mail* in 1909, and he quickly became such a frequent contributor that FPA asked him to lunch one day. That lunch led to jobs on the Washington *Times* (running a humorous column called "This, That and a Little of the Other"), on the New York *Tribune* (as a drama reporter for Heywood Broun, who ran the department) and then on the *Evening Mail* (another column, called "The Mail Chute"). When the *Mail* was sold in 1915, Adams saw that Kaufman got his job back working for Broun on the *Tribune,* where FPA himself was then employed. When Kaufman married Beatrice Bakrow in 1916, FPA was his best man, and the Adamses and Kaufmans became a frequent foursome. Although everyone at the Round Table owed some part of his success to FPA, no one owed him more than Kaufman—except perhaps for Dorothy Parker, who credited Adams with having "raised me from a couplet." But Kaufman and Adams were too alike ever to collaborate, and as Kaufman's desire to be a successful playwright began to crowd out his work as a journalist, a collaborator was what he desperately needed. During the war, he found what he was looking for in Marcus Cook Connelly.

Connelly was an unabashed ham, the progeny of show business folk in McKeesport, Pennsylvania—his father was a singer—and a man without doubt of his interest to other people. No one fit better into the literary vaudeville. In a *New Yorker* Profile of Connelly in 1930, Woollcott wrote: "What? You never heard him give 'Spartacus' with gestures? Never heard him mimic Ruth Draper doing 'A Railway Station on the Western Plains'? Why, I guess you don't get asked out much." Connelly was at his best doing Cleopatra, and he was not above secretly asking someone who was going to the same party he was to request a performance of it. His wit was as sharp as Kaufman's, but where Kaufman's was laconic, Connelly's was exuberant. Kaufman's stories came in a sudden burst—Connelly called his technique "the invisible gun"—but both James

Kaufman resented all charges of logrolling and during his tenure on the *Times* drama desk edited out all plugs for his plays. Toohey, who handled publicity for *To the Ladies,* finally asked Kaufman what he would have to do to get Hayes's name in the paper. "Shoot her," Kaufman said.

Thomas Flexner and George Oppenheimer remember that Connelly told the same stories over and over again, in excruciating detail and at intolerable length.

In 1917, Kaufman and Connelly collaborated on a play called *Miss Moonshine.* It failed to find a producer, but the ubiquitous John Peter Toohey liked what he read and recommended Kaufman to George Tyler. Kaufman proceeded to rewrite two plays for Tyler, both dismal failures—and Connelly tried to adapt an old comic opera for Tyler, called *Erminie,* also quick sinking. What they needed was an idea of their own, or at least one that was not fished out of the melodramatic past to suit a nostalgic present, because the present that assaulted New York in 1920 demanded more. Just then Tyler found himself in need of a vehicle for a favorite ingenue.

Writing a play to order is not exactly dream work, but the play Kaufman and Connelly had in mind turned into something far more than it could have been. For one thing, the actress was Lynn Fontanne, for whom a starring role in America was long overdue, and the character they began to develop for her seemed wonderfully resonant with her own personality. The character's name was Dulcy, and she was an extended, elaborated version of the fictional Dulcinea who turned up regularly in FPA's column spouting clichés: "It never rains if you have your umbrella," she would say, or "When you need a policeman you can never find one." Miss Fontanne was less a Dulcy than a Gracie Allen in real life, but she had just the charmingly dazed quality the lines needed to make the leap from banality to satire. ("Next week," Alfred Lunt once told his wife, "we'll be playing in Minnesota." "If it's in Texas, I'll love it," she said.) The character was FPA's contribution—the authors acknowledged the debt by giving him 10 percent of their profit—and having a Lynn Fontanne to play it was blind luck. What made the play as important as it was, for its authors and for the American theater, was that in *Dulcy,* Kaufman and Connelly struck a rich new vein of topical, local humor that they would work together for the next five years and that Kaufman would continue to mine for the rest of his career. There was a dizzily animated plot: a missing string of pearls, a butler who turns out to be an ex-con, a would-be millionaire who turns out to be an escaped mental patient, an effete screenwriter who goes on at hilarious length about his new

Frazee Theatre

42d Street, West of Broadway
Telephone Bryant 0031
Direction of H. H. Frazee

Manager.....................................Richard E. H. French
Treasurer,.....................................Walter Heyer
Treasurer's Assistant.....................................Lester Worden

FIRE NOTICE

Look around NOW and choose the nearest Exit
to your seat. In case of fire walk (not run) to THAT
Exit. Do not try to beat your neighbor to the street.
THOMAS J. DRENNAN, Fire Commissioner.

BEGINNING SATURDAY EVENING, AUGUST 13, 1921
Matinees Wednesday and Saturday

"DULCY"

A Comedy in Three Acts
By George S. Kaufman and Marc Connelly
(With a Bow to Franklin P. Adams)
Staged by Howard Lindsay
(Direction of George C. Tyler and H. H. Frazee)

The Players
(In the order of their appearance)

WILLIAM PARKER, Dulcy's brother........GREGORY KELLY
HENRY.....................................HARRY LILLFORD
GORDON SMITH, Dulcy's husband............JOHN WESTLEY
TOM STERRETT, advertising engineer.......ELLIOTT NUGENT
DULCINEA.....................................LYNN FONTANNE
SCHUYLER VAN DYCK.....................................GILBERT DOUGLAS
C. ROGER FORBES.....................................WALLIS CLARK
MRS. FORBES.....................................CONSTANCE PELISSIER
ANGELA FORBES.....................................NORMA LEE
VINCENT LEACH.....................................HOWARD LINDSAY
BLAIR PATTERSON.....................................GEORGE ALISON

The scene of the three acts is the living room in the home of Dulcinea
and her husband, near New York City.

Liberty Theatre

42nd Street, West of Broadway
234 WEST 42d STREET CO., INC.   J. W. Mayer, Manager

NOTICE: This Theatre, with every seat occupied, can be emptied
in less than three minutes. Choose NOW the Exit nearest to your
seat, and in case of fire walk (do not run) to that Exit.
THOMAS J. DRENNAN, Fire Commissioner.

WEEK BEGINNING MONDAY EVENING, FEBRUARY 20, 1922
Matinees Wednesday and Saturday

"TO THE LADIES!"

A Comedy in Three Acts by
George S. Kaufman and Marc Connelly
THE AUTHORS OF "DULCY"
Staged by HOWARD LINDSAY
(Direction of A. L. Erlanger and George C. Tyler)

THE PLAYERS

ELSIE BEEBE.....................................Helen Hayes
LEONARD BEEBE.....................................Otto Kruger
JOHN KINCAID.....................................George Howell
MRS. KINCAID.....................................Isabel Irving
CHESTER MULLIN.....................................Percy Helton

PROGRAM CONTINUED ON SECOND PAGE FOLLOWING

CORT THEATRE

Forty-eighth Street, Just East of Broadway
Direction JOHN CORT

BARNARD KLAWANS, Manager

Designed and Built by Edward B. Corey

Telephone Bryant 46

NOTICE: This Theatre, with every seat occupied, can be emptied
in less than three minutes. Choose NOW the Exit nearest to your
seat, and in case of fire walk (do not run) to that Exit.
THOMAS J. DRENNAN, Fire Commissioner.

WEEK BEGINNING MONDAY MATINEE, JANUARY 1, 1923
Matinees Wednesday and Saturday

MERTON OF THE MOVIES

A Dramatization of Harry Leon Wilson's Story of the Same Name
By George S. Kaufman and Marc Connelly
(Direction George C. Tyler and Hugh Ford)
Staged by Hugh Ford

Characters

MERTON GILL.....................................GLENN HUNTER
AMOS G. GASHWILER.....................................EDWARD M. FAVOR
TESSIE KEARNS.....................................ESTHER PINCH
ELMER HUFF.....................................BERT MELVILLE
CHARLEY HARPER.....................................TOM HADAWAY
LESTER MONTAGUE.....................................J. K. MURRAY
THE MONTAGUE GIRL.....................................FLORENCE NASH
CASTING DIRECTOR.....................................LUCILE WEBSTER
SIGMUND ROSENBLATT, a director.......EDWIN MAXWELL
HIS CAMERAMEN..................{ ALBERT COWLES
                                { E. J. CHATTERLY

PROGRAM CONTINUED ON SECOND PAGE FOLLOWING

Helen Hayes (bottom, right) played 128 performances
of *To the Ladies* on Broadway and then toured in the
play for two years. The first three collaborations of
Kaufman and Connelly had a collective run on Broadway of 522 performances, and all were made into
movies at least once, making the authors rich by 1922.

Kaufman, Fontanne and Connelly with the notices of *Dulcy*. They were raves: "a deft and diverting comedy of character—a gay piece written by and for the sophisticated" (Woollcott) ; "an ingenious trick play, and the patter which introduces the legerdemain is even better than the stunts" (Broun).

Lynn Fontanne and Gregory Kelly in *Dulcy*. In considering the play years later, John Gassner concluded that although the satire of her cliché-ridden speech and fatuous emotionality was "barbed," Kaufman and Connelly "withdrew the arrow for the sake of amiability and a full box-office till."

Glenn Hunter and Florence Nash in *Merton of the Movies*. Critical acclaim for both *Merton* and *Dulcy* rested more on the critics' disdain for the same cultural phenomena Kaufman and Connelly were exploring— in *Merton,* the boorish world of movies—than on the merits of the plays. The highest praise Krutch could bring himself to for *Merton* was that the playwrights were satirizing "those typical American institutions that the plain man was inclined to regard with reverence."

epic, "Sin Throughout the Ages." But what set *Dulcy* apart was that it introduced "something novel on the stage," as Joseph Wood Krutch wrote, "satire from a point of view rather 'smart' . . . than universal in its appeal."

Kaufman's journalistic talents and training prepared him uniquely for the observation of those small but telling bits of behavior by which people define themselves, and he had the good journalist's instinct for what was new and noteworthy. Howard Lindsay, who played the play's scriptwriter, told Maurice Zolotow years later: "I played [him] to the hilt as an out-and-out fairy scenarist. In those days, movie writers were still a new butt for jokes, and fairies were unheard of, and so the combination of the two was very funny." The audience's applause for such satire constituted proof of its sophistication.

Dulcy opened to rave reviews in New York in February of 1921. A year and a week later, the two men opened *To the Ladies,* another written-to-order vehicle, this time for Helen Hayes, in which Rotarianism was the foil. Eight months later, they opened *Merton of the Movies,* whose targets were the fan magazine phenomenon and the film world itself. In the span of twenty months, Kaufman and Connelly had three hit shows to their credit.

In *Exiles Return* Malcolm Cowley wrote of his literary generation:

> *We read Wilde and Shaw, who were always mentioned together. From one or the other of these dramatists—or perhaps from Mencken and Nathan, then editors of* Smart Set—*we derived the sense of paradox, which became a standard for judging the writers we afterward encountered. If they were paradoxical—if they turned platitudes upside down, showed the damage wrought by virtue, made heroes of their villains, then they were "moderns"; they deserved our respect.*

Kaufman and Connelly were moderns in that sense, but only to a point. They showed up the conventions and crazes of middle-class America for a fraud; they snookered the careerists; they showed virtue to be a tool of hypocrites. But their audience was no Lost Generation; they were people who could afford tickets, and to make sure to leave them laughing, the playwrights always let their targets get away clean in the end. Merton becomes a star, even if not the kind he wants. Dulcy's husband gets his business deal. Even business is given its due in *To the*

Ladies. "This is what fetches the bacon home," said Parker. "If you have a message," Kaufman's famous advice went, "call for Western Union."

The columnists at the Round Table seem to have felt the same way. In the early 1920s, newspaper columnists were among the city's most celebrated and powerful people, and in 1920, along with Don Marquis and Christopher Morley, Broun and Adams were the most celebrated and powerful of the columnists. "They can turn a mayor to ridicule," Carl Van Doren wrote in *Century Magazine,* "send hundreds to a theater or keep dozens away from it, stimulate the sales of a book, give a clever phrase household currency, fix public attention upon some neglected figure or episode . . . laugh some general hysteria to sleep." There was no lack of hysteria in the immediate postwar years: anti-German xenophobia, the Red Scare, rabid antilabor campaigns. But Broun (then) and Adams (always) stuck for the most part to a secondary role: "to retail the gossip," Van Doren wrote, "promulgate the jests, discuss the personalities, represent the manners of New York. To read them in any distant city is to miss half the points they make, or at least half the freshness of their points. They are the licensed jesters of the town."

Their license was their public profile. They wrote of nothing more often—or better—than of themselves, and part of their success, like that of the Kaufman comedies, lay in their ability to convey a sense of in-ness to their readers, even though, to keep their readership large and loyal, that in-ness was often more apparent than real—FPA's Saturday column, "The Diary of Our Own Samuel Pepys" commonly descended to mere name dropping. Neither Adams nor Broun had formal grounding in the subjects of their pieces—which ranged, sometimes in the same space, from theater to sports to literature to politics—and that was so much the better, because it meant they could never write over their readers' heads. What they had in abundance were personal opinions, the instinct Kaufman had for what was topical and just ready to be remarked on. In the era of the automobile, radio, films, syndicated news and the portentous population shift from country to city—all the instruments of a national culture

Broun in 1922, in a rare moment of tidiness. Usually Broun appeared in mismatched socks with tie and jacket askew (if worn at all), a persistent habit of dress that had once led Pershing to ask him during the war: "Did you fall down?"

—they also had a large market for their product, which was nothing less than an inside line to the new sophistication.

Broun later became something more than a hawker of premium views, but in the early years of the Round Table, he was content to write about anything that caught his attention. In those days, he wrote often of plays and books and Adamsesque peeves ("An Adjective a Day"), but nothing inspired him more than sport spectaculars such as the Dempsey-Carpentier fight, whose elaborations he would spin out with the kind of zeal he would later bring to the plight of Sacco and Vanzetti. This, for instance, an excerpt from his column about the lightweight title match between champion Benny Leonard and Rocky Kansas:

> *Spiritually, Saint-Saëns, Brander Matthews, Henry Arthur Jones,*
> *Kenyon Cox and Henry Cabot Lodge were in Benny Leonard's corner. His*
> *defeat would, by implication, have given support to dissonance, dadaism,*
> *creative evolution and bolshevism. Rocky Kansas does nothing according*
> *to rule. His fighting style is as formless as the prose of Gertrude Stein.*

Broun noted that Leonard, though bleeding in early rounds, remained "faithful to the established order," and when he finally dropped the challenger, Broun concluded: "There is still a kick in style, and tradition carries a nasty wallop." Broun knew less about sports than many of his peers—Ring Lardner and Grantland Rice are the obvious examples—but his columns about it, if wildly embellished, were also vastly enjoyed.

Woollcott also shone more for enthusiasm than substance. His taste was questionable at best. He loved *Abie's Irish Rose,* which every other New York critic saw for the piece of sentimental idiocy that it was. Later, he realized his mistake but only compounded the error by castigating O'Neill's *Strange Interlude* as "that *Abie's Irish Rose* of the pseudo-intelligentsia." Wrong-headed as he could sometimes be, he was unparalleled as a salesman for what he liked, calling no less than three plays of the 1920–1921 season the best ever to appear on the American stage. In 1921, George Jean Nathan, Woollcott's only real competitor for critical and syntactical flamboyance (and conspicuously absent from the Round Table for that reason, among others), attacked Woollcott in *Smart Set,* calling him "the Seidlitz Powder in Times Square":

The Conning Tower

THE DIARY OF OUR OWN SAMUEL PEPYS

Saturday, October 7

A DULLISH gray day, and read hard in the day's journals, in this one what a fine man is Mr. Smith and what a sorry fellow is Mr. Miller, and that one what a fine man is Mr. Miller and what a churl is Mr. Smith, but it did not confuse me at all, forasmuch as I know them both to be good men, and far better than most of those who are going to vote for them and against them. Read this day the worst parody of a thing ever I read, called "If Winter Don't," by Barry Pain, maladroit and without skill or humour, and utterly without any sense of the Hutchinsonian style. Yet very pretentious.

So to the courts, but it come on to rain, so stopped there all afternoon, like a zany, waiting for it to stop, and indulging in footless chatter with M. Wheeler and L. Howard and G. Moran, and so home and with my wife to G. Kaufman's for dinner, which I had too much of, and felt ill,
but not till past midnight, and thence home and lay awake all the night till nine Sunday morning, in great pain and in greater rage at myself for having it.

Sunday, October 8

U P BY eleven, and was in poor fettle, but went to the courts and met there Dr. Coburn and asked him whether it would harm me to play, and he said it would be good for me but bad for my game, and so it turned out, for even M. Wheeler beat me a match, and so home, and felt weak, but H. Ross and Jane come in for supper and my wife cooked me some soup and some chicken and I had some, and was much cheered at the tayles H. Ross tells of the troubles he is having with his new house, what with carpenters and plumbers and plasterers and carpenters' helpers and plumbers' helpers and plasterers' helpers, and so early to bed, but I was stunned to think of the time and pains that are expended by all of us in obtaining food, shelter, and raiment; and the time we put in on all else is much too little, which thought kept me awake, and my vigilance fretted me, forasmuch as I cannot do fair work save I am well rested.

It Seems to Me
By Heywood Broun

We want to add "Tramping on Life," by Harry Kemp (Boni & Liveright), to the list of current books which seem to us worth reading. This is an autobiographical novel by an adventurous person who is happily devoid of self-consciousness.

Nor does Mr. Kemp go in very much for reticence. He manages to be frank without seeming either abject or boastful. The early portion of the book, which deals with a boy's encounters with what are known as "the facts of life," seems to us to be exceptionally good. This should be prescribed reading for all radical young authors who plan to write a novel about sex. Kemp shows that it can be done without either whispering or shouting.

Another book which has interested us is "Shouts and Murmurs," by Alexander Woollcott. This is a collection of essays on plays and players, written originally in the Sunday columns of the Times and in various magazines. Of all American reviewers, Woollcott has undoubtedly the greatest passion for the theatre. He remains a barrier against the argument that no man can go to the theatre three or four times a week throughout a year and fail to become blasé and jaded. With him the magic of the playhouse has persisted. We are informed on reliable authority that during a busy season he saw one particular play which he happened to like no less than fifteen times.

Since our own temperament is much more crabbed we often find the judgments of Mr. Woollcott in violent disagreement with our own. To be sure, he has hates but he is moved to anger more slowly. Moreover, he has a distinct interest in acting as a thing apart from a play itself. A thoroughly bad play leaves us inconsolable, but Mr. Woollcott often manages to cheer himself up with the memory of some particular person in the cast who was not so evil as all the rest. "Shouts and Murmurs" deals chiefly with things which he has enjoyed and it is a zestful book full of grace and humor.

(Top) One of FPA's Saturday columns from October 1922. (Bottom) One of Broun's columns from the same time. Lippmann, on the *World*'s editorial page, considered the Round Table's logrolling on the Page Opposite "a shameful performance," as did other New York journalists. But the likes of Woollcott, Kaufman, Ross and Grant increasingly came to be of interest to the columns' readers.

If FPA was bothered by talk of log rolling, he never showed it.

His style is the particular bouquet I invite you to sniff. It never strikes a mean; it is either a gravy bomb, a bursting gladiolus, a palpitating missa cantata, an attack of psychic hydrophobia, or a Roman denunciation, unequivocal, oracular, flat and final . . . a style, in brief, that is purely emotional, and without a trace of the cool reflectiveness and contagious common sense suitable to criticism. . . . His appraisals of his feminine favorites read like a bewitched college boy writing and beseeching a lock of hair.

Nevertheless, Woollcott's readers reveled in the enthusiasms of his likes and hates, and in the early years of the Round Table, that readership steadily increased. In 1922, Frank Munsey offered him $15,000 a year to leave the *Times* for the *Herald,* and Woollcott happily obliged.

The charge against them all was logrolling, and Adams was particularly defenseless against it. Like Broun and Woollcott, Adams filled his column with more sparkle than light; unlike them, he had no particular subjects to cover. His columns were filled with and by his friends, their contributions to his columns and his accounts of time spent with them. He continually gave favorable notice to the books and plays his friends wrote, and he gave them space in his column to do the same for each other. As Newman Levy wrote in an unpublished biography of Adams: "Within the rules of wit and technical proficiency, the column was the house organ of a congenial coterie." Morrie Ryskind carried on a courtship through "Conning Tower" contributions about his lover. Edna Ferber wrote a poem for the column that was intended solely to plug *The Girls.* Levy himself advertised his friend Gilbert Gabriel's first novel, *Jiminy and Her Lost Sonnets,* by writing a rondeau that ended, "Buy *Jiminy.*" Adams was unapologetic for this aspect of his column, saying only that "friendships are first found through admiration of work, rather than the other way about."

Those first years of the Round Table were inarguably a swirl of success, publicity, mutual admiration and the happy coincidence of various self-interests, for they were all patently in the same business. FPA was far from alone in lending visibility to his friends. Woollcott and Benchley and Parker (filling

The Log Rollers

The Leaning Tower

Whatever greatness you achieve
And though your writings dodge the tomb,
You're out of luck—you get me, Steve!—
If you use who instead of whom.

DIARY OF OUR SHAM PEPYS

Saturday.— Rose early and to breakfast at a publick with Reginald Winerath, the barrytone, and speaking of this and that he said that he wished a notice in the publick journals of his consett, but I said naught until we had settled this boat's reckoning, when I could not loss him, such a softie am I. So in my petrol waggon to Mistress Bridget's, the washerwoman, and she charming albeit chiding me for my tardiness in bringing the wash, the which I deserved. Then to my office but unable to do my stint, what with some thief having made off with my pastepot and shears and leaving me helpless. So to luncheon with A Woolkott, the critick, and about to cast for the account when came Harold Nell Write, the novelist, and joined us so that we did not cast the dice after all. Then to my office again and finding my tools returned quickly despatched my labours. To dinner with H. Un script, the poet, at Mistress Greysa's and a right merry gathering, and all marvelling at his wit which surpriseth even me. Then in a cab with T. O O Loose, the painter, to Webster Hall, where was a reception and ball of the Reformed Second Story Workers' Association, and in a daze at the splendour of the gathering, what with fair ladies and bright jewells. Leaving at four found none who might convey me and so home by publick omnibus and to bed, grieving over my improvidence, the which bids fair to see me end in a poorhouse.

To Who It May Concern

Doubtless there may have been two better books written lately than Don Marquis' "Tom and Jerry" and "Joys of Inland Living" by Christopher Morley, but if there have been any such they have escaped notice—and will continue to escape.

This bard a laurel wreath bestows
On every author who he knows—
Intimately.

DULCINEA SEES THE LIGHT

Dulcinea believes literature has reached its zenith; a renaissance of good will, she calls it, if you get what she means.

"The spirit of noblesse oblige among the writing craft is most significant," she says. "It shows a change for the better in public taste, like the growing popularity of police dogs.

"The Olympian columnists go out of their way to help us everyday mortals in a workaday world, who used to be so puzzled about what to read," she muses.

"F. P. A. tells of every good book Don Marquis writes. And that darling Kit Morley keeps us posted on F. P. A.'s works. And one can find such enthusiastic comment on Kit Morley's books in Don Marquis' column. Isn't it wonderful how those great men appreciate each other? It simplifies everything for us. And so modest! So modest! Never a word about themselves, always someone else. Such good taste! Delightful! Isn't it delicious? But you must excuse me now I have to run along—to Brentano's. Ta' Ta! Don't take any wooden money."

As the log is rolled, so are the saps inclined.

Suggestion for literary tourists: see Park Row first.   *With no apologies to*
F. P. A.

This funny and pointed parody of FPA's column was probably written by a committee of Round Tablers in the *Life* office. As the "To Who It May Concern" item makes clear, the charge of logrolling was not confined to the Round Table. The habit of mutual address, as it were, was established among New York columnists long before the war.

George Jean Nathan, his criticism of Woollcott notwithstanding, was also reputed to have an ingenue mistress to promote on Broadway.

in on occasion) reviewed plays by Kaufman and Connelly and performances by their friends. FPA kept all of the Round Table names in the paper. At *Life,* Benchley and Sherwood returned the compliment with an annual parody of FPA's column called "The Leaning Tower." They also hired Kaufman and Connelly to do a humorous monthly calendar of historical and not so historical events. FPA and Heywood Broun wrote about each other and their mutual friends in the *World* (to which they and Woollcott were eventually lured by higher pay), and they reviewed each others' books. (In what amounted to a parody, Broun finally decided to skip the middle man and reviewed his own first novel himself.) All the while, Pemberton and Toohey were scoring beats every day by shuttling Round Table quips to columnists who were not among the invited—Woollcott's nemesis, S. Jay Kaufman, among them.

In that sense, the Round Table was joined to a grand new reality fabricated for the Twenties by business and its handmaiden, "public relations." According to a selective survey by Silas Bent in 1926, New York newspapers probably drew at least half of all local stories from press agents, often bothering only to replace the publicist's letterhead with a headline. As Bent concluded, editors had grown accustomed to accepting handouts during the war, in which journalism was all but annexed to the AEF's G-2 office. The board of the Associated Press had declared baldly in 1917 that "for the duration . . . the responsibility we have as citizens must outweigh our responsibility as news gatherers." Even before that, with the success of the muckrakers, businessmen had begun hiring press agents to counteract negative publicity and build positive corporate images. By 1920, public relations had become a way of American life and livelihood; ham-fisted Barnumesque methods had given way to surveys and polls, and a newborn "science" began to call itself "the engineering of consent." The patina of science was, of course, just that; in fact, a cynical new game of thought-shaping was born. The press agents learned to sell baking soda by hawking the dangers of self-rising flour, bricks by blasting terra cotta, bacon by urging hearty breakfasts, hairnets by showing the depravity of bobbed hair. Too often the publicists were able to persuade syndicated columnists to devote space to such sophistries for a sizable clandestine fee.

Among the actresses allowed to frequent the Round Table were: Margalo Gillmore (top, left), who was a successful Broadway actress in 1919 and Marc Connelly's girl friend; Ruth Gordon (bottom, left), whom Woollcott had dubbed "ever so gay as Nibs" in the Maude Adams *Peter Pan* of 1915 and who was married to Gregory Kelly; Helen Hayes (bottom, right), who won their hearts in *To the Ladies* and came to parties on the arm of Charles MacArthur; and Tallulah Bankhead (top, right), who was known as the Great Maw for her habit of dancing around the table picking up scraps of food in her lean days of the early 1920s.

FPA played with the Round Table mainly at night and on weekends because of his schedule at the *World,* but he was still able to serve as first trumpet of the Round Table's activities to the outside world.

No one had to pass money under the Round Table to get his name in the papers. That was just one of the privileges of membership. At the same time, the many actresses who came to the Round Table on the arms of press agents were probably not seeking just to match wits. As Ben Hecht wrote in his biography of Charles MacArthur, Woollcott "could snarl, pout, rage, insult everybody like a true monarch and withal . . . could get your name in the paper . . ." David Wallace, the only press agent besides Pemberton and Toohey allowed there, was by all accounts tolerated only for his contacts among actresses—ladies with whom several of the Algonquin men were not averse to going out. One chorus girl who asked Woollcott whether she should have an affair with Broun was advised: "My dear, I can think of no way an aspiring young actress can receive so much free publicity." Which is not to suggest any explicit bargains were struck, only that no one cared to draw the line between private life and public role. If it bothered Percy Hammond and George Jean Nathan that the Round Table critics ate daily with press agents and actors and actresses (and it did), it bothered Woollcott not at all and never had. In 1915, when the *Times* sent him to Europe to educate himself on theater in London and on the Continent, Burns Mantle lectured him at length on the perils of associating with actors and actresses. Next day, Woollcott kept his appointment for tea with Sarah Bernhardt. He maintained then and later that friendships would not color his opinions, that the Algonquin group in particular met for fellowship and fellowship alone. Even to his Round Table friends, however, the drift of his reviews proved otherwise.

Quite naturally, the more the Round Table expanded, the more copy it provided—for their own columns and others'. Less obvious were the increasing personal demands that growing visibility would make.

In 1921, the Thanatopsis Literary and Inside Straight Club was born. John Peter Toohey had already managed to change the irregular, pickup poker game of various Algonquinites into a regular weekly game in his own apartment, and when Frank Case perceived the obvious advantage of having both the Round Table and its gaming annex at his hotel, he gave them free use of

BACK SCRATCHING AT THE ALGONQUIN
FROM AN OLD ENGRAVING BY JOHN HELD JR MADE IN 1926

After seeing *To the Ladies,* FPA gave his readers the Round Table reaction to such charges of logrolling as John Held's (above): In "The Diary of Our Own Samuel Pepys" he wrote, "So to an inn and met G. Kaufman and M. Connelly, and I said, You boys are good playwrights and are doing what Mr. Ade should have done, and I said, Let us set at rest this talk of Logrolling, so I shall say, Your play is rotten, and to show how fair you are, you say in your paper I am a prince. . . . But about Logrolling there is this to be said : that friendships are first formed through admiration of work, rather than the other way about." Edna Ferber, who received little commendation from the Round Table critics, said logrolling had never existed. "Far from boosting one another, they were actually merciless if they disapproved," she wrote in her autobiography. Public disapproval of each other was rare, however, as the authors of "The Leaning Tower" took pains to make clear, and "Fannie Hurst," as Woollcott called Ferber, was one of few who pretended otherwise.

Neysa's real name was Marjorie; she had it changed on the advice of a numerologist, in the interest of her career. She wrote a column on numerology herself for a short time in the 1920s—until she discovered that people were heeding her advice.

a suite on the second floor. The Thanatopsis game thereafter became a Saturday-night event for the players—and a Monday-morning event for New York newspaper readers. This led to a wholly new strain in the Round Table lexicon: readers were treated to accounts of "loser's sleeping sickness, or, Broun's disease," to Kaufman's decision to "fold my tens and silently steal away." Stakes were still fairly low, but the game's public visibility was high.

Also in 1921, the salon of magazine illustrator Neysa McMein opened to the Round Table crowd as it had been open before only to the group's best-known members. Like Woollcott, McMein was an unabashed stargazer who attached herself romantically to H. G. Wells, Charlie Chaplin, Feodor Chaliapin and others both before her marriage and after. Her self-introduction to FPA in 1916 was characteristic: she turned up unannounced at his office and presented him with a bunch of sweet peas. Beginning the next day, she appeared regularly in his column as one of many "young damsels" he escorted to dinner and theater. She was, as a contemporary put it, "a tart . . . a professional beau catcher, that one," and, again like Woollcott, her principal requirement of those she courted or who courted her was born or acquired status. For those she liked, she was not above some revisionism. The man she married, John Baragwanath, was a mining engineer who had worked in South America, and his father had been a Methodist minister. When Neysa described him to her friends, that information was magically transformed. "He's a Latin American," she would say. "His father is a minister to Washington from one of those countries." In a novel about the Algonquin group called *Entirely Surrounded,* Charles Brackett describes his Neysa character as one who "would always be where the sunshine was warm."

Neysa was much more a creature of her decade than Woollcott was. Her pastel portraits caught a distinctive look on canvas—the look of the placidly sophisticated ingenue, a woman whose freedom to be sophisticated Neysa had helped win in the suffrage movement. And no matter who the model, her portraits finally resembled no one more than herself. She was a hard and prolific worker; even during the afternoon gatherings at her apartment, she continued to paint, which proves either that her concentration was extraordinary or that little was

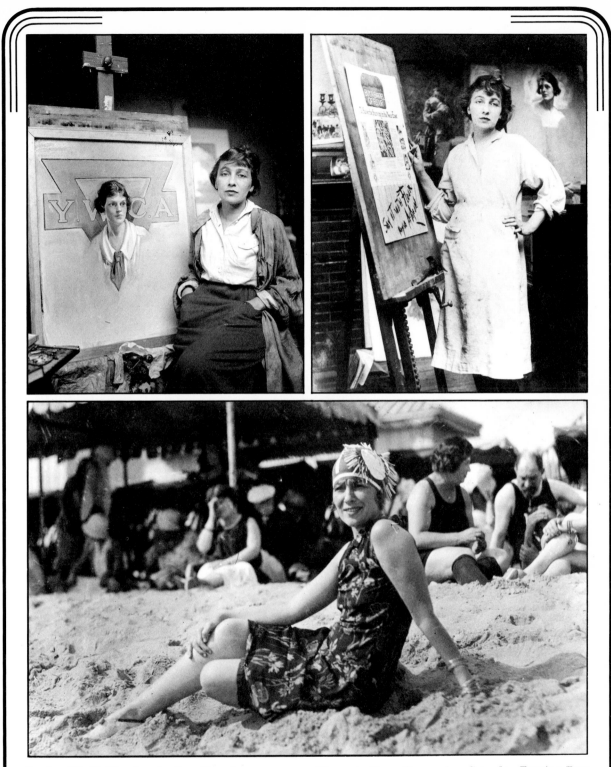

During World War I and after, Neysa's career was leavened by commissions from the U.S. government, the YMCA (top, left), the Near East War Relief (top, right) and U.S. savings bonds. She was also a YMCA entertainer during the war. By 1920, she had established herself as a commercial artist, doing covers for *Woman's Home Companion, Saturday Evening Post* and other magazines. Woollcott credited her with "an insatiable, childlike appetite for life," and she lost none of that appetite after her marriage in 1923 to John Baragwanath. (Bottom) Neysa in a 1924-vintage one-piece bathing suit in Palm Beach.

necessary. No doubt it was her style and the style manifest in her subjects that drew editors' eyes to her work in the first instance, but gradually her signature itself became a sought-after quantity. She was selling not just a picture but a status symbol, a remnant of the frenzied, hair-down playground of her celebrity-filled atelier.

McMein and Woollcott both loved to court the celebrated, but their strategies were opposite. Neysa paid hardly any attention to her guests, except that, as Noël Coward remembered, "when they arrived or left, with a sudden spurt of social conscience she would ram a paintbrush into her mouth and shake hands with a kind of disheveled politeness." Edmund Wilson's "literary vaudeville" blossomed at Neysa's as nowhere else. In a magazine profile of McMein, Woollcott remembered her parties as "wildly variegated":

> Over at the piano Jascha Heifetz and Arthur Samuels may be trying to find what four hands can do in the syncopation of a composition never thus desecrated before. Irving Berlin is encouraging them. Squatting uncomfortably around an ottoman, Franklin P. Adams, Marc Connelly and Dorothy Parker will be playing cold hands to see who will buy dinner that evening. At the bookshelf, Robert C. Benchley and Edna Ferber are amusing themselves vastly by thoughtfully autographing her set of Mark Twain for her. In the corner, some jet-bedecked dowager from a statelier milieu is taking it all in, immensely diverted. Chaplin or Chaliapin, Alice Duer Miller or Wild Bill Donovan, Father Duffy or Mary Pickford —any or all of them may be there.

For those who wanted it, much more than tea could be had on most days. Neysa's bathtub gin was a renowned admixture of grain alcohol, glycerine, distilled water and oils of lemon and coriander. More often than not, the fellowship at some point during the party would accompany Broun as he bellowed out his favorite drinking song:

> The mist on the glass is congealing,
> 'Tis the hurricane's icy breath
> And it shows how the warmth of friendship
> Grows cold in the clasp of death.
> Stand, stand to your glasses steady
> And drink to your sweetheart's eyes. . . .

The season of 1921–1922 was one of seemingly unclouded gaiety and glory for the Algonquin group, to which FPA's Saturday column, "The Diary of Our Own Samuel Pepys," gave a running testament:

> . . . *So to the baseball game with D. Stewart . . . thence to G. Kaufman's, and played cards, and lost so little that H. Ross said it was a moral victory . . . So to H. Broun's, where a great party and merry as can be, and we acted a play, J. Toohey being the most comickal of all; but I loved Mistress Dorothy Parker the best of any of them, and loathe to leave her, which I did not do till near five in the morning . . . then after to R. Sherwood's to play at cards, and an amusing game we had of it save for the long and dreary recital of a story of H. Broun's wherein he told of the high cost of transporting provisions and ended it with "Cartage delenda est," a feeble jape at best . . . so in the snow to where A. Woollcott was having a party for the old A.E.F. and a gay party too . . . So to luncheon and met there John Weaver the poet, and much serious talk, and we cast dice for the reckoning, and he paid for mine and for H. Ross's too. . . . and so to F. Case's, where we fell to cards, and as merry an evening as I ever had, and Rob Benchley come in to watch and did most comickal anticks ever I saw in my life, what with imitating a cyclone and a headwaiter . . . so to H. Miller's again and played till two in the morning, and all very gay on the street and I threw three snowballs at A. Woollcott, who chased me and washed my face in the snow, but not by strength but by weakening me with causing me to laugh at his anticks and crude remarks . . . Saw too Miss Mary Pickford . . . And in came D. Fairbanks . . . and so to dinner with R. Benchley and Mistress Dorothy . . . and I fell in love with Miss Helen Hayes for a few minutes, and so home, at near four in the morning. But I made a vow that I shall go to bed early forever after this.*

It is only a small selection of Adams's entries from the fall to the spring of that year, and a smaller selection of all the accountings of Round Table play to which New York was treated. For the expanding and movable party that was the Round Table, these were heady times indeed. Success seemed assured to those who did not already have it, and success, it turned out, was every bit as much fun as they had dreamed it could be. The Round Table had become a magnet. Edna Ferber, more famous and more successful than any of

Edna Ferber (left, in about 1916) was more prodigious by far than the writers of the Round Table, but all of the Round Table critics except for FPA ignored her writing or damned it with faint praise.

them at the time, became furious with Woollcott when he turned up late for a dinner party, declaring herself "resentful and hurt" with his "crude and disappointing" performance. Then, to a letter of late 1921, after making clear she would expect him to turn up promptly from then on, she added a meek postscript: "Could I maybe lunch at the Round Table once?"

Determinedly now, they were glorying in their public profiles, playing happily to a city and a decade that seemed to be there for them alone. Their clothes were uniforms, emblems of style: Woollcott sported a cape and top hat to opening nights; Dorothy Parker came to be known for her splendiferous spring hats; Benchley and Stewart made an annual harvest-time ritual of buying derbies at Brooks; Marc Connelly bought an Inverness; Neysa played hostess in pastel chalk dust; Heywood Broun made a virtue of his dishabille, which made Woollcott think of him as "an unmade bed." More than ever, they began to honor their ambitions for each other and themselves in mutually beneficial antics outside their inner circle.

It was, for example, to help Sherwood sell a film script to director Rex Ingram, whom the *Life* film critic had befriended, that a dinner party was arranged at Delmonico's restaurant for Ingram, his wife Alice Terry and some of the Round Table regulars—Connelly and Margalo Gillmore, Parker, Benchley and Mary Brandon, a young actress whom Sherwood was courting at the time. Sherwood's co-conspirators were invited in order to show Ingram that Sherwood was well connected and not likely to sell his scenario cheaply—and to win the heart of Miss Brandon, who, however, egocentric and petulant, was nevertheless susceptible to a certain awe of Sherwood's friends and quite aware of what their friendship might mean to her languishing career. Nothing quite worked out the way Sherwood planned: Ingram's wife, at Parker's gentle urging, became terribly drunk on pousse-cafés and kept shuttling off on Parker's arm to the powder room; Ingram, it turned out, had just given up movie making and was going off to the Riviera to paint and relax; Mary Brandon turned bellicose whenever she felt left out of the conversation. Ingram finally fell asleep at the banquet table, and Gillmore joined Terry and Parker in the ladies' room.

Woollcott gloried in his notoriety, as suggested in his pose for James Abbe in 1923 (above). Perhaps his first and best lesson about the value of publicity and a high public profile came when the Shuberts locked him out of first nights before the war. The New York *Times* took the Shuberts to court and covered the case dil- igently, and although the paper lost its case, Woollcott came out of it as the city's most talked-about critic. "They threw me out," Woollcott said at the time, "and now I'm basking in the fierce white light that beats upon the thrown." Later the Shuberts relented—for the sake of publicity.

When Irving Berlin (left) hired Benchley to appear in his Music Box Revue, he prompted not only Benchley's taking an apartment in Manhattan but also his gradual and regretted development into a stage "personality."

To allow Sherwood some privacy in which to calm Mary Brandon, Benchley and Connelly strolled out to the balcony of the restaurant, which overlooked Fifth Avenue. Standing there in the spring air in evening clothes watching dusk settle over the city, Benchley took a puff on his cigarette, gazed at the pedestrians passing by below them, and remarked, "These are some of the peasant class, I presume?" It was all Connelly needed. As he wrote in his memoir:

> *I stepped to the balcony rail, and raising a commanding hand, shouted, "People, people!"*
>
> *Benchley looked at me with only mild curiosity as pedestrians, motorists and bus passengers all craned their necks upward. I cried out, "Your new prince."*
>
> *Without a flicker of hesitation, Benchley stepped forward to the balustrade. He lifted his hands to silence unshouted cheers, then, as smoothly as though he had gone over the speech with an equerry, he assured his listeners in broken German that he did not want them as a conquered people to feel like slaves under a yoke but as chastened human beings aware that their future depended on the acceptance of a regime which they might resent but that would do its best to govern them in a kindly fashion. Benchley promised that as soon as they evidenced self-restraint, he would order curfews lifted, begin freeing political prisoners, and in time restore to qualified Americans the right to vote for local officials.*
>
> *"And now," he concluded, "my prime minister and I will retire to discuss matters of state. And you have all been so cute, next Saturday night I will permit fireworks and dancing in the streets."*

Their legend was made in such moments, and their group life came more and more to be a *festschrift* of them; only the high points counted, the best stories, the heartiest laughs. The rest was repressed or ignored or swept into their famous cracks. Still, their wit, however evasive it could sometimes be, held to a single constant: it reflected nothing better than themselves.

In the weeks and months after Benchley's address to the populace, the Round Table attracted more public attention than ever before. The entire group —actors, actresses, columnists and critics—wrote and acted in a one-night show for select theater friends called *No Sirree,* which other celebrities reviewed for

NO SIRREE!

An Anonymous Entertainment
by the Vicious Circle of the
Hotel Algonquin

49th STREET THEATRE
SUNDAY EVENING, APRIL 30th 1922

(Theatre by courtesy of the Messrs. Shubert)

Spirit of the American Drama .... Heywood Broun

OPENING CHORUS

Alexander Woollcott, John Peter Toohey, Robert C. Benchley,
George S. Kaufman, Marc Connelly and Franklin P. Adams

"THE EDITOR REGRETS——"

Mabel Cenci .... Marc Connelly, '25
George Medeci .... J. M. Kerrigan, '26
A Composer-Author .... Donald Ogden Stewart, '25
Dante .... Harold Gould, '28
An Average Male Reader .... Henry Wise Miller, '22
An Average Female Reader .... Mary Brandon, '30
Venice at the time of Dante. The editorial offices of "Droll Tales," a popular
twice-a-month magazine which flourished at that period.

THE FILMLESS MOVIES
Baron Ireland and F. P. A.

THE GREASY HAG
An O'Neill Play in One Act
CAST
(In the order of appearance)

*Elizabeth Inchcape, known as Coal-Barge Bessie, a retired
water-front prostitute* .... John Peter Toohey
The Murdered Woman .... Ruth Gillmore
First Agitated Seaman .... George S. Kaufman
Second Agitated Seaman .... Alexander Woollcott
Third Agitated Seaman .... Marc Connelly
Scene

Vote for One	Backroom of Billy the Bishop's saloon, near Coentie's Slip, New York.
	Firemen's forecastle on a freighter bound east from Rio.

Time—The present.
Incidental music by Arthur H. Samuels

HE WHO GETS FLAPPED

With Robert E. Sherwood and the following ingenues: June
Walker, Winifred Lenihan, Juliet St. John-Brenon, Tallulah
Bankhead, Mary Kennedy, Ruth Gillmore, Lenore Ulric
Helen Hayes and Mary Brandon.

BETWEEN THE ACTS

The Manager .... Brock Pemberton
The Manager's Brother .... Murdock Pemberton
And the following first nighters: Dorothy Parker, Alice Duer
Miller, Neysa McMein, Beatrice Kaufman, Jane Grant, Heywood Broun, Alexander Woollcott, Robert C. Benchley,
George S. Kaufman, Marc Connelly, Kelcey Allen, Arthur
Bachrach.

"JOHNNY WEAVER," a Ballad
Sung by Reinald Werrenrath

BIG CASINO IS LITTLE CASINO
A Samuel Shipman Play
IN THREE ACTS

James W. Archibald, a Rich Man .... John Peter Toohey
Dregs, a Butler .... Alexander Woollcott
Mr. Harper, a Broker .... J. M. Kerrigan
John Findlay, a Young Attorney .... George S. Kaufman
O'Brien, a Detective .... Franklin P. Adams
Margaret, Archibald's Daughter .... Mary Kennedy
A Convict .... Marc Connelly
The Broker's Boy .... David H. Wallace
The Governor of New York .... Robert E. Sherwood
Guests ...... { Alice Duer Miller / Neysa McMein / Jane Grant }

SYNOPSIS OF SCENES
ACT I—The Home of James W. Archibald.
ACT II—The same. A week later.
ACT III—A Wall Street Office. Two days later.
Offstage Music by J. Heifetz

INTERMISSION

MARC CONNELLY
"That Somewhat Different Cornettist"
—in—
"A NIGHT AT FRANK CAMPBELL'S"
Scene—Frank Campbell's.   Time—Night.

Z O W I E
or The Curse of an Akins Heart
A ROMANZA IN ONE ACT
"Nor all your piety and wit."—*From the Persian.*
CAST
(in the order of appearance)

Marmaduke LaSalle, a stomach specialist ...... John Peter Toohey
Lady friend of LaSalle's .... Neysa McMein
Another lady friend of LaSalle's .... Louise Closser Hale
Dindo, a wandering busboy .... J. M. Kerrigan
Zhoolie Venable, a suppressed desire* .... Ruth Gillmore
Mortimer Van Loon, a decayed gentleman ...... George S. Kaufman
Archibald Van Alstyne, a precisionist ...... Alexander Woollcott
Lemuel Pip, an old taxi-driver .... Harold W. Ross
Scene—A Capitol Lunch.   Time—Printemps, 1922.
* Suppressed in Humansville, Mo., sometime in April, 1908.
Offstage Music by J. Heifetz

MR. WHIM PASSES BY
An A. A. Milne Play

Cynthia .... Helen Hayes
Nigel .... Sidney Blackmer
Uncle Tertius .... J. M. Kerrigan
The scene is the morning room at The Acacias, Wipney-cum-Chiselickwick.

SONG: "KAUFMAN AND CONNELLY FROM THE WEST"

BEATRICE HERFORD
—in—
"The Algonquin Girl"

FINALE
by the entire company

GOLDEN PTG. SERVICE, N. Y.

The *No Sirree* program for some reason does not include the most important act of the night—Benchley's "Treasurer's Report"—and the content of the other acts has been lost, since no complete script was ever written. From Laurette Taylor's review, however, we know that "Ruth Gillmore [Margalo's sister] did a splendid imitation of Ethel Barrymore . . . Helen Hayes gave a splendid imitation of an English flapper . . . Jascha Heifetz played off-stage music off-key . . . Franklin P. Adams gave a humorous impression of an Irish detective called O'Brien." Still, Taylor concluded: "I would advise a course of voice culture for Marc Connelly, a new vest and pants that meet for Heywood Broun [and] I would advise them all to leave the stage before they take it up."

Sherwood with his chorus in "He Who Gets Flapped" —from left, Constance Binney, Helen Hayes, June Walker, Ruth Gillmore and Lenore Ulrich. Missing from the picture are Juliet St. John Brenon, Tallulah Bankhead, Mary Kennedy, who later married Deems Taylor, and Mary Brandon, who married Sherwood. Their number was Dorothy Parker's "Everlastin' Ingenue Blues," which ran: "We've got the blues, we've got the blues/We believe we said before we've got the blues/We are little flappers, never growing up/And we've all of us been singing/Since Belasco was a pup...."

the next morning's papers—Laurette Taylor for the *Times,* Wilfred Lackaye for the *Tribune.* In *No Sirree,* Benchley delivered his now-famous "Treasurer's Report," and Irving Berlin, who was in the audience, hired him to repeat it eight times a week for $500 a week in his Music Box Revue. That success quite literally changed the course of Benchley's life by taking him into the acting career he would always regret and sealing his status as a public entertainer.

There was a good deal of backstairs talk after *No Sirree* about how those Algonquin people were going too far in their mutual admiration and exclusivity. Burton Rascoe wrote that they were getting "unduly exhibitionistic and quite as vulgar as if they had consented to demonstrate fountain pens in drugstore windows free of charge, for the chance it gave them to be seen." But if they were worried about such a reaction, they gave no sign of it; as some of them sailed together to Europe a few weeks later, those left behind, particularly Kaufman, Connelly and Parker, began thinking about doing another Vicious Circle production with the idea of making this one more professional, profit making and even, perhaps, a hit.

The unlonesome travelers—Woollcott, McMein, Deems Taylor, Donald Ogden Stewart and Jane Grant—met Edna Ferber in Paris, and Woollcott took them all for a tour of his beloved battlefields around Château-Thierry, a mad carouse in "a very smart town car (rented)," Ferber remembered in her 1939 autobiography. "This romping was, as a matter of fact, our protection against the dismal sights we saw . . . hundreds and thousands of little white crosses . . . row on row. . . . You had only to read the names to realize that really nothing could be more democratic. Karl Bauers. Tony Mazzetti. Sam Johnson. Leo Cohn. Joyce Kilmer." Even Woollcott seemed subdued by the experience; Stewart found him "more human" than he had seemed in New York and was even inspired to begin an antiwar novel. But the mood of tranquil reflection would not hold. They found themselves rubbing elbows with "the Lost Generation but they were only playing hide-and-seek with life," Ferber concluded. "Berlin was prophetic enough for anyone who cared to read the writing on the wall," she wrote. "But we played craps with Woollcott."

When they came home in July, Woollcott moved into a house at 412 West Forty-seventh Street that he and Ross and Hawley Traux (Woollcott's Hamilton College friend) had begun to remodel around the time of *No Sirree,* and which soon became as much a meeting place for the crowd as Neysa's studio and the Thanatopsis and the Round Table itself had been before. The months of August and September 1922 were given over to the planning of a gala housewarming for all of their friends and, at Woollcott's urging, some of the celebrities he thought could be lured by virtue of the group's enhanced public stature. Jane Grant remembered in her book that Woollcott took over the planning and recruiting of guests from the start.

> *"Let's see now: Bob could start the ball rolling with one of his monologues. He could even do The Treasurer's Report, Irving wouldn't object, but perhaps he'd better do something we haven't heard so many times. . . . Marc can begin with his Spartacus, or Johnnie could read one of his poems or there's [John] Kerrigan—but we've got to have something besides monologues. Well, then, Bob [Sherwood] can sing his Red Robin song, that would be different, and George [Gershwin] and Irving will help out with their songs. We could have a skit about the Thanatopsis—George and Marc were talking the other day about doing one. If they haven't time Toohey can get to work on it and I'll polish it up."*
>
> *"I'd hoped we could have girls," I put in.*
>
> *"My God! Females! Huh*, performing *females," he sneered. "We gave you your chance in the* No Sirree—*and before that."*
>
> *"Your little dream princesses won't be happy if you leave them out of this."* A small but decorative coterie of young actresses resorted to ingenious tricks to beguile Aleck into a mellow mood, the better for him to judge their acting ability. An easy prey to their wiles, he was not unaware of the potency of my remark.
>
> *"All right," and he returned to his list. "Well, there's Ethel [Barrymore]—I'll put her down for that reading from* The Twelve Pound Look; *we might get Bea [Lillie] and Gertie [Lawrence]; and—a wonderful number—Peggy [Wood] and Sidney [Blackmer] will give their Romeo and Juliet. With Peggy doing her scene from your balcony and the guests in the garden, it should be the hit of the evening. . . ."*

Traveling companions Grant and Woollcott. Grant, like the rest of the party, found Woollcott to be nicer in Europe than in New York, but he had elbowed his way into the house that she, Ross and Truax were remodeling, and she returned from that trip with mixed feelings of happy anticipation and dread.

Aleck . . . contracted to snare the Great Neck crowd, which included the Ring Lardners, the Grantland Rices, the Phil Boyers; the group that went on Sunday to Hilda and Crosby Gaige's in Peekskill, or the theatrical and literary people accustomed to motoring out to Lloyd Griscom's in Syosset or Ralph Pulitzer's at Manhasset for croquet, badminton, tennis or other outdoor sports on the beautiful weekends. . . .

Only three weeks after their party, which was a great success—the hit of the evening was indeed Peggy Wood's Juliet, with Woollcott playing the offstage nurse—a second and even more glittering event took place: the wedding of Robert Sherwood and Mary Brandon, at which so many of the decade's great and near great were in attendance that the marriage was moved from the society pages of New York newspapers to the local news pages. The Round Tablers were there in force—Margalo Gillmore was maid of honor, and Connelly, Benchley, Woollcott and Frank Case were among the ushers—but what really drew the crowds to the Little Church Around the Corner on that October morning in 1922 was word that the reigning couple of American films would also be there: Douglas Fairbanks and Mary Pickford, friends Sherwood had made in his role as *Life's* film critic. After the ceremony, Anita Loos and her husband, John Emerson, hosted a reception for the newlyweds, and, according to Sherwood's biographer, John Mason Brown, "among the guests were the Booth Tarkingtons, Mary Pickford, the Louis Evan Shipmans . . . the F. Scott Fitzgeralds, the Morris Gests. . . . To Sherwood's delight, and Mary's, it was all glitteringly *Who's Who*." Unfortunately, and perhaps predictably, the wedding proved to be the high point of their marriage. As happens to those who marry when they are young and on the verge of fame, they both wedded façades: to Mary, Sherwood was the foremost film critic in America, which was true as far as it went; to Sherwood, Mary was the essence of femininity, all flapperish frivolity and alluring egocentricity. It was the kind of marriage Hollywood might have made—and then remade into an epic of fire-and-ice upheavals. In fact, however, Mary became a barely tolerated bore, according to most of Sherwood's friends who knew her at all well, spending all the money he made while saving her own, trading on his friendships quite openly, if without much success, and by her lavish

After the wedding, Sherwood and Mary posed with the most famous of their guests: the Booth Tarkingtons, Douglas Fairbanks and Mary Pickford. The Round Tablers seemed to be on to Mrs. Sherwood before Sherwood was. When she became pregnant, she talked of nothing else, and when she finally delivered a daughter, Parker sent a telegram saying: "Congratulations. We all knew you had it in you."

spending forcing him to hold on to his job at *Life* long past the time he knew he should be moving on to more substantial work. As Benchley and Connelly preceded the bride and groom down the aisle in the wedding procession, they sang softly to each other, "Will she come from the east where the Broadway peaches grow? Will she come from the north, the land of ice and snow?" The answer, for those who knew them both, was already clear, and the wedding, for all its glamour, was more than anything Sherwood's sentence to live out the 1920s in more light than warmth.

The week after the wedding, the Round Table presented its grown-up elaboration of *No Sirree:* a full-scale production called *The 49ers* with skits by Ring Lardner, Parker, Benchley, Kaufman, Connelly, Morrie Ryskind, Howard Dietz and others. The full script has not survived but some vintage fragments have, such as Lardner's unpublished playlet *The Tridget of Greva,* in which the only action is three men sitting in rowboats talking nonsense:

> Barhooter: *What was your mother's name before she was married?*
> Corby: *I didn't know her then.*
> Laffler: *Do they allow people to fish at the aquarium?*

Most of the revue was nonsequiturial. Parker and Benchley collaborated on a one-act "historical" drama called *Nero,* with Cardinal Richelieu presiding and muttering over a game of solitaire such trenchant comments as: "Many a mickle makes a muckle, but only God can make real maple syrup." The piece began with two French popular guards on patrol during the Revolution:

> First Guarde Populaire: *As you know, Citoyen, this is the month of Thermidor and the Place Louis Quatorze is running with blood. What do you make of it all?*
> Second Guarde Populaire: *Only time will tell.*

The playlet ended with the Giants winning the pennant and Generals Grant and Lee repeatedly exchanging swords.

More than anything, the audience was mystified. So completely idiosyncratic and inside was the strain of humor they were working that Frank Crowninshield remarked, "Maybe I missed something, but was it all supposed to be

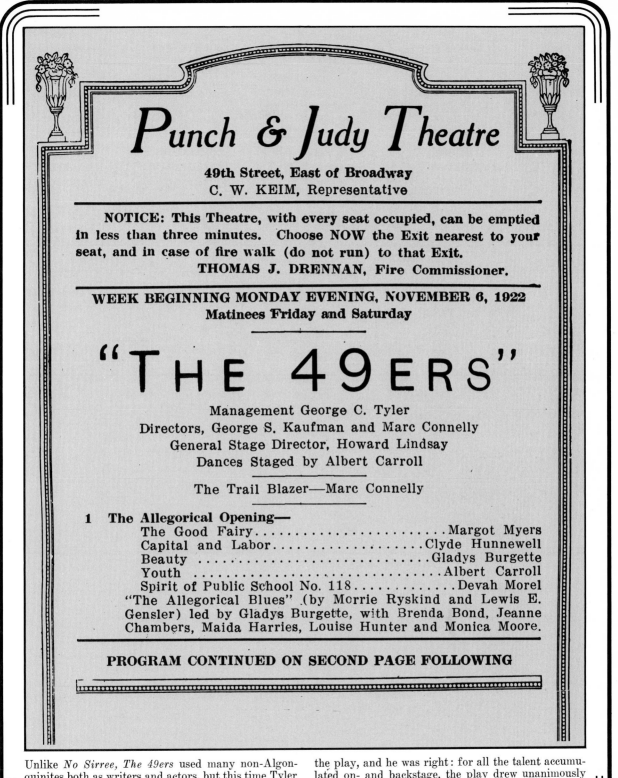

Punch & Judy Theatre

49th Street, East of Broadway
C. W. KEIM, Representative

NOTICE: This Theatre, with every seat occupied, can be emptied in less than three minutes. Choose NOW the Exit nearest to your seat, and in case of fire walk (do not run) to that Exit.
THOMAS J. DRENNAN, Fire Commissioner.

WEEK BEGINNING MONDAY EVENING, NOVEMBER 6, 1922
Matinees Friday and Saturday

"THE 49ERS"

Management George C. Tyler
Directors, George S. Kaufman and Marc Connelly
General Stage Director, Howard Lindsay
Dances Staged by Albert Carroll

The Trail Blazer—Marc Connelly

1 **The Allegorical Opening—**
The Good Fairy......................Margot Myers
Capital and Labor...................Clyde Hunnewell
Beauty ....Gladys Burgette
Youth ....Albert Carroll
Spirit of Public School No. 118............Devah Morel
"The Allegorical Blues" (by Morrie Ryskind and Lewis E. Gensler) led by Gladys Burgette, with Brenda Bond, Jeanne Chambers, Maida Harries, Louise Hunter and Monica Moore.

PROGRAM CONTINUED ON SECOND PAGE FOLLOWING

Unlike *No Sirree*, *The 49ers* used many non-Algonquinites both as writers and actors, but this time Tyler had to pay for the actors' services at their going rates, which were not low. Tyler had been reluctant to back the play, and he was right: for all the talent accumulated on- and backstage, the play drew unanimously bad notices and played to half-empty houses until it closed after fifteen performances.

THE REVIEWING STAND

By Alexander Woollcott

For the Minority, Indeed.

PUNCH AND JUDY THEATER—First bill of the Forty-niners, with sketches by Montague Glass, Heywood Broun, Franklin P. Adams, Ring Lardner, Robert C. Benchley, Dorothy Parker, George S. Kaufman, Marc Connelly, Morris Ryskind, Walt Kuhn, Howard Dietz, Bertram Blochy, Deems Taylor, Lewis Gensler and Arthur H. Samuels. In the company are May Irwin, Roland Young, Beryl Mercer, Sidney Toler, Denman Maley, Howard Lindsay and Ruth Gillmore.

An expectant audience packed the little Punch and Judy Theater last evening for the pre-release showing of "The Forty-niners," due to hold their first public revels there to-night. Here, we said, would be fine fooling. Here were some of the most gifted and most fantastic humorists of their time, summoned, for once in a way, to write their prankful whimsies under the thrall of no dull commercial manager and without a thought for that huge threatening, hydra headed half wit—the public. Here were Ring Lardner, Franklin P. Adams, George Kaufman, Marc Connelly, Heywood Broun, Robert C. Benchley, Dorothy Parker and Montague Glass, turned loose in a little theater and bidden to cut loose. My, what fun! And then it wasn't. It wasn't fun. Not at all.

It is not any too easy to say just why. It is true that there was hit or miss showmanship about it. It is true that, like that precious "Zuleika Dobson," of which any twenty pages was always enough for us, it ran too much in the single vein—rather like a dinner consisting of five courses of perfectly splendid lemon meringue pie. It is true that it seemed depressed rather than buoyed up by the person chosen to be its Balieff—none other than May Irwin, returning to town and floundering around between the scenes, quite hopelessly out of her element. There must have been more than one old timer out front last night who yearned to call out: "Dear old friend, push this foolish little show into the wings,

get a piano hoisted up and clear the old throat for "I'm Looking for That Bully Must Be Found," or "When Mr. Shakespeare Comes to Town."

After this melancholy admission that "The Forty-niners" plunged us into a very abyss of boredom it should immediately be admitted that there were gleams of engulfed and enshrouded gayety on which we stumbled from time to time. There was one patch of delightful nonsense by Benchley—tolerably well delivered by one Denman Maley. Also a moment or two of mad humor in a languid adventure in nonsense by Ring Lardner. Also a passable vaudeville sketch by Mr. Glass which was at least second rate. And a bright morsel of a sketch by Kaufman. Also a fair to middling travesty on all the musical comedies of the last twenty-five years—this last by Franklin P. Adams. But it came at a time when its facetiousness groaned under the extra burden of waking an already hopelessly bemused audience. Indeed it must be recorded that the one thoroughly entertaining episode in all the dozen numbers of the evening was a foolish little nursery imitation of an equestrienne act, done very much à la Chauve-Souris and credited by the program to one Walt Kuhn, of whom we never heard before.

Involved in the proceedings were several excellent actors, of whom Sidney Toler seemed the best equipped for goings on of the sort invoked. His cheerfully idiotic smile could be glimpsed from time to time through the fog that settled over an evening of which we carried away this as our most definite impression—a lot of extremely clever people being given too much rope, a lot of celebrated comedians of the printed page under orders to romp around in an elfin manner and not presenting a too edifying spectacle.

As we sneaked away disconsolate into the drizzling November rain there seemed to come to us across the wet housetops a strange and embarrassing sound. It was the sound of George V. Hobart—laughing himself sick.

Woollcott's rather ungenerous review of *The 49ers* no doubt owed something to the fact that he wasn't in it. (Tyler, unwilling to risk his investment on the performances of amateurs, replaced even Benchley in "The Treasurer's Report.") But the review also served to counter charges of logrolling and reflected the opinion that most critics had of the play: "a lot of extremely clever people," as Woollcott put it, "being given too much rope . . . and not presenting a too edifying spectacle."

A contemporary commentator celebrated the allure of the Round Table in 1923: "What more satisfying to us poor mortals than to gaze upon gods—especially intellectual gods—eating, and while eating, talking? At the Algonquin Round Table, Alexander Woollcott, with finger upraised, holds Horace Liveright spellbound, while to the extreme right F. P. A. listens cynically. Marc Connelly dogmatizes on Americana to Johnny Weaver, who throws up his hands protestingly. Next on the left, Heywood Broun and the spectacled Joe Kaufman, across the table, indulge in sad reflections on the failure of *The 49ers*. Behind, immaculately attired Host Case, explains to the elongated Bob Sherwood the futility of all things, especially of trying to squeeze in another chair at the table."

taking place in an insane asylum?'' The play's problems were only compounded by the fact that the producer, George Tyler, had insisted upon hiring May Irwin to emcee the show, an old-pro vaudevillian whose bag of laff-riot one-liners was precisely the wrong kind of warm-up for their off-the-wall revue. But, on the other hand, nothing could have saved it from collapse. The humor was inbred, manic. Its authors, clearly full of themselves, had all put their skits together in spare time, and some of the skits seemed to have been written in a giddy haze of alcohol, which is more than possible. It closed in late November after a losing two-week run.

In late 1922, the dues demanded by their greater fame began to be called in, as the Sherwood wedding and the failure of *The 49ers* gave partial testament. The boundary between the group's public life and its members' private lives seemed to be growing blurred. The Vicious Circle was no longer a group of talented young men and women reveling in each other's company for the fun of it, or even for the glory. What had been a loose-knit coupling of shared ambitions and insecurities was gathering into a self-propelling force in each of its members' ways of living and working. Few of them seem to have thought much about it then. They were, after all, helping to rid their generation of the tattered creeds of a world whose time had gone—all of them, that is, except for Woollcott, Ross and Adams, who had full calendars when it came to anything so remote. If some of the rest of them were riding the crest rather than leading it, that was nothing to be sneered at either. But as 1922 drew to a close, doubts were beginning to simmer among them about the Round Table's role in their lives and work, doubts that would begin increasingly to darken even the best of their times together.

RAISING ON A PAIR

It was a cold winter morning in January of 1923 when Emil Coué, the much-heralded prophet of positive suggestion, stepped off an ocean liner in New York Harbor and into a crowd of waiting reporters. His reputation had preceded him by months—even during the crossing a *World* headline proclaimed, "Rough Sea Sickens Many, Not Coué: Magic Words Triumph Over Waves"—and in a ten-day tour of the United States he made a small fortune telling throngs of people that everything from colds to nosebleeds to business reverses could be cured if only they would repeat with him a simple phrase: "Every day in every way I am getting better and better." He was feted by statesmen, swooned over by society ladies, touted in headlines; pictures of the kindly, bearded old gent appeared in scores of newspapers along with accounts of his "miraculous" cures. Dorothy Parker loved to fix on such fads—Ouija boards, Mah Jong, one-piece bathing suits, "Yes, We Have No Bananas." She loved them for their fleetingness, almost believed in them. But just then, in early 1923, something somber was settling over the city in general and Dorothy Parker in particular. William Bolitho wrote in the *World* that solo saxophones were taking jazz into a musical region that was "endlessly sorrowful and yet endlessly sentimental, with no past, no memory and no future." Dorothy Parker was suffering a broken love affair with Charles MacArthur, who was now being seen around town with Beatrice Lillie. At first, she was inconsolable; later, she grew resigned, but friends found it harder than ever to drag her away from the bar at Tony Soma's. News from the Coué expedition should at least have been entertaining—"Coué Says He Heals Love's Heartaches," read a *Times* headline— but somehow this new craze failed to excite her the way the others had, either positively or negatively.

On the second Sunday of 1923, as Coué was bringing his message to the American plains, Dorothy Parker found herself alone in her room on West Fifty-seventh Street with her small dog and her canary. Eddie had moved to Hartford not long before, and Parker had refused to go with him. "What in God's name would she do in Hartford?" Stewart asked John Keats years later. "Can you see her going to Hartford with Eddie Parker after she had begun to meet people like Benchley and Sherwood and FPA and Woollcott?" She thought to telephone

WIT'S END

Dorothy Parker in the mid-1920s. By then, she had begun ordering her soaps and perfumes from Cyclax of London, specifying the tuberose scent, which undertakers use on corpses (she must have learned the fact from the undertakers' trade journals to which she and Benchley subscribed). Eddie had gone to Hartford and left her in the apartment with her unhousebroken dog ("It's not *his* fault," she would say of the dog to visitors who wondered how she could live with the mess) and a canary she named Onan ("because he spills his seed upon the ground"). "I was sorry for her about Charley," Donald Ogden Stewart said, "because she did love him terribly. Goddamn it, she was suffering."

The Alps restaurant downstairs to send up some dinner, then went into the bathroom, found a razor Eddie had left behind and slashed both her wrists. The restaurant's delivery boy found her lying unconscious on the bathroom floor.

Only her closest friends in the Algonquin group went uptown to visit her at Columbia Presbyterian Hospital—Benchley, Broun and a couple of others. Those who made the trip found her with light-blue ribbons laced into bows around her wrists, and she showed them off as if they were diamond bracelets. It was all your fault, Benchley chided—you have to cut deep to do it right. Her only recorded comment on the matter was that Eddie hadn't even managed to keep his razors sharp.

Dorothy Parker with her ribbon bracelets: there could have been no more eloquent symbol of the unhappy pass at which the Algonquin wits now found themselves. Their *toujours-gai* spontaneity was unimpaired, but intimacy among them seemed all but impossible. Donald Ogden Stewart sensed it even as he reveled in the group's reflected glory. "I was never really at ease in this company," he wrote in his autobiography, "partly because of the constant strain of feeling obliged to say something funny, and partly because the atmosphere seemed to me to be basically unfriendly, too much of that dog-eat-dog."

For all their talk, there seems to have been little communication. Woollcott complained that Broun was impossible to know, that the death of the entire group would strike him as no more than a good news story. Charles Brackett said the same of Woollcott, that he would never befriend anyone whose life would not make a good magazine article. According to Sherwood's biographer, "Sherwood's friends finally had to admit that, though they had known him long and intimately and prized his friendship, they never quite felt they knew him well." FPA wrote in a magazine profile of Broun: "Although we were office-mates at the *Tribune* for years and I was his best man, I know little about him except for a few facts." And Dorothy Parker perhaps more than any of them suffered the constant fear of being rejected by those she granted access to her private self—a fear she fashioned into such a multifaceted personality that even her closest friends still disagree about what she was really like.

Alice Duer Miller (left, in the 1910s) outraged both her family and society by attending Barnard College and by working as a journalist. She ghosted wartime speeches for Woodrow Wilson and spent her last twenty years in Hollywood writing films for Goldwyn.

In Kaufman and Adams, keeping interpersonal distance seemed almost a matter of principle. Kaufman was as shy of sentiment as he was of physical contact. Marc Connelly remembered in 1975 that during their collaboration, "when it came to a sentimental scene, a love scene or just a piece of poignant dialogue, George would make me write it. Afterward, he wouldn't even give it the kind of close examination he would give to other kinds of scenes. He didn't seem to have the stomach for it." Beatrice, in the summer of 1928 on the Riviera, spent whole afternoons at the aquarium near Cap d'Antibes gazing at a tank of "sensitivos," tiny fish that retreat into a shroud of extra skin at the approach of anything alien. She said to Harpo Marx that they were "like so many people I know."

Adams's absence at Parker's bedside was also characteristic. Two of his closest Chicago friends, Joseph Wise (Rabbi Stephen Wise's brother) and Montague Glass, died of lingering diseases, and though they both asked to see Adams several times before they died, he refused to go. Parker had sensed something of that aloofness from the beginning of their friendship. In his Saturday "diary" column in late 1921, he wrote of a lovely evening with her and added: "She saith ere long I will chuck her aside like a withered nosegay, which is hard to promise one way or the other." In the event, they remained good friends, but given Parker's peculiar personality, their friendship could have persisted as much because of his coolness as in spite of it.

The ritual, Wilde-ish wit of the group and the distance they kept between them despite so much mutuality of interest and play evoke a pattern more Victorian than entirely modern, and that pattern seems to have been as real as it is apparent. Woollcott certainly was beckoned more to the Victorian period than his own time; his literary tastes and his public demeanor both give evidence of the fact. One of his best friends before the war and to the end of his life, and one of the senior members of the Round Table, was Alice Duer Miller, whose husband Henry Wise Miller was a prominent member and host of the Thanatopsis poker game. Mrs. Miller, who later became noted for her poem "The White Cliffs of Dover," had debuted in the social season of 1895. Although her career as a journalist and suffragist (she wrote a column in the *Tribune* called "Are Women People?") recommended her as something more than a socialite, it was clearly as much her pedigree as her rebellion against it that attracted Woollcott to her. In *All Our Lives*, her husband, who had Boston Everetts, Brooks and Frothinghams in his own family tree, wrote of the late-nineteenth-century high society in which his wife came to maturity, the world of her cousins the Livingstons, Van Rensselaers and Gracies:

> *The inner circle was a closed and organized entity. . . You had to be acceptable to a few social autocrats who would make or mar you. The prestige and the training did a great deal for you, and the society of a few hundred people who knew each other intimately and had nothing to do but amuse each other, and who brought that pursuit to a fine art, was a liberal education in itself. They were not intellectuals, they were the reverse of strenuous, but say what you please about them, no one ever had a better time.*

It could as well be a description of the Round Table's public pose.

Victorianism was perhaps the only shared characteristic of the Algonquinites' backgrounds, which were otherwise widely diverse. Woollcott grew up on a New Jersey commune modelled after Fourier's 19th-century phalanxes. Benchley, Broun and Sherwood all came from stolid WASP stock and Harvard educations. Kaufman and Adams were Midwestern Jews without college degrees. Ross was a high-school drop-out whose agnostic father was a failed silver prospector. Parker's Jewish father and bible-riffling Baptist stepmother tried to insulate their daughter with the prototypical upper-class young lady's strict schooling, which could not, of course, include college. But if Adams was most clearly of an earlier generation, all of them—possibly excepting Sherwood—were old enough to remember and to have experienced in full a nation confidently at peace with itself, the America before 1914, and to have been measured against, and chastened to subscribe to, the tenets of that passing era.

In that sense, the Round Table was a lost generation of its own sort. However young they were when they met in the Rose Room, they were a crucial few years older than the widely hailed generation of "flaming youth," which accounts for some of Adams's and Broun's coolness toward Fitzgerald's *succès de scandale, This Side of Paradise,* in 1920—and accounts as well for Dorothy Parker's cutting pieces about the obnoxious, headline-making advance of "flaming youth" in the *Saturday Evening Post* some years later. Not long before 1920, Benchley had been tithing his time to settlement houses, the Big Brother organization and other charitable endeavors, and until 1922 he held almost to a Temperance Union attitude toward drinking. Kaufman, Adams and Woollcott were also impatient with drinkers and remained so. Despite the great apparent commonalities between the libertine behavior of the Algonquin group and the heedlessness of Fitzgerald's generation, the difference between them is equally important. The Algonquinites' play could never be quite as free of the strictures and values of the old order as that of the men and women born just a few years later. However loud their laughter and determined their abandonment of old constraints, their cutting loose was less a generational given than an ominous but beckoning choice they made.

The reaction of the Algonquin men to the Lucy Stone League gives clear evidence of that counter-current. Ross putatively prompted his wife and Ruth Hale to co-found it because he was tired of hearing them tell each other how important it was for women to keep their maiden names. "Go hire a hall," he said, and in 1921 they did. Parker didn't join ("I married to change my name," she said once), but Neysa did, and the actresses of the Round Table, most of whom had kept their maiden names for professional purposes, were sympathetic. Despite all the feminist sentiment at the Round Table, however, and for all the moral support the group provided, the actual plight of women was of little concern to the men in the group, even when that plight was palpably demonstrated to them. Jane Grant, who was still holding her job as a *Times* reporter, was nevertheless saddled with all the cleaning chores at 412 West 47th Street; the Thanatopsis club often met there as many as eight or ten nights a month, leaving behind a heaping mess of full ash trays, half-empty glasses and mouldering food—the remnants of good times in which Grant took no part. Ruth Hale was informed by Frank Case one day that neither she nor any other women would be permitted to smoke in his lobby. "Then this one leaves," she said, but her years-long boycott of the hotel was seconded by no one. Chivalry, if nothing else, would seem to have demanded some sort of protest to Case.

All of the Algonquin men seem to have suffered from the sexual repressions

The infant Woollcott. His birth, he wrote, was "regarded as a family calamity. Aunt Julie told me once that she spent that day crying in her room as the least she could do."

commonly ascribed to the Victorian era, but none more so than Woollcott. The evidence of his homosexuality is presumptive, but he left ample evidence of real sexual confusion: his habit of delightedly dressing in his sister's clothing around puberty; his undergraduate fascination with the works of Krafft-Ebing and the Oscar Wilde scandal—and a confessional session with Anita Loos in the early 1920s. "Suddenly, he began to cry," she remembered in 1975. "He said he had lived with a great tragedy all his life—that he had always wanted to be a mother. He brought out some pictures of a college theatrical in which he was dressed as a woman and said, 'These were the happiest moments of my life.'" Miss Loos is, however, a somewhat biased observer. According to Marc Connelly, she was pointedly omitted from the Algonquin group "because we all knew she was a petty little *arriviste*." She is indeed virulent on the subject of the Round Table and Woollcott. Further, it would not have been beyond Woollcott to undertake such a scene in order to fabricate intimacy with Loos. In college, when classmates gave him the nickname "Putt" (for "putrid"), Woollcott took it as a compliment (or pretended to) and tried to enhance that image by affecting bizarre mannerisms and dress. It became a favorite undergraduate pastime to throw Woollcott into the campus fountain, and he picked fights with several of Hamilton's athletes, never winning and never expecting to. Woollcott's own explanation of his sexual life was that a case of mumps in 1916 had made him forever impotent (which, of course, mumps in adults does not do, although it may diminish sexual ambition or cause sterility).

Whatever his sexual orientation, Woollcott pursued various women avidly and in all apparent seriousness. Before the war, he fell into an arrangement with Jane Grant, then his colleague at the *Times*. She taught him to dance; in return, he took her to Hamilton alumni dances, where she hoped to meet eligible bachelors. For Woollcott, the arrangement became something more; for her, it never did. When she came to Paris during the war as a YMCA entertainer, he began to raise the notion of marriage with her. They were only tentative, half-joking references, and she laughed them off. But Woollcott persisted—until one night at Nini's in Montmartre, when she came with Woollcott and left with Ross. Ross and Grant were married in 1920.

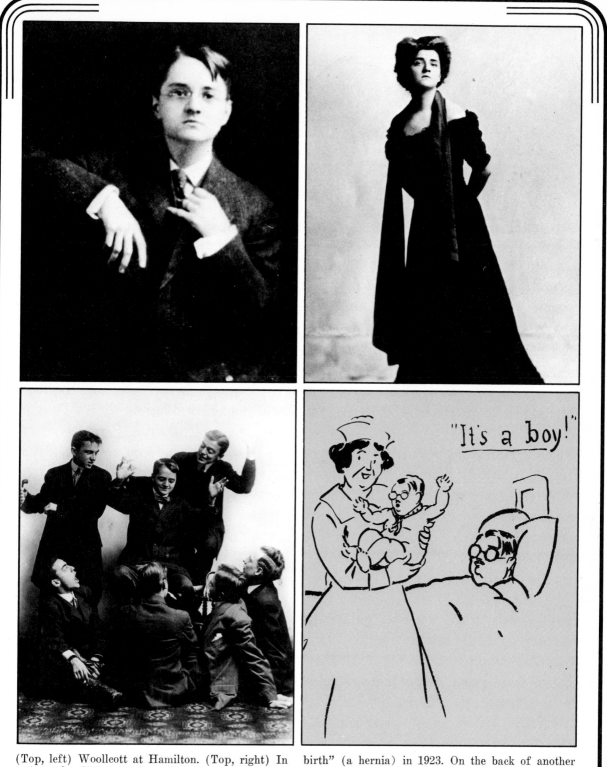

(Top, left) Woollcott at Hamilton. (Top, right) In costume for *Mabel the Beautiful Shopgirl*, the glee-club show he wrote for himself. (Bottom, left) Woollcott performing (middle, naturally) with the glee club. (Bottom, right) A card his housemates sent him when he went into the hospital for "chronic childbirth" (a hernia) in 1923. On the back of another picture of himself in drag at the age of seventeen, Woollcott wrote: "Under the influence of some intuitive yearning and Rose Field—At the instigation of Ivy Ashton Root—And by the Grace of God—THE PHALANX DUSE OF 1905."

Woollcott continued to declare throughout his life that marriage and parenthood were the ultimate proofs of humanity, and each of his several rejected proposals of marriage in later years—to Neysa McMein and at least three others—seemed only to redouble that belief. Perhaps as a recourse, he involved himself in the romances of his friends, helping to estrange them from one another with the same glee he took in getting them together. Parker's tragic love affair with MacArthur was Woollcott's doing, and later he tried to persuade Helen Hayes not to marry MacArthur. Failing that, he became the groom's best man. He was delighted at bringing together his Hamilton friend John Weaver with Peggy Wood. And even when Ross and Grant told him of their decision to marry, he seemed to take great pleasure in helping to pick out the wedding ring at Tiffany's and in planning the ceremony. Woollcott matched his *Stars and Stripes* friend C. Leroy Baldridge with his wife but then seemed to lose interest in them. "We were too happily married," Baldridge wrote Samuel Adams. "Aleck liked it better if a marriage he had fostered went on the rocks, so that he could preside over the break-up as well as over the union." And so it would be when Ross and Grant, after seven years of marriage, began to grow apart. If Freud was right when he said that wit is "the economic expenditure of suppressed libido," Woollcott's waspishness is understandable indeed.

Remnants of Victorianism seem to have plagued the Algonquinites' marriages as well. Ross believed, Jane Grant wrote, that there were good women (wives) and bad women (whores). Although he could and did allow himself such troglodyte remarks as "coons are either funny or dangerous," he could not bring himself to a scatological reference in a woman's presence, at least during his marriage to Grant. He was a rigorous censor of even vaguely off-color references in *The New Yorker* long after the early decade's censorship battles had discredited such prudishness among would-be sophisticates. Kaufman's well-documented extramarital love life, mainly with prostitutes in the 1920s, is presumed to have begun with his perception of Beatrice as a mother figure in the earliest days of their marriage. Benchley's wife, Gertrude, had been a Sunday-school classmate whom he had known since the age of eight, and he was another charge-account customer of the infamous madam Polly Adler in the 1920s.

Ross and Grant in the early Twenties. Woollcott had jumped at Grant's offer to let him arrange the wedding, but when they returned from their honeymoon, Woollcott presented a bill for services that included not only every cent he had spent—seemingly caught up in the spirit of the occasion—but also $100 for "personal wear and tear." Ross and Grant fought bitterly against paying the last item, but finally they did. In certain respects their marriage was modern: they agreed to have separate engagements, Ross agreed to Grant's keeping her maiden name, and he encouraged her to keep her job. In the early years, they lived on her salary and saved his for a publishing venture.

FPA's attitude toward women seems to have been the most patently crude. Newman Levy overheard him at a party one night. "I think, Frank," an ingenue was saying, "that all you care about is my body." "You're damned right," Adams replied, "and a beautiful body it is, and let me tell you, young woman, you'd better take good care of it, because when it's gone you won't have a damned thing left." "I cannot appraise the efficacy of unmitigated rudeness as an amatory technique," Levy noted. "I know that many charming women resented it, but I have reason to believe that Frank's score of successes was astonishingly high." His wife Minna, a chorus girl ten years his senior whom he married in 1903, had resorted by the mid-1920s to a strictly maternal attitude toward him. People who witnessed his marriage in its last days found the experience difficult at best. The Adamses divorced in 1924.

Against that backdrop, the group's notorious mania for games—spelling bees, dice, poker, cribbage, Scenes from Great Plays, Murder, anagrams, and so on—seems less an expression of elation than a means of escape. That mania only heightened in late 1922 and after, as FPA's diary attests, and the games became increasingly intense and consequential. Much has been written about the psychology of people who are willing to play for life-changing stakes, and in the months and years ahead, the Algonquin players did nothing to exempt themselves from that literature.

Thanatopsis—sometimes the Thanatopsis Pleasure and Inside Straight Club, or the Thanatopsis Chowder and Marching Society, or the Young Men's Upper West Side Thanatopsis Literary and Inside Straight Poker Club—was a name FPA had taken from the club in *Main Street* and given to their poker game even before he knew it meant "contemplation of death." The game had started during the war, in the back room of Nini's in Montmartre, where on Saturday nights, after the *Stars and Stripes* was delivered to the printer, Ross, Woollcott and Adams would be joined by Ring Lardner, who was covering the "lighter side" of war for *Collier's;* Capt. Grantland Rice of the *Stars and Stripes* sports page; Lt. Adolph Ochs, Jr., the paper's treasurer; and Heywood Broun, who had taken his honeymoon in Paris with Ruth Hale and was reporting on the war for the *Tribune*. It would perhaps be melodramatic to suppose that

"Thanatopsis" came to FPA unconsciously as a metaphor for the game's original setting, but it seems inevitable to relate the game's origin to the war all of them were missing. It has often been observed elsewhere that the real psychic casualties of World War I were not those who fought but those who never did, and the *Stars and Stripes* jobs in Paris were distinctly behind the lines. "It was not so bad," Fitzgerald wrote of a non-combatant in a *Saturday Evening Post* short story, "except that when the infantry came limping back from the trenches, he wanted to be one of them. The sweat and mud they wore seemed only one of those ineffable symbols of aristocracy that were forever eluding him."

Margaret Case Harriman related an incident at the Thanatopsis table that suggests both its resonances with the war and Woollcott's particular sensitivity about his wartime role:

> *David Wallace turned up for an impromptu game wearing an Army shirt with the Infantry insignia on its collar tabs. Wallace, at that time publicity agent for William Harris, Jr., had been a First Lieutenant in the Infantry during World War I. The reason he wore the Army shirt, he says now, was that his laundry hadn't come back when the Thanatopsis pulled him out of bed to play poker, and he had to put on the first shirt that came to hand.*
>
> *Woollcott began baiting him the minute he came in the door.*
>
> *"I didn't know we were entertaining General Pershing," he said bitterly; and, "Do tell us all about your war experiences in the front trenches." Later he said, "Tell me, are you related to General Lew Wallace, who wrote* Ben Hur?"
>
> *It was Woollcott at his nastiest, but everybody in the room, including Dave Wallace, realized that it was also the Woollcott who had wanted to go to the war and had been turned down by the Army, Navy and Marines as being near-sighted, flat-footed and overweight. . . . It was natural for Woollcott to hate an Infantry man, and since he always took everything personally, it was natural for him to consider Dave Wallace's Army shirt a deliberate, personal insult.*
>
> *The Thanatopsis went on playing, with Dave Wallace taking a hand. But Woollcott was still simmering.*
>
> *"It's too bad you're sitting down, General Wallace," he said presently, "or you might show us your battle scars."*

"Broun was a good poker player," one Thanatopsis player remembered in 1975. "His only problem was that he couldn't bear to break even. He had to be either way ahead or way behind before he could quit."

At this, Dave Wallace lost his temper and threw down his cards. He glared across the table at Woollcott.

"At least I'm not a writing *soldier," he shouted.*

There was a silence. . . . Ring Lardner made his only remark of the evening.

"You sure swept the table that time, Dave," he said quietly.

Wallace followed Lardner's lazy glance around the table. The circle of poker players included almost every "writing" soldier who had been on the staff of the Stars and Stripes in France.

Poker at the Algonquin was far more nearly a "contemplation of death" than it had ever been at Nini's. John V.A. Weaver lost all the royalties he made on his best-selling book of poetry, *In American,* at a single sitting; unlike the others, he stopped coming back. In the game's latter days of astronomical stakes, Broun lost his house, and though he tried to stay away and was advised by his psychiatrist that he played pathologically, sado-masochistically, he never could quit. FPA "would raise and raise with a pair," one occasional player remembered a half-century later, "and then fold on the last round. He always lost, even though he made it sound like he was a first-class player in his column. And even though he was making a good living on the *World,* he often lost a good deal more than he could afford."

Every regular poker game has regular losers, but around the Thanatopsis table the losers seemed to be in the majority. John Peter Toohey lost nearly every time he played. Opinions of Toohey varied at the Thanatopsis table—from kibitzer Peggy Wood's description of him as "a flat know-nothing kind of fellow who was just tolerated by the rest because he'd been there from the start" to Marc Connelly's more generous assessment: "Everybody loved John. His gullibility was long established and we took great advantage of him." The two points of view are not incompatible, however: Toohey was willing enough to play the fool as long as he could keep coming back, retaining his position as the publicity profession's inside line to the wits of the Round Table.

Ross was also a chronic loser and with similar justification. "Ross was a born outsider," Brendan Gill said in 1976, "He lost a great deal in those Thanatopsis sessions, very nearly lost his bankroll for *The New Yorker,* but I'm sure

According to his diary column, FPA played poker an average of three times a week in the early 1920s. After his remarriage in 1925 he played less; one day in 1928 he even wrote of going "to bed, and wondered what ever happened to the silly old Thanatopsis club." It was, of course, very much alive. That FPA went less frequently was due more to his change of lifestyle than to any adverse opinion of his new wife's. On their wedding night she was persuaded to let him play poker with the group—as a condition of their having given the Adamses an expensive set of cards and chips as a wedding gift.

Connelly, who was one of the game's least avid players, once tore up the cards after a lost hand—and later caused Broun to do the same. In a one-on-one betting duel with Broun, John Toohey seemed to be wavering, so Connelly said: "It is the consensus of the group that Toohey call." Broun had been bluffing and so lost the hand.

he considered it a small price to be in the company of those people. He probably considered it a high compliment to be able to lose that money." Of course, his attendance did turn out to be good business: it was at a Thanatopsis session that he met the man who was to capitalize *The New Yorker,* Raoul Fleischmann. In the manner of most Round Table matches, Fleischmann had been invited into the game by Woollcott for that very purpose.

Kaufman was by far the group's best player, and when the inevitable flaps arose over bad checks, lingering debts and precise amounts owed, Kaufman volunteered to become the game's official treasurer, cashing checks with his own cash and taking upon himself the sometimes lengthy procedure of collecting the face value of the bad ones. His desire to see the game continue smoothly can have been his only reason for doing it, and that desire is understandable, given his always more than even chances of winning among such players. His card sense was famous; Charles Goren later said he could have been a professional at bridge. It is therefore understandable too that most of the best witticisms flashing across the Thanatopsis table were Kaufman's: "I have been trey-deuced" and "I will now fold my tens and silently steal away"—they were the words of a happy man.

Woollcott was Kaufman's most resentful prey, and he quit the Thanatopsis game in 1923. On the premise that any game that did not include him would soon naturally wither and pass, he wrote a piece for *Vanity Fair* that year called "The Passing of the Thanatopsis," calling poker "a preposterous waste of time." He said he had been joined in his defection from it by Marc Connelly and Heywood Broun, and while they did not join him in anything but the *idea* of quitting, Woollcott stayed away for nearly a year, his strength of resolve drawn primarily from the strength of his motives for leaving: not only was he losing consistently (cribbage and croquet were his best gambling games), but, what was unendurable, he had ceded center stage to Kaufman.

It was in the same year that he left the Thanatopsis game that he bought an island on Lake Bomoseen in Vermont, where cribbage and croquet became fixed activities for all guests who wished to receive Woollcott's favor. Several of the group were already fanatical about croquet, playing in Central Park when

Woollcott was sufficiently in evidence at Thanatopsis sessions in the late 1920s to allow Paul Hyde Bonner, who commissioned the Thanatopsis portrait (top), to have him painted into it. But it is safe to say he spent a great deal more time and made much more money playing cribbage on the island (bottom). Alice Duer Miller once accused Woollcott of making her his "cribbage pimp" on the island—a role she might have doubly resented for the amount of money he was willing to take from the unsuspecting.

they were not at one or another country estate, and in fact part of the reason that Woollcott was able to persuade some of his Algonquin friends to become partners in the island was that they would have their own croquet course throughout the summer. Woollcott also hoped that the island would be a place where all his talented friends could find a retreat hospitable to hard work and good talk. In the 1930s and after, work actually did get done there: Cornelia Otis Skinner practiced lines walking around the island, MacArthur and Hecht finished their filmscript for *Wuthering Heights* there, Joseph Alsop finished *The 168 Days* in the guest house and both S. N. Behrman and Moss Hart found the place ideal for revising scripts. If Woollcott believed in holding court, he also expected that his friends work hard and succeed. But in the 1920s, before the Depression made work so much a prerequisite for play, no one worked at Neshobe, and Woollcott was less a benign patron of their work than a ringmaster of their ritual play.

There was a mandatory morning dip at 7:00 A.M. and a seemingly interminable communal breakfast shortly thereafter, at which Woollcott read excerpts from his stack of daily mail. After that came a few minutes of free time and a long lunch. What had begun as a partnership of equals quickly became another Woollcott proprietary, and he stood no competition. One night in the late Twenties, by which time his island rule had been firmly established, Noël Coward proposed to read aloud from his yet unproduced new play. "Where?" Woollcott explained.

Ruth Gordon, whom Woollcott considered—and who considered herself— a discovery of his, wrote a story in her memoirs that, for all its roseate hindsight, does convey the tenor of Woollcott's reign:

> "*Wake up, Blossom. Northern Lights! Slip on something indecent, you're going to have competition.*"
>
> "*I don't—*"
>
> "*Do you want me to tear this door down with my bare hands and make suet of you?*"
>
> "*What?*"
>
> "*Two minutes flat or Dr. Crippen will be in there with his bag of lye.*"

Shortly after buying the island, Woollcott began building a house for himself (top), which he appointed grandly. All entertainment that included Woollcott took place in his house rather than the original house on the property, which was used for guests. (Bottom)

A typical after-dinner scene in Woollcott's dining room. The game was Murder, and Woollcott, as usual, was the District Attorney. To his left, island habitués Alice Miller, Raymond Ives (an insurance executive and one of Woollcott's oldest friends) and Neysa.

"Oh God."

"That's my dated ingenue!" He knocked next door. "Stout Cortez?"

Bea Kaufman groaned. "I'm asleep, Dream Boy."

"Get that upstate charm into something shapeless not to bedazzle poor sensitive Howard Bull [the island's utility man]."

There was a sound of feet on the floor. . . .

People stumbled out in anything from a raincoat to a Charvet dressing gown or an Emma Maloof or Boue Soeurs. . . .

"We're going out in the gondola."

"Oh, no!"

"Acky, no!"

"Please, Acky!"

"Why go out? Can't we see the goddam Northern Lights through the window?"

"Bull, drench any renegade not aboard in two minutes."

To understate the matter, not everyone in the Algonquin group took to his whip so well. Kaufman almost never went, in part because Beatrice and George Backer carried on their long love affair there, in part because he had his own pursuits, amorous and theatrical, in the city. Peggy Wood was never invited. "I wouldn't have gone anyway," she said fifty years later. "I knew too much of their private lives and what went on up there, and I didn't need to be involved in all that." She also felt that "it was not my business to cultivate a critic—it would have been fatal." Neither reason is entirely convincing. She was, after all, a regular at the Round Table, where, she said, she felt ill at ease much of the time, and while libertine exploits were indeed relished by Woollcott—a Hollywood couple, engaged but not married, romping in a creaky bed upstairs known as the "informative double," Dorothy Parker spending an entire weekend in nothing but one of her picture hats, Harpo Marx scaring visitors and boaters on the lake by jumping nude out of the bushes—Miss Wood's disapproval was probably more the reason she was never invited than the reason she never went.

Benchley had the best reason of all for staying away: he hated games almost as much as Woollcott's overbearance. In his review of John Eliot's book *At Home with H. G. Wells,* Benchley quoted a passage that suggests how alike were Woollcott and Wells, whom Woollcott idolized. "For a distance of ten or

Woollcott on Bomoseen with his unfaithful dog Cocaud, who was named after one Mme. Cocaud, the owner of a bistro near Woollcott's base hospital in Savenay during the war. "Considered as a one-man dog," Woollcott said, "she is a flop. In her fidelity to me, she's a little too much like that girl in France who was true to the 26th Infantry." He had similar problems with his German shepherd: "In the company of any large male dog," he wrote, "she suddenly becomes almost unbearably ingenue, developing the most winsome mannerisms, and somehow managing something equivalent to baby talk."

Howard Dietz (not pictured here) was Harpo's partner in this game with Beatrice Kaufman and Woollcott, and when he and Harpo won, Woollcott was furious. "Good-by to you two Jews," he said as he left for the mainland in a huff. "I hope I shall never see you again."

twenty miles round," Eliot wrote, "folks come on Sunday to play hockey and have tea. Old and young . . . Tories, Bolsheviks, Liberals, or men and women of no political leanings, Can you play hockey? is all that matters. If you say No you are rushed toward a pile of sticks and given one and told to go in the forward line; if you say Yes you are probably made a vice-captain on the spot." To Benchley, that sounded perfectly awful. "I can't imagine a worse place in which to spend a weekend," he wrote, "than one where your host is always boisterously forcing you to take part in games . . . about which you know nothing. A weekend guest ought to be ignored, allowed to rummage about alone among the books, livestock and cold food in the refrigerator whenever he feels like it, and not rushed willy-nilly . . ."

What hockey was at the Wells estate, croquet was at Woollcott's—a command performance. The course itself, like all the courses Woollcott set out before those who would be his friends, was rutted, utterly unpredictable. Woollcott alone had all the gullies and impassable places carefully mapped out in his memory. "It is no game for the soft of sinew and the gentle of spirit," he wrote of croquet on the island. "The higher and dirtier croquet can use the guile of a cobra and the inhumanity of a boa constrictor." Woollcott happily averred that of all his playmates, he most closely fitted those characteristics, and at the other required island game, cribbage, he was also unchallenged and unforgiving master. Given the frequency of games on Neshobe, even though the stakes were kept low, playing with Woollcott was an invitation to slow financial ruin. Woollcott never forgave a gambling debt, and some who felt they had been coerced to play when they could least afford it never forgave Woollcott. Looking through Harold Ross's library one day in the 1950s, Benchley's elder son Nathaniel came across one of his father's books which had been autographed for Woollcott. The inscription read: "To Alexander W Woollccoott, who stole the first dollar I ever earned."

In New York in 1923, Neysa McMein's salon was the Round Table's principal parlor-gaming annex, and in June of that year Woollcott impulsively got aboard the ship on which he knew Neysa was sailing for France to propose marriage to her. The match would surely have been attributed to the muse of

WIT'S END

"My doctor forbids me to play unless I win," Woollcott once told his playing companions, and after Neysa suggested there should be no boundaries on the rutted acreage where they played, the advantage he accrued by spending the entire season among its gullies and hazards became almost insurmountable.

Neysa with Jascha Heifetz, Woollcott and another man on her honeymoon trip to Paris. The man behind the camera was Marc Connelly, who was in Europe with his mother.

charades, but Neysa had, as it happened, been married secretly only days before to Baragwanath. Friends thought it typical of her that her new husband was off on a mining expedition during what was to have been their honeymoon trip. Woollcott was dejected when she told him about her marriage, and she was sincerely sorry for him; to the end of his life, she was quite solicitous of his affection, addressing him as "Moonglow" and "Pretty" in her letters. But at the Round Table, little attention was paid to Woollcott's having cut short his trip, or to his patent depression. Luncheon conversation and the headlines were full of McMein's odd honeymoon. "Famous Artist Marries . . . Spends Honeymoon with Four Other Guys," read one, and the *World*'s read: "Neysa McMein Secretly Wed. Lucky Bridegroom Sulks at Home." Marc Connelly offered, "Marry McMein and See the World," and Swope, the *World*'s executive editor, said later his paper's headline should have been "A New Groom Sleeps Clean."

Baragwanath was not much enamored with parlor games—except, in accordance with his "thoroughly modern arrangement" with Neysa, the pursuit of other women on what he and his cohort George Backer called their "freedom weekends"—but after their marriage, the round of games at Neysa's continued unabated and, as elsewhere, grew increasingly consuming. Charades particularly came to seem a proving ground of one's worth as a human being. Perhaps inevitably, as the competition at such games intensified, the games themselves had begun to change. In the last month of 1922, FPA reported in his column that the group had found a new one.

> So to Neysa's and found a great crowd there, in earnest discussion of this one's and that one's personal allurements, and giving everybody we knew a ranking, as in a crowd of 100 men how many would not be indifferent to this woman, or in a crowd of 100 women how many could not be indifferent to that man; and some terrifick disagreements in our estimates of various persons, but all of us trying to be fair and impersonal about it, in especiall . . . H. Broun and I.

On New Year's Eve of 1922, he wrote, the game at Neysa's reached a certain refinement:

Woollcott wrote of Neysa: "Because she has often allowed her pastels to be reproduced by thrifty processes that drain them of half their color and character; because she will cheerfully draw for a department store or a soapmaker; because of the newspaper reports of her judging beauties at Coney Island, or playing tunes or singing for wounded soldiers, or opening a new movie house in Toronto, or swimming impromptu in the Marne, she arouses suspicions either that she lacks the apocryphal virtue called dignity (which is quite true) or is a schemer for publicity (which is not true at all)." Neysa said of her relationship with Woollcott: "We got under each other's skins."

*Seven of us played a game, rating various qualities of the seven of us,
such as intelligence, sex appeal, honesty, and so on, on a scale of ten. And
my mark was not so high as I thought it would be.*

Adams was not specific about which quality had failed him, but Broun sulked
and complained openly for weeks about his own low mark for sex appeal.
Whether or not as a direct result of this evaluation, he devoted much more time
and energy to his extramarital relationships in the years that followed, and
though Ruth Hale felt bound by her word and finer thoughts not only to tolerate
but to encourage his affairs, a growing tension between them was the understandable and probably inevitable consequence.

No one was counting casualties, however; more than ever, membership in
the group was an insistent invitation to games—at Neysa's, on Neshobe, around
the Thanatopsis table and at their various apartments, newly appointed by now
and designed for parties. Marc Connelly and Deems Taylor, who shared an
apartment on East Eighteenth Street, were exempted from the regular demands
of entertaining, although everyone was expected to host an occasional poker
game on week nights. Dorothy Parker, living on her free-lance income, could
never have competed with Neysa's parties across the hall even if she had
wanted to. FPA did not entertain in those days because he and his wife were
living almost entirely separate lives. But for the rest of them, home was where
you were quite likely to be interrupted at any time by a band of people with
nothing better to do than barge in and play. The Kaufmans had by now outfitted
a luxurious apartment, the Pemberton and Toohey households were seldom used
but always fair game and the renovated Ross-Grant-Woollcott commune on
West Forty-seventh Street was rarely quiet. Traffic was so constant there that
neighbors were convinced the house was actually a speakeasy. For that, of
course, they had Woollcott to thank and blame; he was just as much the play
maker of Forty-seventh Street as he was of Neshobe.

Grant and Ross hadn't wanted him as a partner in their house. Back in
1921, he had burst in on a meeting between Ross, Grant and Woollcott's Hamilton friend, Hawley Truax (who was the original third party to the living
arrangement) at which they were going over plans for renovating the house. They

tried to squirrel away the blueprints before he saw them, but he had heard about their project and was not to be deterred. "I'm joining this little intrigue," Jane Grant remembered his announcing, and while she tried to stay on good terms with him and commemorated him fondly in her memoir, the event also left her firmly convinced that "Aleck made possessions out of people, quite without caring if they liked it, and entered with gusto any of their activities that interested him."

If the Woollcott mystique faded somewhat for Jane Grant during her life with him on Forty-seventh Street, it is a small wonder.

> *Solitude, to him, was agony. In the years that followed we were generously treated to his need for companionship. No one's privacy was inviolate. Late at night Ross and I came to dread the sound of the taxicab that deposited Aleck beneath our window. We tried turning out the light when we heard him but that got us nowhere.*
>
> *"I saw the lights go out, can't fool Uncle Aleck," and he would burst into the room. . . .*
>
> *"Come on, Ross, three games—that's all I have time for," and Ross would groan, get up and drag himself to the living room.*

He held huge parties in Ross and Grant's quarters when they were out of town—quarters he had encouraged them to decorate lavishly at a time when they could scarcely afford it so that (Grant later realized) he would have an appropriate space larger than his own in which to entertain.

Woollcott also demanded—and it was conceded by the rest—that the house be open, that anyone of their circle would be welcome at any time for any meal. As a result, Grant once served dinner to thirty-one extra people. While Woollcott was by then earning $2,000 a month, Ross was making only half that and Truax, whose father's death had forced him to leave law school, had himself and his mother to support in separate households. Furthermore, Grant wrote, "Woollcott made no secret of his impatience with the foibles of Ross and Hawley, both on diets for queasy stomachs. Aleck relished rich food, and had the true fat man's interest in our menus. . . . He hated green vege-tables, and when there was soup flatly refused to come to the table until it was finished. If Aleck happened to arrive in the dining room before the meat course, he would stride into the garden or sit at a nearby table, glaring at us through his thick glasses."

All of his demands were by way of galvanizing his court around him, and inevitably, as Neshobe and the Round Table had become, the house on Forty-seventh Street became a Woollcott fiefdom and a playground. George Gershwin played *Rhapsody in Blue* before its formal première on their piano, Edna Millay read the new poems of hers that were appearing in FPA's column, Irving Berlin's new songs were sung, Scott Fitzgerald read his latest work aloud. It became, in short, a gallery of much of the latest and best in American culture. The draw of Forty-seventh Street was probably less Woollcott than those he had gathered around him. One didn't, after all, have to be a regular of the Round Table to delight in a Benchley monologue, in Sherwood's rendition of "Red, Red Robin," in courting Dorothy Parker or Neysa McMein. For those seeking pleasant diversions from work, such company guaranteed at a minimum that they would not be bored.

The house on Forty-seventh Street, like the Algonquin crowd itself, had the further, simpler allure of being always available, like the welcome succor of a late-closing bar, a place one decides to patronize even at some cost in quality or company because it can be counted on not to be closed when it is needed most. Whatever the Round Tablers were not, they were always "on." At the same time, as Ring Lardner's years in relative proximity to the group make clear, the succor they gave could be far from genuinely enlivening.

Before 1922, although Lardner had joined the poker game in Paris and, infrequently, the Thanatopsis game in New York, his only close acquaintance in the group was Adams, in whose column his name regularly appeared before the war and after. He was, of course, already a formidable figure by the time the Round Table began, and even though he never lunched with them, he was a presence among them from the first. While the "amazing whelps" were still just that, Lardner was an acknowledged master, lauded by the city's best critics. T. S. Mathews defended him from the inevitable charge that his wide following was proof of slack standards by invoking Chekhov and Shakespeare in the

New Republic; H. L. Mencken and Edmund Wilson acclaimed him lavishly. Lardner, moreover, had no apparent personal investment in the acclaim; like the Round Table writers, his principal goal was to make money, and if some of his pieces made it into the big leagues according to the critics, that was fine with him but of little moment.

Lardner's detachment—and particularly that he so staunchly eluded Woollcott's anxious grasp—had great appeal at the Round Table. Lardner always deferred in verbal jousts. At a party Dorothy Parker gave in the mid-1920s, the story goes, he pretended to be a recent immigrant from Poland so that no one would expect him to speak, and at the Thanatopsis table he rarely said a word unless it was to raise, fold or trade in cards. Edmund Wilson noted in his postwar journal:

> *I was struck by the enormous reverence that the Algonquinites felt for [him]. He never mingled with them. He lived at Great Neck, Long Island, and came into town only for business; I never saw him at the Algonquin. He was somehow aloof and inscrutable, by nature rather saturnine, but a master whom all admired, though he was never present in person. It may be that all any such circle demands is such a presiding but invisible deity, who is assumed to regard them with a certain scorn.*

But beginning in late 1922, Lardner showed up with some frequency among the Algonquin crowd, if not at the Round Table itself, and at the same time, his drinking redoubled and his work fell off drastically. In the years of his closest association with the group, 1922 to 1925, he wrote no short stories. Like them, he submitted himself to the conveyer-belt schedule of periodical deadlines: for his syndicate, a daily comic strip and a regular feature article; for the magazines, a few modernized fairy tales retold in Lardnerian Americanese and some nonfiction pieces about travel in Europe—all odds and ends. Fitzgerald got to know Lardner in late 1922, when he rented an estate in Great Neck, and although he admired Lardner's work immensely, he despaired for the man he met. "As he struggled to fulfill his contracts," Fitzgerald wrote later, ". . . it was obvious that he felt his work to be directionless, mere 'copy.' . . . The truth back of it was that Ring was getting off—he was a faithful and conscien-

F. Scott Fitzgerald, who found much to admire and much to rue in the Ring Lardner he knew in 1922. The two men were as much drinking companions as anything else in the two years that they were neighbors in Great Neck, and when Fitzgerald went to Europe in 1924—so he could accomplish some important writing, he said—he left Lardner in doldrums.

Edmund Wilson recalled for Donald Elder an evening with Lardner (above) and Fitzgerald in 1924, when Fitzgerald was talking of leaving: "There was great talk on Lardner's part of going to the Red Lion or some other roadhouse, but when we did leave—all the liquor now gone—we simply went to Lardner's, where we drank Grand Marnier—he insisted on presenting each of us with a little bottle—and more Scotch."

tious workman to the end, but he had stopped finding any fun in his work.'' Fitzgerald put a good deal of Lardner into Abe North, the popular composer in *Tender Is the Night*. ''Why does he drink?'' he has Nicole Diver ask. ''So many smart men go to pieces nowadays.'' ''And when haven't they?'' Dick Diver replies. ''Smart men play close to the line because they have to—some of them can't stand it, so they quit.'' Abe North was a finished artist, and Lardner was more than that; he did some of his best work after 1925. Yet Fitzgerald's observation of Lardner in these spirited but aesthetically barren years was otherwise acute.

Lardner persisted at his lifelong effort to write for the theater, but the best he could do was nonsense playlets of the kind he did for *The 49ers; The Tridget of Greva* was, in fact, his first such skit. If such works mystified their audiences, the critics mined them for all they were worth—and more. Edmund Wilson connected their formless form to dadaism, speculating that they derived from similar and related sources: ''in France the collapse of Europe and the intellectual chaos that accompanied it; in America what is perhaps another aspect of a general crisis: the bewildering confusion of the modern city and the enfeeblement of the faculty of attention. It relieves some anxiety to laugh at pointlessness.'' Perhaps. But perhaps Wilson would have come closer to history's judgment on such works had he applied the phrase ''enfeeblement of the faculty of attention'' to the author rather than his characters. Clearly, what Wilson found to recommend in Lardner's ''dada'' plays was less a reflection or articulation of intellectual chaos than the haphazard effect of one notable result of it—that is, Prohibition and, more specifically, the uproarious Twenties' breaching of it. Lardner wrote another playlet called *I Gaspiri* (''The Upholsterers'') for Connelly, Stewart and Benchley to perform at a raucous Author's League dinner. It was even more nonsensical than *The Tridget of Greva* had been, and Lardner must have been at least a little amused when Ben Hecht published it in his Chicago *Literary Times* and when the *Transatlantic Review* in Paris republished it in 1924 and suggested that it accomplished and surpassed what the French surrealists and dadaists had tried but failed to do.

The influence was, of course, two-way; some of Lardner's Round Table

friends, particularly the original cast of *I Gaspiri,* also dove into the non sequiturial genre and the same liquid inspiration. The evidence of the connection between dada humor and alcohol is abundant. Not until Stewart got Benchley off the Prohibition wagon in 1922 did Benchley venture into such work, and in one of his earliest examples of it, a story called "Do Insects Think?", he leaves little doubt of the nature of his muse:

> *One evening I had been working late in my laboratory fooling around*
> *with some gin and other chemicals and in leaving the room I tripped over*
> *a mine of diamonds which someone had left lying on the floor and knocked*
> *over my card catalogue containing the names and addresses of all the*
> *larvae worth knowing in North America.*

Stewart makes the connection between "crazy humor" and alcohol quite explicit in his autobiography. The idea to do a whole book in that vein seemed quite natural to him. He wrote: "I had first begun to get laughs with nonsensical non sequitur shortly after college, usually with the help of alcohol." The characters in the book he wrote, *The Crazy Fool,* were modeled on himself and his friends Benchley and Parker.

The interplay between work and play among the Algonquinites was inevitable and inevitably telling, but for many of them in this period of heightened group mania and lionization, the effects were not as benign as they were for the crazy-humorists. In 1923, George Kaufman and Marc Connelly were still basking in the afterglow of their three hits on Broadway and succumbing to increasing demands on them for Dutch Treat and Little Revue skits. Just then came their first and worst failure, *The Deep Tangled Wildwood* (it had five other titles before this one was settled on). Everything about it was predictable from their previous work, even if it was still of a novel strain in the theater: a successful New York playwright returns to what he hopes will be the intact innocence of his small upstate home town only to find it struggling to become bigger and not so innocent; for the happy ending, the playwright wins the girl and the town sheepishly recovers its smallness. The critics thought it was a love story without enough convincing romance, which was true and not surprising, given Connelly's involvement with Margalo Gillmore and Al-

The heroes of *The Sun
Field*, Babe Ruth and
Ruth Hale. Even FPA
panned the book, allow-
ing some surcease from
back-scratching charges.
As Woollcott said at
the time, "You can see
Frank's scratches on
Heywood's back yet."

gonquin intramurals at the time. Connelly said later it failed because he and
Kaufman listened to all the advice they got from their Algonquin friends.

Their next project was probably their grimmest experience in the theater
—a musical called *Helen of Troy, N.Y.*, commissioned by a hucksterish agent-
turned-producer, backed by bootleggers and George Jessel and written to for-
mula. Neither of its authors ever liked the play. Though it did well in New
York and on the road, again Connelly was the less visible partner, and again
the worry was that it was a love story lacking in love. What saved it was
Kaufman's unflagging accuracy at crossfire dialogue and sense of pace; what
could have been another miserable remake was kept alive with paste and pyro-
technics—and Kaufman, always alert to the scent of failure, knew it.

Broun confided to the group one afternoon over lunch that he was going
to try his hand at fiction again; his first novel, *The Boy Grew Older,* had been
treated generously by the critics, but it was clearly nothing that would shine
brightly on his reputation for long, and Broun was sensitive to the charge that
he would never be anything but a journalist. Someone commented that Broun
had enough commitments to keep anyone else at the typewriter twenty-four
hours a day: his drama criticism for the *World,* five columns of opinion and
rumination a week under his banner "It Seems to Me," a syndicated book
column for the Sunday edition and regular freelance contributions to *Collier's,
Judge, Vanity Fair* and the *Atlantic Monthly.* With his dauntless speakeasy
schedule at night, Algonquin lunches at noon and time out for the group's
poker games and parties, facile and quick as he was with his column, how
could he possibly have the time for a work of fiction? His answer was that he
still had his Friday afternoons open—and when it came out in late 1923, *The
Sun Field* read as if it had indeed been written in borrowed time; it was a
rambling patchwork of old columns, his life and his knowledge of baseball, with
some ill-disguised portraits of Famous People thrown in for good measure. His
Algonquin friends liked the cryptic profiles especially. For instance, of a character based on Walter Lippmann, who then dominated the *World's* editorial
page, Broun wrote: "We were in college together and even then it seemed to me
that he was all finished. There wasn't room to put any more education on him.

The bags beginning to develop under Broun's eyes in this 1922 photograph owed something to the demands of his professional obligations: drama criticism and "It Seems to Me" for the *World,* and monthly articles for *Collier's, Vanity Fair, Judge* and *Atlantic Month-* *ly.* He was also writing *The Sun Field*—and acquiring his reputation as a womanizer. "The ability to make love frivolously," he wrote, "is the chief characteristic which distinguishes human beings from the beasts."

As Kaufman began to sense that he and his collaborator were slipping into unprofitable diversions, he also began to see that their days together were numbered.

That is one of the things there ought to be a law about. A city ordinance or a federal statute should lay down the principle that nobody should be educated above the twenty-third story." Babe Ruth, Ruth Hale and Broun himself (a sports writer with a heart condition) were the major characters, but after the references were unveiled and the book mined for baseball color, there was nothing to recommend it.

Woollcott, too, was in doldrums, although he attached less importance and more readily accepted limits to his writing than any of the others. His contract gave him four summer months off, but he quickly found that he had nothing to write about but his friends and theatrical favorites. He wrote about them all and became infamous at the Round Table for it; Richard Ben-Ami, Minnie Maddern Fiske, Irving Berlin, Helen Hayes, Neysa McMein and the Lunts were treated to what journalists today derisively call "big wet kisses" from Woollcott in these off months. When he was not doing that, he was rehashing yet again some of his *Stars and Stripes* battlefront stories for Harold Ross, now editor of the *American Legion Weekly*. If any doubt remained that Woollcott, however prominent a figure *in* the Twenties, was never quite *of* it, his stories for the American Legion magazine, coming at the time when the first great antiwar books by Dos Passos and cummings were being published, gave flagrant and positive proof of it. Although Woollcott's top-of-his-voice flag waving had subsided in favor of *sotto voce* poignancy, his persona was still that of the unredoubtable warrior, glad and brave at his post. To his credit, Ross got stomach ulcers at the job.

Life at *Life* was hardly more inspiring. Benchley was still appearing in the Music Box Revue eight times a week, and keeping up his weekly drama criticism. Dorothy Parker began writing for other magazines, especially for the *Saturday Evening Post*'s "Short Turns and Encores" page, and she began doing some prose for the women's magazines, most of it about middle-class pretensions and all of it greatly padded out to fit her editors' word-length requirements. Sherwood, while writing about films and the people who made them for his weekly department, "The Silent Drama," began to write film subtitles to supplement his income. His ultimate goal was still to sell a scenario

Life

Burlesque EFFICIENCY *Number*

CIRCULATION

I AM THE SPIRIT OF AMERICAN MAGAZINES:

I am dedicated to the proposition that all men are created equally stupid.

I know What the Public Wants and, safe in this knowledge, I dictate my commandments to the makers of our national literature.

In my realm—

No stories shall end unhappily.

Each shall contain a lesson, preferably of how the hero made fifty thousand dollars and was promoted to the Sales Managership.

Omnipotent shall be the presence of the "half a million women subscribers in the small towns of the Middle West." What they like, goes.

Any illustration which has a pretty girl in it is the kind of Art we want.

On such occasions as it is necessary to use the word "hell," it shall be printed "h---."

There shall be no direct mention made of biological functions in a serious manner, but a row of asterisks in a spirit of romance never hurt anyone, and often helps circulation.

Readers like to laugh, but not to be laughed at. Satire is too promiscuous and might hit some of our readers.

No one shall poke fun at any public superstition which is of more than fifty years' standing.

It is just as well not to irritate an advertiser.

I am the Spirit of American Magazines, dedicated to the proposition that all men are created equally stupid.

And the worst of it is, I am right.

The young Marc Connelly could have been the model for "the spirit of American magazines," and his update on Joseph Gonnick's Cantilever Bridges was among the high spots of the fall 1923 "Burlesque Number." "We had a wonderful time on those issues," he recalled in 1975, still able to laugh at a mock news photo whose caption he had written: "Convention-Crazed Dentists Haul the Largest Gold Tooth in the World."

to the movies, but, perhaps fortunately for him, that never happened.

Sherwood and Benchley did manage to bring some of the Rose Room mania to *Life,* bringing on Stewart, Connelly and Kaufman at various times for various projects. One was "Life's Calendar," which Connelly and Kaufman did monthly during 1923 and part of 1924, even as they produced three plays and while Kaufman kept his job as editor of the *Times* drama page. Another was the "Burlesque Number" parodying current magazines—*Photoplay, Everybody's,* confession magazines and the tabloid newspapers—an idea derived from the *Harvard Lampoon's* parodies of *Life* and *Vanity Fair.* Such lines as Connelly's advertising slogan, "Your Daughter Is Safe on a Gonnick Cantilever Bridge," were hardly more than the kinds of cracks he might make over lunch, and yet, while Connelly and his friends were loath to admit it, both kinds of humor took time and energy to create—time and energy they enjoyed spending but nevertheless the time and energy of people busily depleting themselves on enormously unimportant matters. Their work at *Life,* that is to say, was more of a piece with games and lunches and gatherings at Neysa's than with their "serious" work—and more of a piece with what they had already done than with that new, better thing most of them claimed to want to do.

That is not to denigrate what they had already accomplished, which was formidable. In the five years since the Round Table began, they had published dozens of books, written a half-dozen plays, run several magazines and published in nearly every important magazine then existing. By the end of 1924, the Round Table was indeed, as their compatriot Frank Sullivan's Dr. Arbuthnot might have said, a Force to Be Reckoned With. Their readers numbered millions, and even if their books would not last—we read Broun today for historical interest, Woollcott for the boomings of a bygone style and Adams not at all—they spoke directly to the readers of their generation, and a few, chiefly Dorothy Parker and Robert Benchley, wrote pieces then that speak to ours.

It is at the same time true that their effect on each other, no doubt a stimulant, was not necessarily a healthy one. They certainly helped sell each other's books. Of Woollcott's collection, *Shouts and Murmurs,* FPA wrote: "Lord! This man hath the power to make whatever he writes of seem so interest-

ing that . . . when he writes of a play it seemeth to me that not to have seen it is a dereliction of duty." When Broun's *It Seems to Me* collection came out, FPA called Broun "one of the greatest journalists of all time." And when FPA's collection, *Something Else Again,* was published, Benchley gushed:

> *If any one had told Mark Twain that a man could run a daily newspaper*
> *column in New York and amass any degree of fame through translations*
> *of the Odes of Horace into the vernacular, the veteran humorist would*
> *probably have slapped Albert Bigelow Paine on the back and taken the*
> *next boat for Bermuda. . . . And yet thousands of American businessmen*
> *quote FPA to thousands of other American businessmen every morning.*
> *. . . In FPA we find a combination which makes it possible for us to*
> *admit our learning and still be held honorable men. It is a good sign that*
> *his following is increasing.*

FPA did have a positive effect of American poetry to the extent that he provided poets with some degree of visibility, good poets like Edna Millay and and Countee Cullen and Dorothy Parker. But a great alikeness developed in some of the poets who wrote for him as well. FPA's most prolific contributors are now, at least as poets, forgotten imitators of imitators—Baird Leonard, Carolyn Wells, Deems Taylor, Newman Levy and scores of others. Never have so many writers in New York written so much alike, and not only for FPA's column. Benchley and Parker wrote almost the same piece about meeting summer-hotel people in the city. The evidence is lacking to show who wrote which of the following poems first, and Lardner was certainly not known (or even likely, given his special talent) to imitate anyone, but it is hardly likely either that, however depressed and self-destructive both he and Dorothy Parker were at the time, they would have arrived at these poems independently. First Lardner's re-frain from a song lyric he wrote (but did not use) for *All at Sea:*

> *But cyanide, it gripes inside;*
> *Bichloride blights the liver;*
> *And I am told one catches cold*
> *When one jumps in the river.*
> *To cut my throat would stain my coat*
> *And make my valet furious.*

> *Death beckons me, but it must be*
> *A death that ain't injurious.*

And Parker's well-known "Résumé":

> *Razors pain you;*
> *Rivers are damp;*
> *Acids stain you;*
> *And drugs cause cramp.*
> *Guns aren't lawful;*
> *Nooses give;*
> *Gas smells awful;*
> *You might as well live.*

Parker stayed at Lardner's house for several weeks in 1925. The ostensible reason was to find some peace in which to work (Lardner complained later that she had only made it impossible for him to work). Perhaps the poems were conscious extrapolations of one another, undertaken for fun between the two of them. Such an explanation would, however, make much the same point. If they were not lifting from each other, neither were they being completely themselves.

In their work and in their play, the Round Tablers were only giving what their public demanded of them, which was more and more connected to the legend they were creating for themselves—a legend demanding greater and greater "debunking," more and more daring, higher heights of defiance for which the honest writer would have to pay a private cost.

In a book Stewart compiled in 1940 called *Fighting Words,* Parker wrote that her work had changed for the Twenties, along with that of her "hundreds, maybe thousands" of peers doing light verse. At first, she said:

> *. . . we chose for our subjects our dislike of parsley as a garnish, or of*
> *nutmeg in rice pudding . . . All you can say is, it didn't do any harm,*
> *and it was work that didn't roughen our hands or your mind . . . Then*
> *something happened to the light-verse writers—especially to the ladies*
> *among us . . . We let it be known our hearts broke much oftener than the*
> *classic once . . . We were gallant and hard-riding and careless of life.*
> *We sneered in numbers in loping rhythms at the straight and the sharp*
> *and the decent. We were little black ewes that had gone astray; we were*

a sort of ladies' auxiliary of the legion of the damned. And, boy, were
we proud of our shame! When Gertrude Stein spoke of a "lost generation,"
we took it to ourselves and considered it the prettiest compliment we had.

But a quarter-century earlier, the pitfalls of that drift into chic, audience-thrilling misbehavior were far from readily apparent. Everyone knew about the Round Table's drunken, hilarious galas and their quick, morning-after wits, and in the age of public relations, everyone's knowing anything was a compelling virtue. So if Parker's first suggestions at the time that something was faintly off about it all were tentative, half-hearted, that is understandable. As it was, she was considered faintly hysterical by her Round Table friends, and when she sent her poem "For R.C.B. [Robert Charles Benchley]" to FPA for his column, it was considered, at least by her, an act of rebellion. FPA ran it:

> *Life comes a'hurrying,*
> *Or life lags slow;*
> *But you've stopped worrying—*
> *Let it go!   .   .   .*
>
> *Some find it fair,*
> *Some think it hooey,*
> *Many people care;*
> *But we don't, do we?*

The theme kept coming back to her, usually with reference to Benchley or herself: "And let her loves, when she is dead/Write this above her bones:/No more she lives to give us bread/Who asked her only stones." She wrote a story called "Such a Pretty Little Picture" about a Benchley character, no good with tools or furnaces, who stood trimming his hedge in suburbia and thinking how to tell his family to go to hell, how to get out of the box he had made for himself. From that, in 1924, she wrote a play called *Close Harmony* with Elmer Rice about the same thing. A similar character, whose wife no longer enjoyed his mandolin playing, almost but not quite leaves her for the woman next door, who encourages his music; instead, he settles back into a nettling home life and raises his voice around the place. (The play got good reviews but folded after a month. Dorothy

Parker sent a wire to the Algonquin: DID A COOL NINETY DOLLARS AT THE MATINEE. ASK THE BOYS IN THE BACK ROOM WHAT THEY WILL HAVE.)

Parker tried to kill herself again, this time in a room at the Algonquin and with pills, and before she passed out she threw a drinking glass through the window. By then, she was in psychiatric treatment with Dr. Alvan Barach; by this time, so was Heywood Broun. In her hospital room, Benchley made his famous remark, "Dottie, if you don't stop this sort of thing, you'll make yourself sick." Broun's reaction, Barach recalled in 1976, was patently infantile. "She was already a pathological drinker, and a great deal of our time together was directed at eliminating that symptom," he said. "Of course, when I had her in the hospital that time I could keep her sober, at least at first I could. Then, after a couple of days, on my four o'clock visit she would be fine but at six she would be tight. I couldn't figure out what was going on, how she was getting any liquor, until I found out that at five every day she had a visit from Heywood. And despite the fact that he knew she should get over it, despite his ideas, he fed her his gin from five to six. Such an interesting part of Heywood's character—so idealistic and yet so willing to play the little boy and try to outwit me. I think, in a way he was testing my affection the way a child would: love me no matter how bad I am."

By now, Dorothy Parker's second thoughts about the Round Table were not only her own; she and Broun were getting Barach's opinions on the subject every week—opinions the more well-informed for Barach's close social association with the group as a whole. "They were all living lives of extreme casualness," he said—and said he told them then. "They always had to be witty, playful, entertaining. They never spoke about anything for more than a minute, and never in depth, and so they were being forced to sell short on the other side of their nature: the purposeful, striving side. They wrote to make money or to be witty and, knowing instinctively that something was missing, they needed the security the group gave them. The exclusiveness of the group, the amount of time they spent together—I saw that, and still do, as an index of how insecure they all were. One of the results was a terrible malice. Nearly all of them had a terribly malicious streak."

One would be hard-pressed to find malice in Benchley, but Barach's ob-

servations about the group were otherwise applicable. More than anyone else at the Round Table when it began, Benchley showed all the signs of a sustaining and important talent. Even in his first contributions to the *Tribune*'s Sunday magazine—one would call it early Benchley except that there was never any late Benchley—there are elements of a style of writing that have persisted in some of the best writers of a later generation. He began his career with a rich and righteous disdain for a culture taken over by big business. This, for instance, his parody of an advertisement in the *Saturday Evening Post:*

I Am the Strength of the Ages

☆ I have sprung from the depths of the hills.

☆ Before the rivers were brought forth, or even before the green leaves in their softness made the landscape, I was your servant.

☆ From the bowels of the earth, where men toil in darkness, I come, bringing a message of insuperable strength.

☆ From sun to sun I meet and overcome the forces of nature, brothers of mine, yet opponents; kindred, yet foes.

☆ I am silent, but my voice re-echoes beyond the ends of the earth.

☆ I am master, yet I am slave.

☆ I am Woonsocket Wrought Iron Pipe, "the Strongest in the Long Run" (trademark).

Send for illustrated booklet entitled
"The Romance of Iron Pipe"

But in his first collection, some of the best and most incisive of his satiric writing was missing. It was hard not to conclude that his social and aesthetic conscience had given way to his allegiance for an audience full of businessmen. In the *New Republic,* when the collection came out, Edmund Wilson wrote a review of it addressed not only to Benchley but to the whole Round Table group:

Mr. Benchley and his companions amount to something like an antidote to the patent medicines administered by the popular magazines. The great function which they perform is making Business look ridiculous. It is not enough that people should laugh at Mr. Addison Sims of Seattle; they must also learn to laugh, as Mr. Benchley teaches them to, at Window

Edmund Wilson (above) wrote of Benchley: "I used, in the day I first knew him, to urge him to do serious satire, but he proved to be incapable of this. His usual character for himself was that of an unsure suburban duffer who was always being frightened and defeated, and this, even in his Hollywood shorts, seemed to be the only role in which he was able to appear."

Benchley in Scarsdale in 1925 with sons Nathaniel (right) and Robert, Jr. In his role as a householder, Benchley bore an uncanny resemblance to characters in Dorothy Parker's story "Such a Pretty Picture" and play *Close Harmony*, men for whom any break from obligation proved finally impossible.

Card Psychology, and the Woonsocket Wrought Iron Pipe—nor must
they forget Mr. Joseph I. Gonnick and his Cantilever Bridges. . . .

    But why does Mr. Benchley stop here? Why isn't he more savage?
Why does he cling so long to the pleasant nonsense of the Harvard
Lampoon? We know that he can write first-rate satire from his sketch
The Making of a Red (Why has he omitted it from the book, by the way?).
Why does he never let his private indignations get into his humorous
work? . . . What self-consciousness, what timidity has divorced his
convictions from his jokes?

    The truth is, I suppose, that if Mr. Benchley and his friends do not
set out to écraser l'infame, it is because they are not sufficiently detached
from it. In spite of the fact that they make fun of it, they still identify
themselves with it. In order to attack it effectively, they would have to
tear themselves up by the roots. . . .

The review was written in 1922 and proved all too true. Benchley turned from
the plague of a business-dominated society to the minor infections he was coming to know better as a householder in Scarsdale: "Facing the Boy's Camp Problem," "The Church Supper," "Kiddie-Kar Travel" ("In America, there are
two classes of travel—firstclass and with children. . . .") Benchley knew the
problem—"The trouble with me is I can't take anything seriously," he said.
"Damn it, I try to worry and I just can't"—and as he saw himself slipping
deeper into drink and his celebrity, he told Parker in a moment of insight, "Each
of us becomes the thing he most despises."

    But for all his gathering doubt, for all that of Parker and others at the
Round Table, little would change as long as the group was whole, and Wilson's
exhortation would stand unchallenged as a last reminder of their broken promise
to the Twenties.

WIT'S END

PERFORMING SEALS AND FLYING FISH

Talk of politics, economics or social problems at the Round Table in the early 1920s was like so much loose change—noisy, vaguely annoying and disposed of with little thought. Even the Philistinism of big business was a target of satire among them more for extrinsic than intrinsic reasons—more, that is, because it stood so grossly prominent than because of what it stood for. It was available, a sitting duck, and far from damaging the structure underpinning it, their punch-pulled parodies even lent a certain validation. That they would finally end up in the court of the Philistines was probably inevitable, given their time and their singular place in it, but it is all the same astonishing with what breathtaking ease they slipped from one side to the other in the decade's continual skirmishes between vision and capital.

Donald Ogden Stewart is a case in point. In 1919, at the age of twenty-four, with Exeter, Yale and a wartime captaincy in Chicago just behind him, he became a business protégé of Harold Talbott, who was trying to manage the enormous profits he had made selling airplanes during the war. Behind a desk at Talbott's office in Dayton, Ohio, as papers swirled in and out under his absentminded auspices, Stewart found himself wrapping Alexander Hamilton Business Course dust jackets around the latest copies of *Smart Set* and *Vanity Fair* and wondering what a life among the New York literati would be like. He deeply resented the forced sociability of the country club, the humiliation of trying to make himself, as he put it, "persona grata within a hierarchy . . . I had watched myself losing self-respect in a struggle to deserve four thousand dollars a year." Talbott fired him just before Christmas 1920, and on three months' severance, Stewart moved to Greenwich Village. He still had less a desire to write than to be a Writer, but after he proved himself a likeable companion at the Coffee House (a forced sociability among more congenial people, at least), he quickly achieved the success in writing that had eluded him in business. The irony—and the point—is that four years after his *Vanity Fair* debut, and just after delivering what he considered a scathing attack on war profiteers in *Aunt Polly's Story of Mankind,* he was back in the court of Harold Talbott, not now as a war-profit manager but as an invited guest at Talbott's Long Island estate, one of several to which the Algonquin crowd was often invited and always wel-

Donald Ogden Stewart (top, left) and some of the
most avid croquet players of Long Island: Howard
Dietz (top, right), Harold Guinzburg (bottom, left)
and Averill Harriman, the latter two pictured on the
Swope course, which was the scene of two four-hour
matches every Saturday and Sunday. Other regulars
of the game were George Abbott, John Baragwanath,
Raoul Fleischmann and several of Swope's business
associates. Swope and Woollcott were tagged the Kat-
zenjammer Kids on Long Island for their frequent
and noisy contentions during play, and it was an argument over croquet that eventually made them enemies.

By the crestfallen look on Dietz's face, one may assume that George Abbott's assault on his ball succeeded.

come. Talbott's estate was particularly prized for its glass-smooth croquet court. One evening in the late 1920s, in a scene worthy of Gatsby, several of the Round Table's diehard croquet fanatics fought off falling darkness by driving their cars through shrubbery to the perimeter of the course. In the crosshatch of beams their headlights threw on the lawn, they played all night. Parker watched a similar scene at the Swope estate from Ring Lardner's porch. "Jesus Christ," she said, "the heirs to the ages!"

Several factors conspired to bring together the Algonquin set and their once and future targets in high society, prominent among them their motives for writing. However diverse the Algonquinites were in personality, they were unanimous in writing mainly for money. None of them took up the solitary life of the exiles, subsisting on small remittances from home. They came to writing as a business from the beginning, and so it remained for all but a few of them. Woollcott and Broun, of course, were journalists from the start and to the finish, but even Dorothy Parker could answer instantly that she wrote out of "need of money, dear." Benchley gave up writing when performing on stage and in films offered more money, and FPA frequently told of getting the "call" when, as an insurance salesman in Chicago in 1903, he had tried to sell humorist George Ade a policy one February noon and found him just settling down to his breakfast of strawberries. "Nor," he admitted to his diary, "has my desire to write often been borne of any less material inspiration." For Kaufman the only motivation stronger than profit was the ever-lurking possibility of loss, and Sherwood had only money to console him for his increasingly unsatisfying work at *Life* until he was fired in 1928. Even the few among them who were doing their most serious work then—notably Lawrence Stallings (*What Price Glory,* 1924) and Deems Taylor (*The King's Henchman,* 1926)—were only lured by virtue of their successes into better-paying, more popular forms. Stallings went to Hollywood in 1924 and ended his days there without fulfilling the promise all the critics saw in the antiwar play he wrote with Maxwell Anderson, and Deems Taylor, widely considered (and by no one more than himself) to be one of America's best hopes for serious indigenous music, eventually became a distinctly middle-brow music commentator on the radio.

Stallings (top, at left) and Anderson at the time of *What Price Glory?* (Bottom) Deems Taylor and Edna St. Vincent Millay collaborating on *The King's Hench-man*. Such early peak works were an invitation, in the 1920s, to slide into new and more lucrative media: for Stallings, the talkies; for Taylor, radio.

"IT'S THE WORLD'S FIRST *Sensible* MOTOR CAR"
— ALEXANDER WOOLLCOTT

None of them was sanguine about his work; quite the opposite, they could be self-deprecating in the extreme. FPA continually apologized for his poetry, calling one collection "the tawdriest stuff ever wrote"; Dorothy Parker denigrated her work, too. Broun was never satisfied with his writing, Kaufman thought every play he wrote, no matter who the collaborator, was the worst yet, and Woollcott knew nothing he had ever written would outlast him.

Their self-doubts were not without justification. Of the city's pre-eminent critics—by 1925, FPA, Broun, Woollcott and Taylor were all on the *World*—one might have reasonably expected better taste. Adams regularly excoriated writers of free verse, holding up Edgar A. Guest as a suitable model, and his eyes glazed over at Stravinsky and *L'Histoire du Soldat* ("I like my music neat," he said). Taylor was scarcely better; during a major public-relations push on behalf of player pianos, he wrote a column declaring that he had heard a live recitalist and a player piano do the same piece consecutively and had discerned no significant difference, and he determined at the U.S. premiere of Mahler's *Das Lied von der Erde* that it was an inferior work. Woollcott wrote that reading Proust was "like bathing in someone's dirty bath water," and he reserved his greatest enthusiasm for unadulterated mawk. In the 1920s, however, it mattered little that Adams or Broun or Woollcott knew virtually nothing about drama and literature when they became critics. In a sense they were salesmen, not so unlike the prewar theater critics who were expected to solicit advertising from producers whose plays they reviewed. Brooks Atkinson told Howard Teichman that Woollcott "lit the lights over Broadway as no other critic had before." Put another way, he sold tickets—and, quite as important, newspapers. It seems now only natural that in 1925 Woollcott undertook his first testimonial contract for Muriel cigars. He called testimonial endorsement "a faintly discreditable business"—FPA frankly called it "dishonest"—but Woollcott pursued it very profitably indeed on behalf of Chrysler automobiles, Seagram's whisky (after Repeal, of course) and Pullman cars, the last being the only product in the group for which he had any known fondness.

There is still a fine line between journalism and press-agentry, and given the fact that public relations was still new and objectivity in journalism often

How to Pick Out a Hat—*By Bob ("Best-Dressed") Benchley**

1. "Now this shape brings out the Benchley you all know...the man among men; busy, affable...dominating his circle and his affairs...the captain of his ship, master of his soul...Benchley, the successful, the envied, the admired!"

2. "Now here's a shape that brings out the old Benchley buccaneering blood... the sportsman, the dare-devil...quick to resent a slur, or to compliment a pretty woman...Buck Benchley, and will he head them off at Eagle Pass!"

3. "Now this shape emphasizes the Benchley nobody knows...scion of the banking Benchleys...cool, far-sighted...a man with a flair for figures and telephone numbers...a man of integrity...definitely a high-class guy."

4. "I like all three shapes...but can't decide...don't want a hat anyway...just... er...dropped in...*what!!!*...it's the same hat!...the Stetson 'Three-Way'...one hat with three shapes?...why, certainly, I'll take all three of it!"

5. "And look at this three-sided, Stetson-stamped box!...Why, the simon-pure, true-blue Benchley, lover of the beautiful, would carry the hat and **wear the** box...and by golly, as soon as I get out of sight of that hat store, I will!"

* *Author and Star of the Current Series of Paramount Shorts*

Woolcott was not alone in doing testimonials, as this ad Benchley did in the 1930s makes clear. On the other hand, Benchley's ad was a good deal less serious. After having seen himself in the snap-brim ("Benchley the successful, the envied, the admired"), then in the brim-down ("that brings out the old Benchley buccaneering blood") and last in the brim-up ("scion of the banking Benchleys"), he finally decides, as "the simon-pure, true-blue Benchley," to wear the box.

Reflecting the frenzy and clutter in which he lived, Broun's columns had a spirit of dizzy intellectual eclecticism, which meant he was often wrong but never dull.

secondary to the visions of Writers posing as reporters, it is not surprising that the Round Table critics danced over that line at will. They were not alone in that —Grantland Rice was as much a salesman for baseball and boxing as Broun was, in contrast, say, to Ring Lardner, who after the "fixed" 1919 World Series considered every major sporting event suspect. Certainly the corruption of journalists was a commonplace. There is no evidence that any of the journalists at the Round Table were ever bribed, but if fight promoter Tex Rickard could not peddle Broun his line about Tunney or Dempsey, he could at least depend on the fact that Broun would wring the fight for all the drama it was worth and more. Just as no censors were needed at the *Stars and Stripes* office, no bribes were necessary to insure that, whatever their opinion of individual events, the Round Table critics generally would boost the industries it was their task to monitor.

By sending nightlife underground to the speakeasies, national Prohibition did more to weaken certain class barriers than anything before or since. Beginning in 1923, when the stock market was recovered and rising, many young rich men like Harold Talbott, born to their riches or just a generation removed from the fortune's making, found themselves happily free to attend to more than money and eager to sample something of the moral and actual ferment they had read and heard so much about. If the rich men's private clubs retained their devotion to class distinctions, the city's growing number of speakeasies did not— and increasingly it was to the speakeasies rather than the sedate house and club parties that the young rich were being drawn. At Tony Soma's, the Round Table's favorite, or at Jack and Charlie's (later "21") or the Club Durant or practically any other building between Fifth and Sixth Avenue on Fifty-second Street, a new social hybrid was bred in the common soil of alcohol. Such demimonde types as Texas Guinan, Polly Adler, gangsters and gangsters' molls found themselves on even footing with Mackays and Pulitzers and Whitneys. Prizefighters, celebrities of Broadway and the silent movies and the city's literary figures—Round Table and otherwise—found delightedly that they had a great deal to talk about. As Donald Ogden Stewart has said, social boundaries then were "merging together in the interests of having a good time. I think it was partly the breaking down of the barriers after the war, but certainly that stuffy Belmont-Newport thing

Twenty One West Fifty Second Street

ELdorado 5- { 8285 / 8286 / 8287

(Top) A card of admittance to Jack & Charlie's (later "21"). (Bottom) Tony Soma's, the Round Table's favorite speakeasy, after Repeal. People who were wealthy enough could get a prescription for whisky from their physicians, but the speakeasy subculture had more than alcohol to offer the wealthy.

Swope once bet FPA $100,000 to one dollar that the last line of a play they had both seen was "You son of a bitch, stand up" and not, as Adams said, "Stand up, you son of a bitch." Adams, for once, was wrong, and his inscription for *Ask Me Another* was: "To Herbert Bayard Swope, who might have dictated the answers..."

was dead, and young Al Vanderbilt and Sonny Whitney didn't draw any particular lines. The speakeasy was a kind of club where what counted was not social position but whether the people one met were fun to be with." It is no wonder that neighbors of the Ross-Woollcott ménage on Forty-seventh Street habitually mistook their house for a speakeasy: the guest list for the two institutions in the mid-1920s was almost identical.

Being invited into the manses of the rich was, of course, quite another matter. Their first such exposure came at Condé Nast's house during and just after the war, when Parker, Sherwood and Benchley were still on the *Vanity Fair* staff and Broun was one of the magazine's regular contributors. Nast kept a meticulous file of names from which he compiled his guest lists for parties, and the file was divided into three parts: "A" was for those with social pedigree, "B" was for celebrities and "C" was for attractive women, especially chorus girls. Some of the Round Table's actresses still fell into the "C" category just after the war, but the others were charitably classified as celebrities, even though their fame was far from its peak. The fact is that the Algonquin crowd was considered and considered itself a group of perfect guests: they knew enough of fine manners to write books parodying them (Stewart's was called *Perfect Behavior;* Parker's, written with Crowninshield, was called *High Society*), they were already ranking practitioners of the art of indoor entertainment (FPA compiled several question-and-answer books, anthologies for reading aloud and books of games) and their gifted conversation could be relied upon to enliven any gathering. For the Round Tablers, the returns in food and good liquor were plentiful. They cemented important connections with publishers and editors and, as time went on, they compiled from these parties a roster of angels for their work and play.

As executive editor of "their" paper, the *World,* Herbert Bayard Swope was their most beneficent patron, giving parties first in his glittering twenty-eight-room apartment on West Fifty-eighth Street, then at his Great Neck, Long Island, estate—and it was through him that they made their way in the mid-decade into the legendary parties of millenial extravagance that made Fitzgerald think of the decade as "the greatest, gaudiest spree in history."

The "tinge of the tarbrush" remark to Swope has also been attributed to Robeson himself. Although Robeson was a frequent kibitzer at Thanatopsis sessions and partied at the Ross-Grant-Woollcott house, he apparently never visited the Swope estate.

While it lasted, the society of Great Neck especially was, as Margaret Swope put it, "an absolutely seething bordello of interesting people." Ring Lardner had moved to Great Neck in 1921, Pulitzer and Talbott had huge estates close by, Swope moved there in 1922, Neysa and Baragwanath in 1925, and from 1922 to 1924, Scott and Zelda Fitzgerald rented there. Within party-jumping distance were Ed Wynn, Eddie Cantor, W. C. Fields, Fanny Brice, John Golden, George M. Cohan, Laurette Taylor and Jane Cowl. Lardner, whose porch faced the Swopes' front lawn cum croquet course and who never much liked his neighbor, complained that Swope ran "an almost continuous house party. A number of other neighbors do the same. There are guests in large numbers roaming these woods all the time. Apparently they become confused occasionally and forget at whose house they are really stopping, for they wander in at all hours demanding refreshment and entertainment at the place that happens to be nearest at the moment."

Swope's parties were not only frequent and lavish, but ran weekend long. Dinner was rarely over before midnight, and Swope boasted that "no one in my house goes to bed before 3:00 A.M." At any hour, whatever food or drink anyone wanted would be served. In his biography of Swope, E. J. Kahn wrote that one guest who asked for a stick of gum was served a selection of six different packs on a silver tray, and another who asked for something sweet in the middle of the night was served an entire chocolate cake and a bottle of champagne. The household staff seemed legion, and each servant was impeccably trained to manage a scrambled routine, sometimes serving breakfast, lunch and dinner to various guests simultaneously. Yet however different a weekend at Swope's could be from the Round Table's somewhat more modest life in the city, he shared with them their love for games and was, if such a thing was possible, even more obsessive than they were about winning. His furies over a missed wicket were notorious, and no one but Adams could match him in question-and-answer games. He was like some of them, too, in that his generosity was driven to a certain extent by social and professional ambition. His concomitant ambivalence about being Jewish was one of Woollcott's favorite targets. At a Thanatopsis session one night, Swope offhandedly said, "Did you boys know that I have a little Jew-

Ruth Gordon and Gregory Kelly were regulars at the Swope estate, and in Gordon's play, *Over Twenty-One,* she wrote of her Swope character: "Type-casting for a President of the United States? The world has been nice to him, and he acknowledges this by constantly giving it a graceful smile."

ish blood?" Woollcott's famous answer was, "Yes, and Paul Robeson's got a tinge of the tarbrush."

But Swope was also of a different order from his Algonquin protégés (he always called FPA, Woollcott, Broun, Stallings, Taylor and the other op-ed writers "my boys"), and he was careful to keep it that way; he joined their Thanatopsis game because he enjoyed poker and their company—and because he often won—but he would never have eaten with them at the Algonquin: that was Woollcott's territory, and wherever he was it had to be his ground alone. Most places in those days welcomed Swope humbly. He had police escorts to sporting events at Madison Square Garden. He hired an entire railroad car to transport him to the Dempsey-Tunney fight in Chicago (where Tex Rickard, whom Swope befriended despite his reputation for lining journalists' pockets, presented him with sixteen $100 front-row seats). The Whitneys kept a suite of rooms for him at their mansion in Saratoga during the racing season.

He was generous in his patronage of the Algonquin writers under him at the *World;* by 1925 they were all making $30,000 or so annually, and they were guests at his house nearly every weekend. Some stayed longer: Ruth Gordon stayed for months after her husband Gregory Kelly died; Dorothy Parker stayed for weeks at a stretch. His food bills alone ran into the thousands of dollars a week. Even on his ample income from the *World* and with investment tips from his good friend Bernard Baruch, he lived always at the edge of his worth. He lived that life and paid the bills for it because he was a gambler, in spirit and in fact. His Thanatopsis winnings could not have helped him much; even when the stakes became astronomical to the others, with winners taking home up to $10,000, they were still low compared to the stakes in games he was used to playing. According to Kahn, his record-making game was played in Joshua Cosden's private Pullman car in Palm Beach in 1923, and it went on for forty-eight hours straight. When it was over Cosden had lost $443,000, Florenz Ziegfeld had lost $294,300, J. Leonard Replogle had won $267,000 and Swope had won $470,300. The books never were cleared for that game—Ziegfeld died without paying his debt—but when a journalist on salary takes the pot in a game of millionaires, it settles a score of one sort. As Broun wrote of his Swope character in *The Boy Grew*

WIT'S END

Dietz first caught Jerome Kern's attention with his contributions to FPA's column, and after his collaboration with Kern in 1924 he was finally admitted to the Round Table.

Older: "Maybe you got the impression from what I said that he's just a big bluff. That's only about ten per cent right. He is a big bluff but in addition to that he's got the stuff."

Through their connection to Swope, the Algonquin group came into the full hue of the socially chosen. Suddenly they were dining with national politicians and financiers, and taking their place in New York's social hierarchy. Woollcott was, of course, thrilled by the fact and began recruiting new members of the inner circle with redoubled vigor and changed standards. Howard Dietz, for example, who had been outcast until his collaboration with Jerome Kern on *Dear Sir* in 1924 and his appearance as a connected businessman at the Swope estate, was warmly admitted to the Round Table. Noël Coward, who captured Woollcott's affection with his Broadway hit *The Vortex* in 1925 and a one-word critique of a play they both attended—"teejus"—was also welcomed under the red-velvet rope that Frank Case had installed to set off the Rose Room from lunchtime celebrity watchers. Irene Castle, the Astaires, the Barrymores, of course the Lunts, Katharine Cornell—in short, every prominent figure of the stage—was by now welcome at the Round Table and at Neshobe. If more of them came to the island than to lunch, it was because of their demanding schedules in the city and because less verbal play and more reverence was the rule at Neshobe, but both settings changed to accommodate them. The unwritten membership rules of the Round Table were waived to allow for nontalkers, and on Neshobe there came what was called "the Revolt of the Classes against the Masses," the classes demanding electricity and running water, the masses holding out and, of course, losing. Initiation fees were raised to $1,000, and members were found who could afford to pay—Raoul Fleischmann of the yeast family and Harold Guinzburg, founder of the Viking Press, among them.

The high-social life that was mother's milk to Woollcott, however, felt toxic to other members of the group. Broun complained that they were being cast in the role of "performing seals" in Swope's company, and Kahn related a story that shows in a general way what he meant, how it was done. The scene was a Swope-sponsored party given by Taylor's replacement as music critic of the *World,* Samuel Chotzinoff:

Barton captioned his caricature of FPA: "Franklin P. Adams—Who, after having masqueraded for years as the ugly duckling of journalism, has blossomed forth in a dashing mustache which reveals him as a handsome Rajah . . ." The new growth came with his courtship of Esther Root.

The high spot was an endurance contest featuring five of the greatest living violinists—Joseph Fuchs, Jascha Heifetz, Paul Kochaniski, Albert Spalding and Efrem Zimbalist. They all played simultaneously Paganini's showy, accelerated Moto Perpetuo. *As soon as each got to the end, he was supposed to begin again. Marc Connelly started off the gifted quintet by firing a blank pistol, and as they all sawed dexterously away, the other guests egged them on by throwing money on the floor, as a prize for the survivor. . . . Fuchs prevailed, fiddling for twenty-one minutes. It was days before any of them was ready again for Carnegie Hall.*

Algonquinites, too, were stretched thin by the demands of their Long Island hosts; party going, game playing, prank pulling and crack making came increasingly to be expected of them, and with varying degrees of reluctance, they complied.

Woollcott recruited Harpo Marx to the Round Table in 1924, and Harpo proved a willing, even enthusiastic, "performing seal"—collecting the Swopes' silver in his sleeves and letting it drop at a propitious moment, inviting all of Hell's Kitchen to a party at the Forty-seventh Street house without letting the proprietors in on it, and delighting other Algonquinites, as he wrote in his memoir, by making Woollcott nervous: "Instead of giving him my hand, I gave him my leg, the old switch gag . . . He pushed my knee away in disgust. 'See here, Marx,' he said with the full hoity-toity treatment. 'Kindly confine your buffoonery to the stage. Off it, you are a most unfunny fellow.'" He picked pockets at Swope's weekend parties and otherwise brought his stage character along wherever he went.

FPA despaired of the demands of Swope weekends not at all; such socializing was his work (it would ornament the Saturday column) and, in any case, his delight. FPA was, moreover, newly in love. The woman was Esther Sayles Root (Smith '15), and she had all the looks and schooled charm and good nature he felt were missing in his wife—and the hereditary stock he envied. As he waited for Minna's divorce to become final, he saw his life and its charms as new through Esther's eyes.

Broun, however, could not shake the vision of himself as a paid prankster in the court of the rich, a sensitivity perhaps explained by the fact that he had

Among the most willing "performing seals" were Heifetz (caricatured top, left), Harpo, and Noël Coward (pictured with his more reticent friends, the Lunts). Of the three, however, Harpo was the only one to register misgivings upon first meeting the group. The night Woollcott went backstage at *I'll Say She Is* to introduce himself, he took Harpo to a Thanatopsis game. It was a difficult initiation. FPA said of Woollcott to the players: "He wants the world to think he invented the Marx Brothers, and he brings one of the acrobats in here like he was presenting a favorite son at court." "I hope you fry in hell," said Woollcott. Harpo lost one hundred dollars that night, and after agreeing to play the next Saturday, as well, he left, wondering "whether I would ever have made it [into the group] if I had been a winner...."

been virtually abandoned to the speakeasies. It was his new assignment—from Swope—to cover the city's nightlife under his banner "It Seems To Me," but however well he did it, the longer nights and shorter days and the necessarily frothier columns he was turning in left him feeling professionally unfulfilled and physically hung-over. In 1925, just months away from his notorious break with the *World*'s editorial council over the Sacco and Vanzetti case, he joined the Racquet and Tennis club, one of the most exclusive private men's clubs in New York and one relying more on wealth than on achievement as its criterion for membership (Broun's father was a member). Also in that year, he vented disillusion with such attainments in a third novel, *Gandle Follows His Nose,* an improbable and unsuccessful fantasy in which the hero finds a magic lamp, loses it and is consoled by the genie:

> *It's my belief that nobody ever got much out of the lamp. Somehow none of them could think up many things to wish for. A girl, a palace, a bag of gold and that's the end of it. Wanting things is fun. Getting them ruins your appetite.*

In a way, the conflict suffered by Broun and some Rose Room colleagues was like the conundrum of Carl Sandburg's flying fish: adaptability to two elements and a resultant discomfort in both. As Woollcott busily recruited, as Harpo and other theatrical friends played happily on, Broun withdrew a step. Ruth Hale was delighted. When she had bought herself a farm in Connecticut in 1923, she hoped it would lure him away from New York and what she perceived as the frittering away of his talent and compassion on speakeasy conversation and pointless love affairs. Broun cherished both his chosen roles—as the disciple of disorder in the Racquet and Tennis and as the blue-blooded champion of the masses—but it was apparent to him, too, that a reckoning was inevitable. His flask of gin and bitters was still at the ready in his rear wallet pocket, but as often as his schedule would allow, he sampled it alone and at Hale's Sabine Farm, so called for Horace's retreat from Imperial Rome.

In 1924, Kaufman and Connelly wrote their last and best work together, *Beggar on Horseback,* a play about the plight of an artist in a rich man's keep. The

protagonist is a composer of high- and middle-brow music who seems to be able to make a living of neither. In a dream sequence, he marries a rich industrialist's daughter and goes into the family business in order to underwrite his serious work, but frenetic rounds of office busy-work deplete his creative energies, and finally he contrives to murder all his in-laws, wife included. After a harum-scarum dream trial, he is sentenced to end his days writing music to order in his father-in-law's Consolidated Art Factory. When he can stand it no longer and resolves to strike, a guard cracks a whip across his face and chants:

> *You take our money and you live our life.*
> *We own you. We own you.*
> *You take our money and you live our life.*
> *We own you. We own you.*
> *You take our money and you live our way.*
> *We pay the piper and we tell him what to play.*
> *You sold your soul and you can't get away.*
> *We own you, we own you.*

The hero decides not to marry the industrialist's daughter when the dream is over, but (Kaufman's characteristic finesse) he decides to finish not his serious work but a popular, orchestral pantomime called "A Kiss in Xanadu," which he thought even the rich girl's father would like. (It was written for the play by Deems Taylor.)

In what one hopes was an inside reference to their own collaboration, Kaufman and Connelly wrote in this conversation between a visitor to the Art Factory and one of the writers:

> *"I see you're writing a new one."*
> *"Of course. I'm under contract."*
> *"What's that?"*
> *"That's my last one."*
> *"But weren't you just dictating from it, for your new one?"*
> *"Yes. They like it that way."*

Both men felt, after *Beggar,* that they had been together too long, that they were writing and rewriting the same play, and both felt the other's next idea was too close to the ones they had written before. Kaufman told Howard Teichman he

"Satire is what closes on Saturday night" was perhaps Kaufman's most famous saying— but *Beggar on Horseback,* a brilliant satire of American philistinism that Kaufman and Connelly fashioned from a German play, had a Broadway run of 144 performances.

also wanted to end the professional relationship because Connelly was playing harder than he was working. "Margalo Gillmore always had a dead cat to bury," Kaufman said, "or someone was always arriving and had to be met. Or someone was always sailing and a bon voyage party was being held aboard ship. Finally, I told him, 'Marc, someday New York Harbor will freeze over and you'll write the best damn play anyone's ever seen.' " They resurrected a play they had written long before, aptly retitled it *Be Yourself,* and presented it to mixed reviews. Then they embarked on solo projects—not the first for Connelly, but for Kaufman, the first and last.

Both works were concerned with the perils to integrity of a Philistine world. The hero of Connelly's *The Wisdom Tooth* is an office clerk who has lost the fervor of youth in the exigencies of getting along, and in the third act he wins back his spirit by bucking the System and losing his job. Kaufman's hero in *The Butter and Egg Man* is an outland naïf hoodwinked by shysters into bankrolling a play. His lost virtue is retrieved when he outwits the big-city hucksters and quits show business. Of the two, Connelly's was by far the better play, richer in plot and character than Kaufman's rapid-fire, stick-figure creation. In that sense, the plays reflected the playwrights' nearly opposite future courses. Connelly would buck the theatrical system of turning out topical comedies and turn inward for future themes while remaining unreconstructedly playful in life. Kaufman, on the other hand, would soon be working harder than ever before, and he would stay with the course he depicted in *The Butter and Egg Man* as unrelievedly grim: plays are worked-over, patched-up dry goods, the play implies; Broadway producers are insensate cretins; the theater itself is corrupted and corrupting. Russell Lembke once wrote that the "amazing achievement of the Kaufman plays" was that "we laugh heartily at what amounts to severe criticism of ourselves," but his work of this period seems intensely self-critical as well. Reading the plays in the black and white of typescript, it is easy not to laugh, to see in them a documentary light. In the best satire of all the Algonquin writers, there is a volatile, shifting quality; now the comic touch is obvious, then suddenly it is gone, and the authors slip in and out of the picture like fireflies, never alighting, always avoiding the vulnerability of

Variety laid the professional divorce of Kaufman and Connelly to Connelly's rigidity, but it was more nearly the opposite: Kaufman's intense devotion to work and Connelly's more casual approach. Connelly's *The Wisdom Tooth* was a hit, but he later went into such a fallow period that, when Simon and Schuster published a newly discovered manuscript by Charles Dickens titled *Life of Our Lord,* Kaufman said of his old collaborator: "Charles Dickens, dead, writes more than Marc Connelly alive."

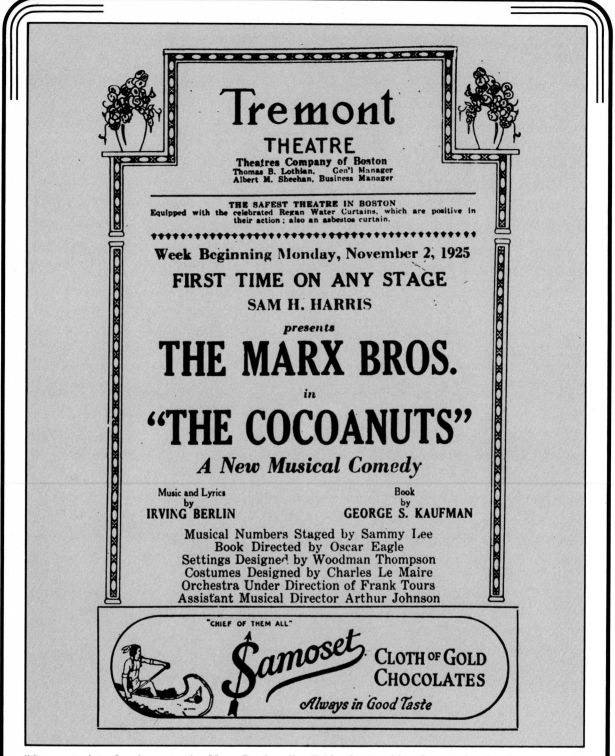

Tremont
THEATRE
Theatres Company of Boston
Thomas B. Lothian,   Gen'l Manager
Albert M. Sheehan, Business Manager

THE SAFEST THEATRE IN BOSTON
Equipped with the celebrated Regan Water Curtains, which are positive in their action ; also an asbestos curtain.

Week Beginning Monday, November 2, 1925

FIRST TIME ON ANY STAGE
SAM H. HARRIS

presents

THE MARX BROS.
in
"THE COCOANUTS"
A New Musical Comedy

| Music and Lyrics by **IRVING BERLIN** | Book by **GEORGE S. KAUFMAN** |

Musical Numbers Staged by Sammy Lee
Book Directed by Oscar Eagle
Settings Designed by Woodman Thompson
Costumes Designed by Charles Le Maire
Orchestra Under Direction of Frank Tours
Assistant Musical Director Arthur Johnson

"CHIEF OF THEM ALL"

$amoset CLOTH OF GOLD CHOCOLATES
Always in Good Taste

"*Cocoanuts* introduced me to the Marx Brothers," Kaufman said. "*Cocoanuts* was a comedy, and the Marx Brothers are comics, but meeting them was a tragedy." Kaufman took a lot of ribbing at the Round Table about writing for people who threw away the script, and he even encouraged the idea, once hushing a spectator backstage during a rehearsal to say: "I thought I heard one of my lines."

The preponderant evidence is that Kaufman's lines were some of the best ever written for the Marx Brothers and that they used his scripts as written—or, as Kaufman would have had it, as rewritten. Groucho tried to get one personal piece of business into *Cocoanuts* and argued for it by telling Kaufman, "they laughed at Fulton and his steamboat, too." Kaufman's rejoinder: "Not at matinees."

a fixed position. But there, inescapable in the only play he ever wrote alone, is Kaufman, the prodigy of Broadway, abjuring his accepted fate. Pitted against the security lust that kept him still at the *Times* drama desk as he earned as much as $50,000 a week on box-office alone, the wish in his work of the mid-decade that writing for the theater could be more than it was for him never had a chance. He went on to write scripts for the Marx Brothers (*The Cocoanuts* and *Animal Crackers* among them)—work for which he will be long remembered and rightly praised. The point, of course, is not that he cheated his talent, only that he glimpsed for a moment what might have been and the dark side of what would be. As he said of himself over some poker table: "I'd rather be a poor winner than any kind of loser."

Kaufman's dilemma was in a way *the* dilemma of the writer in New York in the 1920s as the fireworks display of business in all its distracting, exhilarating variety came to outshine natural light. But if the social ascendance of the Round Table writers and the attendant tug of material success pulled some of them into an exquisite sort of purgatory, the new order of things came to Harold Ross much as the war had come—as an answered prayer.

It is one of the persistent puzzles of publishing history that Harold Ross could found and edit a magazine as sophisticated as *The New Yorker:* the man who popped into a conversation James Thurber and H.L. Mencken were having about Willa Cather to say, "Willa Cather, Willa Cather, did he write *The Private Life of Helen of Troy?*"; the man Edna Ferber first met at Kaufman's apartment shooting craps on a blanket and thought he was some poor boob Woollcott and Adams had dragged out of the war for their private amusement; the man Kaufman at first thought "had a good chance of starving to death . . . a complete misfit"; the man who was editor of two ridiculous postwar military magazines.

But perhaps that was exactly his strength; what posed an exquisite dilemma to subtler, more vulnerable minds struck Ross as a gold mine, a cinch. In 1924, he successively scuttled his plans for a newspaper of the shipping industry, for a tabloid with a full-color advertising insert and for a cheap paper-

back publishing house, and chose to devote full time to what he then conceived as a high-class humor magazine exclusively for and about New York.

That he was able to capitalize on the new speakeasy mix of classes by providing them with a house organ of sorts—indeed, that he was able to capitalize a magazine at all—owed everything to the social education and connections he was given at the Round Table. Likewise, the magazine's everything-be-damned light touch owed everything to the sensibility of the group that gave it birth. The magazine's few causes were distinctly Adamsesque—the no-smoking regulations in the New York Public Library, for example, and the lack of sufficient gallery space above the city's squash courts. As Thurber wrote of the first few issues:

> *The amiable periodical tiptoed away from disputes and disturbances, since it had nothing particularly in mind to prove or disprove, to attack or defend. Now and then it jostled the celebrated, or thumbed its nose at the powerful, but all in a spirit of gay mockery.* The New Yorker *was not really angry. It just didn't give a good goddam.*

Though Ross later said that listing five Algonquinites as advisory editors for the first year was "the most dishonest thing I ever did," it is appropriate that the only editors' names ever to appear on a *New Yorker* masthead belonged to members of the Round Table.

The New Yorker's early issues of 1925 seem more symptomatic than reflective of their times. In contrast to Mencken's *American Mercury* and Crown-inshield's *Vanity Fair, The New Yorker* was resolutely middle-brow. It intended to put its readers in touch with the Pulse, as *Vanity Fair* did, and it promised to weed out the dull and mindless, as the *Mercury* did, but its sights were set decidedly lower than either of those magazines. News events, Ross promised, would be treated "in a manner not too serious. . . . *The New Yorker* will present the truth and the whole truth without fear and without favor, but will not be iconoclastic." Its main purpose, his prospectus continued, was to apprise readers of "what is going on in the public and semipublic smart gathering places—the clubs, hotels, cafés, supper clubs, cabarets and other resorts . . . the comings, goings and doings in the village of New York." While Mencken

Hirschfeld's interpretation of the unreconstructable hayseed Ross, whose most prized line was quoted around New York with considerable relish: "Don't think I'm not incoherent."

pricked the booboisie, while Crowninshield cooed over cubists, Ross printed bootleg liquor prices at the end of each "Talk of the Town" section. This, *The New Yorker*'s review of Kaufman's *The Butter and Egg Man:*

> The Butter and Egg Man, *then, is not for the artistically inclined. By finding out what plays the artistically inclined propose to patronize, however, and by staying carefully away from them, the readers of* The New Yorker *can have a merry, entertaining season.*

Ross received little editorial help from the Round Tablers on his masthead: in 1925, Dorothy Parker sent in only two poems and a small piece of prose; Benchley sent in one piece; Woollcott, Connelly, Kaufman and Miller nothing. Adams did come in once a week to choose poetry (most of *The New Yorker*'s poets were also "Conning Tower" contributors), and Marc Connelly went to the office once in a while to do something clerical that he cannot now recall. But the group's influence was stamped on virtually every page of the magazine, its practical help advanced at every critical turn. John Peter Toohey suggested the magazine's name. Woollcott arranged for Ross to meet Raoul Fleishmann over a Thanatopsis poker game, and at FPA's wedding to Esther Root in May of 1925, Fleischmann was convinced by Murdock and Brock Pemberton, among others, to continue financing the flagging enterprise. As Ross struggled to rid himself of the "he-she" editors who populated the early issues with predictable gags, it was Alice Miller who sent over two relatives—Wolcott Gibbs and Ellin Mackay—to help out, and Minna Adams who sent over Ward MacAllister's nephew, Ralph Ingersoll. Several of the Round Tablers appeared in full-page newspaper advertisements endorsing the magazine.

Whatever debt Ross may have thought he owed the Round Table was more than repaid in the first eighteen months. As unabashedly as any "Conning Tower" column, the magazine's critics gushed over Algonquinites' works— from *The Wisdom Tooth* to Deems Taylor's *Circus Days* to FPA's "Conning Tower" collections. If the citizens of New York were already convinced that the Rose Room was *the* locus of urban sophistication, *The New Yorker* did nothing to dissuade them. In Lois Long's column on nightlife, the reader could learn what Bea Kaufman was wearing, how Dorothy Parker was arranging

In *Here at The New Yorker*, Brendan Gill describes Ross's official portrait (above), which still hangs in the magazine's editorial offices: "Miserably aware that he is having a formal portrait taken, he stares into the camera with the air of a small-town crook arrested for having tried to hold up a bank with a water pistol." Most pictures of Ross are distinctly unflattering, and pictures of Ross are few indeed.

her hair and what lunch at the Round Table was Really Like. It is of course reasonable to suppose that in order to cover "the comings, goings and doings in the village of New York" Ross had to cover the Round Table, except that in mid-1926 he declared and partially enforced a moratorium on further anecdotes about or by the group. By then, of course, the magazine was aiming higher than it had before.

The beginning was a series of compromises to attract the attention of Park Avenue—and Madison Avenue, in the process. Ross said there were two things he would never do when he had his own magazine: run a column about pets or a column about fashion. He had done both before the first year was out. He confided his reasons for hiring Ralph Ingersoll rather abashedly to James Thurber: "He knows what clubs Percy R. Pyne belongs to, and everybody else. He has entree in the right places. He knows who owns private Pullman cars, and he can have tea with all the little old women that still have coachmen or footmen or drive electric runabouts. It's damned important for a magazine called *The New Yorker* to have such a man around."

One of his most significant compromises, which turned into one of his most fortuitous ones, came over an article sent him by Ellin Mackay. Mackay was Alice Duer Miller's niece, Bea Kaufman's friend and the daughter of Clarence Mackay, one of the wealthiest men in America. Known principally for her parentage, she was a writer of small distinction for the women's magazines and *Vanity Fair* whose identification with both Flaming Youth (she was twenty-two in 1925) and High Society was just the sort of imprimatur Ross's magazine needed. Nevertheless, when Ross opened the leatherbound, elegantly scripted manuscript she sent him, his enthusiasm curdled. He sent the manuscript, byline deleted, to Ralph Ingersoll for his opinion. Ingersoll thought it dreadful but likely to elicit strong reaction, so Ross asked Fillmore Hyde to rewrite it. Miss Mackay, with the officers of the Social Register behind her, protested the revised version, and Ross was forced to print it in the original or not at all. Buckling to such pressure for one of the first and last times, he printed it as written under the title " Why We Go to Cabarets: A Post-Debutante Explains."

As written it was one of the most obliquely snobbish pieces of journalism ever published. Its point was that modern socialites preferred public cabarets to private parties because they preferred chosen company to the imported stag line of tradition. The main corollary to her argument, and the publicity-making point, was that many men in the stag line were actually not Harvard or Yale men at all but West Siders pretending to be. "We do not particularly like dancing shoulder to shoulder with gaudy and fat drummers," she admitted. "We go [to cabarets] because, like our Elders, we are fastidious. We go because we prefer rubbing elbows in a cabaret to dancing at an exclusive party with all sorts and kinds of people." In a second installment, in December of 1925, called "The Declining Function: A Post-Debutante Rejoices," she enlarged on the point. In the old days, she wrote, "functions" featured concert artists singing or playing the piano or harpsichord. Her lament was that talents of such caliber were now scarce and that hostesses were turning to celebrities— rude things!—to perk up their parties. She contemplated how topsy-turvy the world had become when people who had only fame to recommend them were paid obeisance by their social betters.

In the same article, somehow, she commended the young for their revolt. "Modern girls are conscious of the importance of their own identity," she wrote, "and they marry whom they choose, satisfied to satisfy themselves." Six months later, the reason for the addendum was apparent. The dark rumor about her that had been circulating whisper by whisper in the drawing rooms of Park Avenue came flashing true in the headlines: Miss Mackay had married the songwriter (and millionaire) Isador Balin (Irving Berlin) against her father's explicit wish and despite a cooling-off trip through the Continent. It was one of the greatest scandals New York society had ever suffered and perhaps as great a boon to *The New Yorker*'s image as Miss Mackay's articles had been. Irving Berlin was, after all, one of the most prominent of the Algonquin group's peripheral members, Ellin Mackay was a *New Yorker* intimate, and the daring young couple, hiding from the press while waiting to sail on their European honeymoon, had chosen none other than the Ross-Grant-Woollcott house for their refuge.

Adams, temporarily without mustache, with Esther aboard the *Mauretania* and bound for their honeymoon in Europe. Esther was introduced to FPA in the spring of 1923 by Edna St. Vincent Millay, who wrote for FPA's column under the name Nancy Boyd and who lived downstairs from Esther on Waverly Place.

"You know, it's pretty nice here," FPA is supposed to have said on first meeting Esther. "I think I'd like to move in." After a two-year courtship and his divorce, they were married in Connecticut with all the Round Tablers in attendance, and in the next six years, they would have four children.

Irving and Ellin Mackay Berlin after the honeymoon. Their doings after the wedding were as closely held as state secrets by their friends. The New York *Times* seemed to have a line on their activities and whereabouts, but Jane Grant, who hid them in the Forty-seventh Street house, surely was not responsible for the newspaper's report that Mackay's first act after the wedding was to telephone Ross. As the *Times* reported it, Ross answered, "Hello, Miss Mackay," and she replied: "Oh, no, it's Mrs. Berlin. I'm no Lucy Stoner. The fact is, I shan't be able to get my piece in on time. I'm leaving town in twenty minutes." The information was obviously wrong, but it was widely disseminated—and just the right sort of publicity for the young and struggling *New Yorker*.

The national and local press seemed to find in the Berlin-Mackay wedding a topic of extravagant importance. *The New Yorker* itself made no mention of the event except to run on its Heroes of the Week page a drawing of Berlin over this caption: "Mr. Irving Berlin—whose marriage to Miss Ellin Mackay last week crowded the popular science story off the front page of the New York *Times* for three successive days. This quiet development, in fact, established a new international record of newspaper lineage and leaves the daily press practically nothing to look forward to but the marriage of the Prince of Wales —if and when." All very breezy, but no one benefited more from the lineage than *The New Yorker*. The magazine had been getting better all along; its coverage of the Scopes trial was magnificent, for example. But it was the work and marriage of Ellin Mackay that earned the magazine a new regard in the upper reaches of society—and among advertisers looking to that group as a market—and it was only with that prestige that *The New Yorker* was able to take a firm and lasting hold. By the early spring of 1926, some of the magazine's major advertisers were Rolls-Royce, Pierce-Arrow, Rajah silks, the French and Cunard Lines, Saks Fifth Avenue, Altman's, Brooks Brothers, Croydon Cravats, Bonwit-Teller and the marketers of such products as yachts and silk pajamas.

Ross's position on the question of courting the rich was obviously unequivocal; although he found that most of his readers were lower-ranking regulars of the speakeasies, he used the Social Register as his circulation-promotion list. Coming at the time when other Round Tablers were nursing doubts about stepping out of class and character, the direction taken by Ross and *The New Yorker* thus signified a widening rift in the Algonquin group: on the one side, those who questioned the wisdom of their social ascendance and its concomitant demands; on the other, those who turned blank stares to such questions.

Ross was, some believe, too boorish or naïve to be successful at social pretense himself, but the same was not true of others in the group. As the Round Table's network of social connections grew, from 1924 to 1926, the press agents particularly found themselves at increasing distance from their old friends. David Wallace suffered most notoriously. Several of them wrote imaginary quotes as

column fillers for *The New Yorker,* intended as belittlement for Wallace's lack of wit. One was: " 'It,' quoth gnomic graybeard David H. Wallace, 'never rains but it pours.' " Another: "As David H. Wallace says, 'Tea and coffee are good to drink, but tennis is livelier.' " Wallace had got all the mileage he could out of his connections among actresses, and his role at the Round Table was increasingly confined to laughing at the jokes of others and bearing those at his expense.

Murdock Pemberton got even ruder treatment, considering that he was *The New Yorker*'s art critic in 1925 and was in large part responsible for the group's inauguration. He remembered the change decades later. "It was becoming more and more like a social register," he said. "I still went there for lunch, because I really enjoyed their company. But—I'll give you one example. Frank Adams was sick up at his home in Stamford one weekend, and since he'd been invited to Swopes', he called me and asked if I'd drive him down. I was living over at Broun's place nearby, so I said sure, and figured that I'd finally get to see this place everybody raved about. I guess I thought I might finally get to belong in that group, too. To make a long story short, when I got him there, he didn't give me a chance to even get out of the car. He just said 'Thanks,' and I felt all I could do was drive away—that was the feeling he gave me. A few of us were frozen out that way, not so much from the Round Table as from those other places."

One who helped with the freezing was Beatrice Kaufman, whose teas on Fifty-eighth Street joined the other Round Table adjuncts as a fixed institution in 1924. She enjoyed her husband's success more easily than he did, and she became one of the city's most fashionably dressed women and most elegant hostesses. Her closest friends in New York were two of the city's richest women —Marjorie Oelrichs, who inherited a vast fortune and married Eddy Duchin, and Ellin Mackay Berlin. The summer she joined Woollcott in a villa on the Riviera, they entertained like a royal couple such renowned figures as Otis and Cornelia Otis Skinner, Shaw, Maugham, Frank Harris, Grace Moore. When she and Kaufman moved to Hollywood in the Thirties, she wrote her mother letters replete with Names: "It's like old home week," she wrote in 1935. "The Swopes arrived yesterday, and Oscar Levant is coming on Wednesday. The party at the

Donald Ogden Stewarts' was great fun the other night, and my evening was made for me when Chaplin sat down beside me and stayed for hours. Or did I write that; I can't remember. Paulette Goddard was there, too—very beautiful; everyone says they are married. So were Joan Bennett, the Frederic Marches, Dotty Parker, Mankiewiczes, etc.'' For Beatrice, the early years of such associations were heady, and Kaufman was unbothered; he could focus and work in any clean room with a typewriter.

But for others in the group, the social exertions were exhausting and enervating. Edna Ferber chastened Robert Sherwood one weekend at the Swopes' in 1925: if he really wanted to do serious work, she said, he ought to get away from the Round Table and all its social annexes. Dorothy Parker was given the same warning by her editor at Boni & Liveright when that firm contracted for her first book. Donald Ogden Stewart was warned away by his editor, Eugene Saxton of Doran, that year. The Round Tablers in the care of Dr. Alvan Barach were given the same advice and were quick to agree. But even Barach found that the enticements of Long Island parties were luring him away from his work, and he credits a talk with Bernard Baruch with pulling him back.

Baruch had always been a patron of the Round Table. He handled Neysa McMein's finances before she was married. He had various members of the group down for hunting at his estate in North Carolina. As one of Swope's best patrons and friends, he was a frequent participant in Swope weekends. He was not, however, one of the leading players. In fact, he worried about what incessant socializing was doing to his friends, Swope most of all. One morning in early 1926, when he and Dr. Barach were the only ones awake in the household, Baruch asked Barach to take a walk with him. "He took me by the arm as we walked up a hill," Barach recalls, "and it was obvious he had something special on his mind. Finally he got around to it. I remember, he said, 'Dr. Barach, you are a man of considerable accomplishment, and you surely have a remarkable career ahead of you. Seneca once said that a man has many hazards, and that popularity is the most hazardous of all. Now, Mr. Swope is one of my best friends, and otherwise I wouldn't say this, but if you spend all your time here at the Swopes' parties, you will lose the energy and drive to develop yourself. Now that's enough said; let's go back and get some coffee.' "

It was *ur*-Baruch, of course, quoting Seneca on the hilltop of a great estate, and Barach never forgot the advice. He tried in years that followed to pass it along to his patients, who included both Herbert and Margaret Swope, but he found that despite his counsel, neurotic symptoms were blossoming in the group like wildflowers in spring. Georges, the Rose Room headwaiter, said, "It must be a boom. They're ordering ice cream on top of everything." Benchley replied, "Yeah, and then they grab their lollipops and pitter-patter over to their psychiatrists."

Perhaps the most palpable of all the symptoms was that of Ed MacNamara, the "singing cop," a onetime boarder of Broun's and one of the few students Enrico Caruso ever coached. In 1925, he developed a persistent lump in his throat, which Frank Sullivan traced directly to the Round Table: "He had one of the first inferiority complexes," Sullivan remembered. "He could never get over the wonder of being accepted into that magic circle, the Round Table. . . . I guess it got to be a strain on him trying to be bright all the time instead of just singing as God made him to do."

In the same year, Broun's chronic claustrophobia became so acute that he found it impossible to sit inside a theater for more than an act, which resulted in his giving up drama criticism. Broun's groundless worries about his heart also escalated dangerously; several times, Barach had to rush over to his apartment when Broun thought it was going to burst out of his chest. "He couldn't walk as far as the corner once he got outside the building," Barach remembered.

One day over lunch, Broun told his friends about a recurrent dream he had been having, and since it was a fashionable pastime in those days to analyze each other's dreams, Murdock Pemberton took Broun's to his own psychiatrist, Dr. Edward Hiram Reede in Washington, who was also treating Ruth Hale. Pemberton related what Broun had told him, that for several nights running, he'd dreamed that a huge bear came pounding on his door, that the pounding scared him out of his wits and he tried everything to hide from the beast, fearing it would break through. "When I told Dr. Reede about it," Pemberton recalled half a century later, "he thought about it for a minute and then lit up. 'It's so simple,' he said. 'In German, bear is *broun*. It's only himself he hears pounding at the door. Tell him next time to open the door and welcome the bear inside.'"

BEYOND THE RED VELVET CORD

In the high winds of fame and social ascendance after 1925, Broun and others began in various ways to grasp for some kind of ballast. A sense of self-reproach had been gathering in these few for years, and since self-reproach was one of the least attractive attitudes possible at a Round Table now more self-possessed than ever, the search necessarily took place at a distance from lunch. No one was ready to give up old acquaintances in early 1926, but the group was undergoing a distinct splay of interests and attitudes, and as some of them began asserting individuality, the seams that held them together as a group began to come undone.

Ernest Hemingway came to New York to change publishers in February of 1926. Benchley and Parker of course knew him by reputation (although only *In Our Time* had then been published) and from the stories that Stewart had told them about his summers with Hemingway in 1924 and 1925. Stewart and Hemingway had made American newspapers as "bullfighting Americanos" in Pamplona in 1924, and when *The Sun Also Rises* was published in 1926, Stewart was mystified by the praise lavished on it; it seemed to him only an accurate journalistic account of what had actually happened during their trip to Pamplona in 1925 with Lady Duff Twysden (Brett Ashley in the book), Pat Guthrie (Mike Campbell), Bill Smith (Bill Gorton) and Harold Loeb (Robert Cohn). Hemingway also knew Benchley and Parker by reputation and through stories Stewart and Fitzgerald had told him. After he met them at a party that winter of 1926, he wrote Dos Passos that he found them to be "obviously attractive people." By that time, Parker was a writer even by her own demanding definition of the word; she was in the process of collecting her first book of poems for Boni & Liveright. Both she and Benchley were anxious to meet the hosts-in-exile Gerald and Sarah Murphy, in whose apartment in Paris and villa in Antibes Stewart had met many of the pre-eminent writers and artists of the day. Benchley seemed, in fact, to be looking for any escape from his enervating work at *Life*. When Hemingway settled finally on a date to sail back to France, Benchley and Parker accepted his invitation to go along.

Parker went with more romanticized expectations of Europe than Benchley did, in proportion to her more romanticized view of writing and the Writer,

(Top, left) Benchley, shipboard. (Top, right) On the beach of the *Hôtel du Cap* in Antibes. (Bottom) Gerald and Sarah Murphy (left and right) on the same beach in the mid-1920s. Hemingway sensed that the Murphys changed the good things their money touched —such as a favorite Swiss skiing village. But his visits and trips with them were discreet experiences. Parker and Benchley were coming increasingly to live among the wealthy, and their visit with the Murphys that summer was not much unlike their life in New York.

but both were conscious of abruptly leaving their New York world. The expatriate writers generally spoke of the Algonquin group derisively when they deigned to speak of it at all. Dos Passos called it a "cesspool" and never took lunch there, even though he stayed at the Algonquin at least once in those years and would have been welcomed eagerly at the Round Table. Hemingway's jaundiced view of New York and New York writers ("all angleworms in a bottle") was and is well known; his tolerance for the likes of Woollcott ("that fat capon") was exactly zero. American writers abroad seemed to respect the Algonquin critics only in the grudging way art respects business for doing its bidding; FPA's status in France rose and fell with his latest review, and Fitzgerald never liked Broun from the time he carried on a minority-of-two campaign (with FPA) against *This Side of Paradise*. (He called it "callow" and suggested that all the moral laxity in it was nothing more than an undergraduate's wishful thinking.)

In part it was the war that had come between the Algonquin writers and those in Paris (and, indeed, some other writers in New York). The Round Table writers had been happy warriors almost to a man, while the vision of most of their literary peers, especially those who served in ambulance units in the years before the U.S. joined the war, was war-sick. The great distance between close-up horrors of trench-and-gas warfare and the grandiloquent prose in justification of those horrors has been credited with shocking American writers abroad into lower-case letters and leaner prose. The *Stars and Stripes* Algonquinites had been, of course, among the foremost retailers of the war. However much a symbol of the literary life the Round Table became for later generations, among the best of what John Peale Bishop called the "first literary generation in America," it was regarded with a signal disdain.

If Benchley and Parker expected to be changed in the light of Paris and in the company of brighter talents, they were disappointed. The Murphys were only more genteel and genial versions of their hosts in New York—quite as wealthy (thanks to Mark Cross, Murphy's family leather goods company, and his wife's fortune), just as consumed by conversation and entertainment, more tasteful in their choice of friends and wiser and more willing about art as a result, but as

socially voracious and determinedly playful as the most ambitious hosts of Long Island. By 1926, Gerald Murphy, who had quit actively running Mark Cross in order to paint, had quit painting. The only surviving story about Benchley's short stay with them that year concerns a trip they all took to an Alpine skiing village, where he and Parker spent one late and tipsy night walking arm in arm through cobbled streets singing "With the Crimson in Triumph Flashing" in case some broken-legged Harvard boy might feel homesick.

Benchley's stay was short. Jesse Lasky wanted him to come to Hollywood that summer and write subtitles. Benchley was as reluctant then as he had been in 1917. John Weaver, Stallings and Mankiewicz were all there now, but to no result he particularly wanted for himself. But then Stewart asked him to be best man at his marriage to a California debutante named Beatrice Ames, whom he had met in Paris in 1924. To be at a good friend's side for such an event was just the sort of justification Benchley needed for what would otherwise have seemed too clearly another postponement of serious work. In June, he left Parker in the care of the Murphys, Hemingway and her current lover, Seward Collins, editor of the *Bookman,* and started off for his first job in Hollywood. One of his first recorded comments when he met Stewart there was his reaction to the Pacific Ocean. It only *looked* peaceful, he said, and sooner or later it was bound to rise up and wash over everything. From his own perspective on his own life, he was not far wrong.

By the time Benchley arrived, the town was Stewart's. He had ensconced himself in the familiar manner. While working for MGM on *Brown of Harvard* for $250 a week, he befriended studio stars like Jack Gilbert and Lew Cody, and through them was invited to their friend Marion Davies's lunches at the Hearst castle, San Simeon, to which they were all shuttled by private railroad car from the Pasadena station. Other frequent luncheon guests of Marion were Charlie Chaplin, King and Eleanor Vidor, and young Harry Crocker, Stewart's room-mate at Yale and a former fiancé of the girl Stewart was to marry.

The Stewart-Ames wedding was all-star; the Algonquinites in Hollywood, all of the Marion Davies luncheon group and a number of other movie stars pulled up in limousines as newsreel cameras rolled outside the chapel in Monte-

159

The Stewarts not long after their wedding. "God, I was nervous about meeting Parker," Beatrice recalled in 1976. "I stayed in the bathroom on the train for about half an hour after we had pulled into the station."

cito. (Benchley did his stint with his leg in a cast; he'd broken it during a pre-wedding party for Stewart when he fell down some basement stairs while looking for a bathroom.) After the reception, Mr. and Mrs. Stewart boarded the Twentieth-Century for that long but lovely ride to Chicago, where *Tribune* photographers posed them for the Sunday rotogravure, and on to New York, where Beatrice nervously met but passed muster with all the Algonquinites who were not in Hollywood or Europe. "Bea was young and beautiful, and I was happy," Stewart wrote in his autobiography. "She was a gay, 'fun' girl, loved parties and dancing, understood my kind of humor and had plenty of her own. . . . My New York friends and speakeasy owners liked her, and she liked them. . . . I was indeed a lucky fool, on an extended leave of absence from infelicity." After two days at the Plaza, the Stewarts boarded a ship for France, happily anticipating the celebrity-glittered nimbus of the Murphys and Antibes, brightened for them by the presence of Dorothy Parker.

Beatrice was accepted instantly and wholeheartedly by everyone there, as she was in New York, but Stewart felt at once that Antibes and his friends had changed. The environs of the Murphys' Villa America, he complained, was a "celebrity circus—the Place-to-be-Seen-at. Grace Moore had a villa, as did many other Big Names of stage and society." (Woollcott would be renting there in the summer of 1928 as well.) Stewart felt that even Hemingway seemed stricken by celebrity, and while such a sensation might have been acutely pleasurable in Stewart's movie friends, in quasi-aesthetic Antibes and in Hemingway, it was singularly distressing. Parker told Stewart when he got there how much she hated the rich, how nervous they made her. (As Hemingway reflected on the Murphys' effect on a favorite Swiss skiing village in *A Moveable Feast:* "Then you have the rich, and nothing is ever as it was again.") Nevertheless, they all did love the rich too, and Stewart's reaction to his friends' absorption by them is notable only because he had himself urged the exiled writers to meet "people who mattered"; now, he was reflecting for the first time on the fact that doing so had changed them permanently for the worse.

The summer was a long party with Scott and Zelda Fitzgerald, the Archibald MacLeishes, the Gilbert Seldeses, the Murphys, the Stewarts and Dor-

(From left) Parker, Benchley, Honoria and Gerald Murphy. Joining their party on occasion were the MacLeishes, who had rented an apartment for the summer in Antibes from Pierpont Hamilton, a Long Island friend of the Lovetts, as well as the Hemingways and Fitzgeralds. But neither Benchley nor Parker ever wrote about that trip to Europe, and Stewart's recollection of it was not entirely happy.

"Here's to Dorothy Parker," went Hemingway's toast, in her absence, at a party in Paris just before she left. "Nothing so became her in life as her almost leaving it."

othy Parker—sometimes a not very good party, but a nonworking summer nevertheless. The Fitzgeralds were at their then worst. As the whole group of couples emerged woozily from a dark restaurant in Antibes one sunny afternoon, they knocked over a street vendor's elaborate display of nuts, which Fitzgerald for some reason found immensely funny and no one else did. "Look, wasn't that funny?" he kept repeating to blank reactions. Finally he gave the vendor a 500-franc note as if to make it up. "There," he said, "I've given him 500 francs. Wasn't that funny?" Perhaps in New York or Hollywood it could have been, but here, and in Scott Fitzgerald, it rankled. Parker found it as impossible as ever to work; the Murphys even tried locking her in her room, but she only got quietly drunk and fell asleep. There was what could have been a memorable trip by Hemingway, Parker and others to Pamplona for the running of the bulls and to see a bullfight, but it ended predictably when Parker became nauseated and ran from the arena. While Parker's feeling toward Hemingway the writer devolved into the most uncritical kind of hero worship, he never returned her obvious affection for him, even once ridiculing her cruelly, in her absence, at a party in Paris.

John Keats has remarked on the fact that Parker never wrote about her trip to Europe or used her experiences in fictional work, which he explains by pointing out that Europe for her was plush villas and hotel rooms and private railroad cars and drinking and parties. Perhaps it was also that Europe seemed, not only to her but to Benchley and Stewart as well, so much like New York— the forced humor, the consciousness of renown, the loss of genuine spontaneity and intimacy to the exigencies of role and play. In Stewart's *Mr. and Mrs. Haddock in Paris, France,* one character says of Americans: "You're all over here looking for something—something you're not getting in America. You don't know what it is but you think maybe it's over here in Europe, and then you get sore when you don't find it." Perhaps that explains Parker's lapse into old ways; where she hoped to find inspiration she found only more spirit-draining enervation. Anita Loos sensed something of the Round Table's self-made prison after that trip, although in *But Gentlemen Marry Brunettes* she added a dash of undue rancor:

Sherwood at work—with thanks to Edna Ferber for "what was unquestionably a shove in the right direction," *i.e.,* away from the Round Table.

So they all started to tell about a famous trip they took to Europe. And they had a marvelous time, because everywhere they went, they would sit in the hotel, and play cute games and tell reminiscences about the Algonquin. And I think it is wonderful to have so many internal resources that you never have to bother to go outside yourself to see anything. . . . And I really do not know why the geniuses at the Algonquin should bother to learn about Europe any more than Europe bothers to learn about them. So they came back, because they like the Algonquin best after all. And I think it is remarkable, because the old Proverb tells about the Profit who was without honor in his own home. But with them, it is just the reverse.

By the time Parker, Benchley and the Stewarts returned to New York, the Algonquin group was changed—more sparsely attended than before and vaguely dispirited. Hollywood had taken Connelly by this time, as it had claimed the others before, but even some of the original Round Tablers who were still in New York came less frequently to lunch or brought conversation-stopping concerns with them. Ross was busy with *The New Yorker,* and when he came to the Algonquin for lunch it was with editorial or business associates, and he sat apart from the Round Table. Adams's first child was born that year, and he consequently spent more of his free time at "Villa d'Esther," as he called their new home on West Tenth Street. Broun still came, but his columns and his thoughts were elsewhere. It was that autumn that Eugene Debs died in prison. "The Debs idea will not die," he wrote in a memorable obituary. "There can be a brotherhood of man." On the horizon was the last appeal of Sacco and Vanzetti. But from Broun's first articulations of a burgeoning activism, it was clear that his Rose Room audience was less than completely receptive.

Sherwood was absent for a similar reason in that fall of 1926; he had taken Edna Ferber's advice to leave the Round Table and work, and by November of 1926 his first play, *The Road to Rome,* was in production and a second, *The Love Nest,* was in his typewriter. He wrote Ferber from *Life:*

A year ago last summer I was engaged in conversation with you at the Swopes' summer White House, with crap games to the left of us, chemin-

Hirschfeld's Woollcott. Thurber called him "Old Vitriol and Violets," but in the late 1920s, vitriol seemed to have the upper hand.

de-fer *games to the right of us, Irving Berlin in front of us and the usually jolly round of volleying and thundering from our host. You said to me, "The best thing that could happen to you would be to have you snatched out of the Algonquin and exiled to Kansas City for two years. At the end of that time, you'd come back with some fine work." That casual observation so impressed me that I left the Hotel Algonquin, where I had had lunch practically every day for six years. I didn't go to Kansas City, but I did go to work and wrote two plays. Furthermore I feel a great deal better because I wrote them. The object of this letter is not, presumptively, to suggest that your glowing prophecy has been fulfilled—but to thank you for giving me a shove in what unquestionably was the right direction.*

Sherwood told a reporter that he wrote *The Road to Rome* because of "a house and two mortgages," and he was indeed $14,000 in debt, but his writing them in fact signaled his independence from Mary and the obligations he felt toward her. On his first New York opening night, January 31, 1927, he went backstage with Mary and gave Jane Cowl, the leading lady, a kiss of gratitude. Mary, characteristically, became enraged, and Sherwood snatched the corsage from her dress and presented it to Cowl, making a histrionic gesture as he did so that literally knocked Mary off her feet. At a party later, Mary announced so everyone could hear, "Bob, I always knew it would succeed." To that, with a few drinks' worth of confidence, he replied, "Don't be such a goddamned liar," and slapped her. Had Sherwood chosen to capitalize on it, he could have been the hero of the Round Table for weeks on the strength of that incident, but by that time Sherwood's investment in the group's approval was much diminished.

Perhaps the greatest change in the Round Table was in Woollcott, whose animus seemed redoubled. He had been driven from the Forty-seventh Street house in a putsch from which his relationship with Ross and Grant would never wholly recover. The reason they gave for asking him to leave was space, but as Grant admitted later, the fact was that Woollcott was becoming increasingly difficult to live with, seeming to feel more keenly than ever the need to run or overrun the lives of those close to him. Ross asked Grant to give Woollcott notice, and thereafter Woollcott began trying to come between them, inviting Ross to first nights and parties and pointedly excluding Grant. Grant was not the only

In a benefit for the Society for the Prevention of Cruelty to Animals, Woollcott played Henry VIII to Madge Kennedy's Anne Boleyn. The audience was made up in large part of Broadway insiders, and when Woollcott made his entrance, the story goes, they broke out in a chorus of jeers and hisses that lasted five minutes. As he came offstage, he said to one of the grips, "I can't understand why Madge should be so unpopular."

target. Neysa coquettishly sidled up to Woollcott at a party at Efrem Zimbalist's and asked him how he liked her dress. He said it seemed to have been "dipped in gumwash," and as he turned away, she began to cry. Beatrice Kaufman's reaction was better when her turn came during a dinner at the Algonquin. Woollcott suddenly turned to her and said, "Your problem, my dear, is that you are married to a cuckold." She threw her drink in his face. It is a small wonder that when Woollcott threw a housewarming for his new apartment at the Hotel Des Artistes in the fall of 1926 and asked his friends for linen, china and silver, FPA brought him a handkerchief, a mustache cup and a dime.

Woollcott was so insufferable in Dorothy Parker's perception that she began disowning him to Beatrice Stewart, who to this day is of the opinion that "Dorothy hated Woollcott. She thought him to be a petty and cruel person and held the Round Table in similar esteem. She never went there as long as I knew her and she told me she never went there before"—this despite abundant and public evidence to the contrary.

Parker and Benchley and Stewart did tire of the Round Table at about this time. Benchley thought the group "had become self-conscious," as Nathaniel Benchley explained it. "Woollcott especially began thinking of the group as some kind of Parnassus, a convocation of wits, and my father just said 'the hell with it.' It wasn't any great feud or break; he just stopped going to lunch there as much." Stewart explained his own disaffection to John Keats: "Everybody was waiting his chance to say the bright remark so that it would be in FPA's column the next day, and there was a kind of—well, it wasn't friendly."

Parker entered into an exquisite ambivalence about the Round Table that would persist well beyond the end of the group. Parker also told Lillian Hellman that she'd never been to the Round Table, though as late as 1934 Parker wrote "A Valentine for Mr. Woollcott" in *Vanity Fair,* and in the mid-Thirties she was still accepting invitations to Neshobe. Nevertheless, Parker joined Stewart and Benchley in at least a spirit of defection. The three of them opened a joint checking account so that none of them would have to worry about overdrafts (the principal beneficiaries of the arrangement were the Stewarts). Benchley and Parker occasionally slept (singly, so far as is known) in the nursery-to-be of the

Stewarts' new Sutton Place apartment, and when the Stewarts' child was born, it was Benchley and Parker who stood at the christening as godparents.

Their break with the Round Table resulted in no noticeable sobering of their lives. If anything, Benchley, Parker and Stewart played harder than the still-loyal Algonquinites, even as they worried jokingly together about where it all would lead. Parker's drinking had redoubled in Europe, and Benchley and Stewart kept up with her in New York. When Edmund Wilson saw her in that fall of 1926, he found her "fat and bloated, puffy-eyed."

Wilson's journal entry about an evening at that time describes just how far Benchley had come from his days of Prohibition and Big Brotherhood.

> *"Do you mind going up to Tony's?" (It was inevitable that she should insist on going to one of their regular hangouts: they didn't know how to get along with anybody but one another.) "Mr. Benchley is sunk tonight, and I promised I'd go up there and see him" (it was one of their affectations that she always called him Mr. Benchley)—his girl and awful little whore, unfaithful to him, made him give her money (Mrs. Benchley busy with children's tonsils), he was getting worse and worse in debt (his syndicate stuff began to show it—overdrafts on Scarsdale bank), he would rush out to Chicago, where the mistress was playing, to lecture; the girl had been a waitress, then on the stage, he had met her in Music Box Revue; he would say, "She enters the room like a duchess!"—When I finally met her, she was quite a pretty blonde with thick ankles, who, however, I thought, had something of that hard-eyed prostitute stare, the result of there being no coherence or purpose in a woman's emotional life. —We drank a great many Tom Collinses. When we first came in, we had found Benchley, with his red grossening face, leaning against the wall in the hall—talk of going down to the cellar to sing—he had got to a point where he no longer went at all to plays he reviewed for* Life. . . .

Wilson noted that Parker's only mention of Paris that night was a Sentence Game feat: "Paroxysmarvelous city."

Stewart's personal life was in better outward order than Benchley's or Parker's, but his professional situation was fairly dismal. His contract for weekly columns in the Chicago *Tribune* had run out, no title-writing jobs were

Whatever the intramural conflicts in the Round Table, the group was good for business in the Rose Room (top, a table setting of the period) and the hotel itself. Case (bottom, with his wife and Jack Whiting) bought the hotel in 1927, as well as a pear-shaped diamond for his wife, a mink for his daughter and a Rolls-Royce for himself.

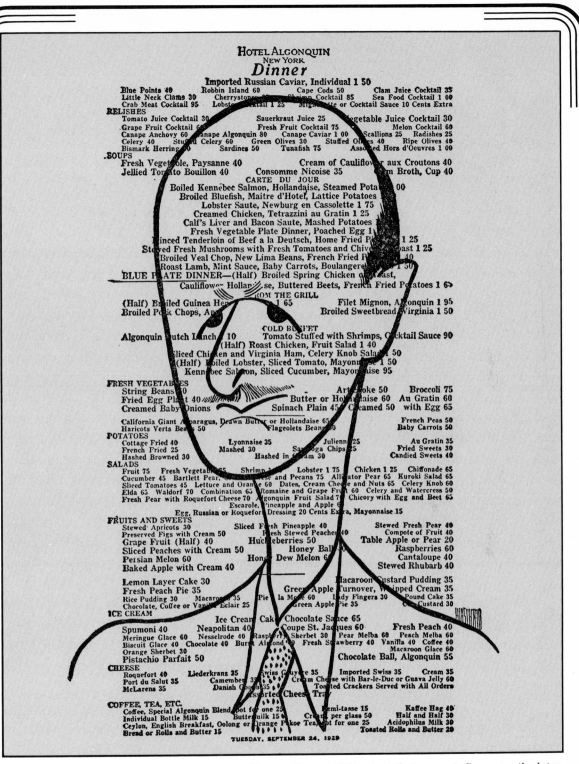

Hirschfeld's rendering of Case on a dinner menu. Murdock Pemberton handled publicity for Case's purchase of the Algonquin, which made the front page of the New York *Times*. He asked Case only for his expenses, which came to about fifteen dollars. To his chagrin, Case paid him just that amount. Some months later, Case told Pemberton he would have to pay an extra week's rent before he could move out of the Algonquin to an apartment. Pemberton lodged a pained protest but had to pay.

Ross by Rea Irvin. The drawing, done for a parody issue marking *The New Yorker*'s first anniversary, shows Ross, an unbuttoned Eustace Tilley, examining his "butterfly in heat" through a monocle—presumably with some disdain.

in the offing in Hollywood, and just as he finished work on his new apartment, his father-in-law's brokerage house collapsed.

For surcease from their multiple problems, the Round Table defectors followed courses of little resistance for which they were uniquely prepared: they all took writing chores at *The New Yorker* and began cultivating socially the Bright Young People of North Shore society—Charles and Joan Payson, Jock Whitney, Alexander and Pierpont Hamilton, Robert and Adele Lovett, and others. Given the social currents of the time, it is appropriate that they were introduced by writers Philip Barry and Archibald MacLeish, in Antibes, and that they reciprocated invitations to Long Island's great houses with evenings at Tony Soma's and the Dizzy Club and the Club Durant. "The effect on me was slightly disastrous," Stewart said in his memoir, "for I once more came to associate the friendship of Society and the Rich with the security which from childhood had been associated with Big Names." The immediate rewards, however, were material. Stewart eventually was given a house on the Payne Whitney estate at nominal rent. Various Wall Street friends gave him stocks and money. He was accepted for membership in the Racquet and Tennis as well—"a dream I'd had ever since Talbott had given me his guest pass in 1920." Benchley was taken by Jock Whitney, who was then a senior at Yale, to the Grand National race in England in the spring of 1927. When he returned, he said he had had his binoculars trained on what he thought to be the final jump only to discover, when a great cheer signaled the end of the race, that he had been watching the neck of the man in front of him. It was not a bad metaphor for the turn he saw his life was taking.

By the time they went to work for *The New Yorker* in 1927—Stewart with his occasional short pieces, Benchley and Parker with their respective columns about the press and books—the magazine had begun to outgrow its first purpose of upward mingling and genial dilettantism, and whatever maturity the magazine eventually achieved owed little to the Algonquinites who finally worked for it. Stewart's short pieces were predictable and slight. Benchley's "Wayward Press" column was full of obvious observations articulated better and often before elsewhere; his drama criticism later was lackadaisical and amateur. Dorothy

THE ENQUIRING REPORTER

EVERY WEEK HE ASKS A QUESTION OF FIVE PEOPLE SELECTED AT RANDOM.
THIS WEEK THE QUESTION IS: DO THE CRITICS AND WRITERS WHO LUNCH
AT THE ALGONQUIN HOTEL LOGROLL FOR EACH OTHER OR IS THAT JUST
ANOTHER LIE OF THE INTERESTS?

THE ANSWERS

ALEXANDER WOOLLCOTT, dramatic critic and *boulevardier*, of West 47th Street: "Stuff and nonsense! There is no such thing as an 'Algonquin group,' and if there were, they would never have a kind word for each other. Isn't Heywood Broun always saying nasty things about Franklin P. Adams's superb writings in 'It Seems to Me,' Broun's magnificent daily column in the New York *World*? And isn't Adams's brilliant 'Conning Tower' almost completely devoted to roasting Broun's epoch-making novels?"

HEYWOOD BROUN, art critic and novelist, of Park Row: "I don't know anything about logrolling, but I know what I like. It is true that I drop in at the Algonquin Hotel now and then at lunch time. After all, it is the centre of life and culture and one is likely to meet there all the people in the world worth knowing. Then, too, anyone who hates a boiled shirt as much as I do likes to be among friends. A fellow can't get his back and shoulders into untidiness when there is company."

FRANKLIN P. ADAMS, columnist and poet, of Park Row: "Whom are you to ask me such a question like you suspected me of logrolling? I have looked up all the statutes, local, state, and national, covering the subject, and I have searched through the Index Expurgatorius, the Code Napoleon, the Corpus Juris Civilis, and the Ten Commandments, and I didn't find a word in any of them that would force anybody to listen to logrolling if he didn't want to hear it."

GEORGE JEAN NATHAN, dramatic critic and essayist, West 45th Street: "That question is *la plus* Brussels sprouts of the present *Sauregurkenzeit*. I permit myself a polite you-know. However, to put an answer to it: certainly the Algonquin House runs a *rathskeller* for no other reason than to afford shelter to a logrolling *verein*. To which *lustig* answer I might add a respectful 'Thank God!' For, were it not for this *verein*, I might have nothing to write about on the dull days when the theatre offers me no particularly luscious bit of flapdoodle to record."

GEORGES, head-waiter at the Algonquin Hotel, West 44th Street: "I am only a head-waiter, but it seems to me, from all that I have heard on the subject of logrolling, that the principal objection to logrolling held by those who object to logrolling is that the log is not being rolled for the right person."—RALPH BARTON

Not long before Ross enforced his moratorium on further coverage of the Round Table, Ralph Barton took up the subject of logrolling, and, except for the fairly charitable response he wrote for George Jean Nathan, his answers were very like the ones the principals often gave.

Parker's "Constant Reader" criticism was often unhelpful to both writers and readers; "when she feels admiration," Woollcott cogently observed, "she can find no words for it," and she reviewed a disproportionate number of bad books as a result. By 1927, Janet Flanner, E.B. White, James Thurber, Frank Sullivan, Corey Ford and Wolcott Gibbs were already writing for the magazine; Katherine Angell was bringing her considerable skills to editing and the recruitment of new talent. The coming of Algonquin writers to *The New Yorker* in 1927 seems now less a measure of the magazine's stature than a reminder of its original limitations.

In the early months of 1927, Heywood Broun stopped playing poker and went on a diet. Neither resolve was permanent, but making them signaled a change in Broun. Dr. Barach was disappointed that he could never get Broun to curb his drinking habit, but he was having his effect. Broun was exercising (jogging around his apartment) and painting in oils (mostly land- and seascapes, which he sold as "early Brouns" for five dollars apiece). He was spending less time in the speakeasies and more time on Sabine Farm. His columns showed a difference as well: in the six months then past, he had mustered real spirit only for Eugene Debs, otherwise doing uninspired variations on nightlife and sports themes. Now, as he undertook a compact for the reform of himself, he turned to a cause even more compelling to him than the death of Debs in prison. It was, of course, the case of Sacco and Vanzetti, whose six years' appealing their conviction of murder were then drawing toward a finish.

Opinions of the case at the Round Table were mixed. Woollcott said they probably were guilty, and Neysa stopped speaking to him for several weeks on that account. (It is probable that Woollcott said it only for effect; he was an apolitical man, but he knew an affecting story when he heard one and stayed fastidiously to the left on most issues.) Parker and Benchley picketed for them; Benchley also testified that a friend of his had overheard their judge make some prejudicial remarks on the case in the locker room of a golf club he patronized near Boston (the friend recanted the story). FPA was sympathetic to Broun and regarded the cause as worthy, but he took little note of it in his own column.

Sherwood, still editor of *Life,* ran a spoof of the custodians of justice in Massachusetts, pricking them for their self-righteousness. Over the Thanatopsis table in Broun's absence it was widely supposed that Broun was just nearing forty and in quest of lost youth, an opinion not wholly without merit.

Broun began writing about Sacco and Vanzetti as early as 1925, their fifth year in prison, but it was not until a trial review commission was convened in 1927 that he began devoting himself wholeheartedly to the case. Among other things, he declared that Governor Fuller's asking Harvard President A. Lawrence Lowell to chair the three-member review board was simply a device to spread the political burden of executing them in the face of resounding international calls for clemency. Long before Broun's famous break with the management of the *World* over their refusal to publish anything more he wrote about the case, his columns on the subject were cut and edited. That power was seldom used at the *World;* Swope and the newspaper were noted for that. But this particular issue raised so many ugly memories—of the riots in Union Square, the bomb found in Governor Fuller's mail, the Red Scare itself—that even Broun's early pleas for Sacco and Vanzetti were perceived as dangerously provocative. Sometimes his pieces were only dampened judiciously; at other times, they were cut wholesale or omitted.

Dwight Taylor, Laurette Taylor's son, was at Swope's house the night in 1927 when Broun came to complain. As it happened, Swope was hosting a game of the Thanatopsis that evening. Having sworn off poker (temporarily, as it turned out), Broun waited for Swope to finish a previous appointment in a reception area across from the game in progress, and as he watched his *World* and Round Table colleagues play their cards, Taylor watched him. "He seemed to be looking over at his fellow clowns with an air of fresh appraisal," Taylor wrote in 1959. "And yet there was a grudging jealousy in his eyes, too— of the warm apartment, the easy laughter and the comparative security of their positions in contrast to his own." He was on collision course with the *World* by then, and he knew it. So did his friends at the game, even if no one offered support for his coming confrontation with Swope. They ignored him until finally he went over to the table with a joke prepared. "If Will Durant should go up to

Sacco and Vanzetti
being brought from
prison to court in 1924.
Broun was sure from
the convening of the
review panel that the
verdict on them would
not be overturned.

Elmira [a reform school for delinquent girls] to give a lecture on French philosophers, do you know what I would say?" No one did. "I would say that Will Durant is putting Descartes before de whores." As often happened when Broun told one of his jokes, someone suggested airing out the room, and the game continued. When Swope finally called Broun into his study, he probably reiterated that the paper would not tolerate a man on op-ed taking pot shots at the paper's official position, which was supportive of the authorities in Massachusetts and, in the abstract, of the idea of mercy. No one knows what Swope actually said, because none of Broun's friends thought to ask him when it was over how it had turned out, but when Taylor said goodnight to Broun and called him "sir," it was clear that his good nature was gone. "If you ever call me 'sir' again," Broun snapped, "I'm going to punch you right in the nose."

Perhaps part of it *was* age. Like Dorothy Parker and her sarcastic stories about the cult of flaming youth for the *Saturday Evening Post* a few years before, Broun's outlook was tinted by the notion that he had been passed over by his own times. As revenge against his opinion of *This Side of Paradise,* Scott Fitzgerald had taken him to lunch back in 1920 and told him it was a pity he'd got to thirty without tasting life. Mike Gold of the radical *Liberator* had stung him with the same charge when Broun criticized O'Neill's *The Hairy Ape* as an elaborate pamphlet; "once a man definitely takes sides," Broun had written, "he begins to see a little less of the world." Gold told him he should go out and get a real job—a laborer's job—and find out what life was really all about.

In a sense, too, Broun's stand-taking for Sacco and Vanzetti was a stand-taking against Harvard—a battlement of unfeeling reason, in Broun's thinking, and of self-perpetuating moral authority. Walter Lippmann, a symbol to him of that institution, was writing the *World*'s editorials on Sacco and Vanzetti. Lippmann had been president of the Socialist Club on campus; Broun hadn't even become a member until his senior year. Lippmann thought the logrolling of the op-ed writers "a shameful performance"; Broun thought Lippmann an overeducated prude, as suggested in the portrait of him in *The Sun Field,* Broun's second novel. Whatever obliquies Broun aimed at the *World*'s editorial position were thus aimed at Lippmann by implication, with the further implica-

Broun (with John Barrymore) in Palm Beach in the year of his break with the *World* over Sacco and Vanzetti. The high-stepping, fun-loving, gregarious half of

Broun's double life was down but not out. The two sides of his character would be battling literally to the last moments of his life.

tion that Broun's passion and compassion were more significant by far than Lippmann's overdetermined notions about ethics and civic behavior. "Take care of concretes," Broun wrote, "and abstracts will take care of themselves."

The columns he wrote from Boston when Sacco and Vanzetti lost their final chance for mercy in the late summer of 1927 were masterpieces of unreasoning frustration and rage, certainly among the best writing he had ever done. And if they did not persuade any but the already persuaded, they did accurately reflect the desolation of liberals after their seven years' war for clemency:

> *They are too bright. We shield our eyes and kill them. We are the dead, and in us there is no feeling nor imagination nor the terrible torment of lust for justice. And in the city where we sleep, smug gardeners walk to keep the grass above our little houses sleek and cut whatever blade thrusts up a head above its fellows. . . . From now on it is our business to make them toss and turn a little, for a cry should go up from many million voices before the day set for Sacco and Vanzetti to die. We have a right to beat against tight minds with our fists and shout a word into the ears of the old men. We want to know, we will know—"Why?"*

Of the four columns Broun wrote after that, only two ran in the *World,* and when Sacco and Vanzetti were given twelve final days before their execution, the *World*'s editorial council decided no more columns from Broun about the case would be accepted for publication. Swope took no part in the decision; he was in Saratoga—it was the racing season. After a few days' thought, Broun decided to strike against the decision. He went to Sabine Farm.

Reaction to the incident among his contemporaries was mixed. John Dos Passos wrote Hemingway from New York: "It was damn decent of H. Broun to lose his job over Sacco-Vanzetti—don't you think so? Besides, he delivered himself of four or five excellent sentences and was as firm in the path of prejudice as the feet of a Lowell ambling to a hanging, etc. . . ." Ben Hecht grumped later that such radicalism was only chic: "You crucified yourself on billboards and came down for bows." Broun himself was aware that his position had been taken more by intuition than any ideological commitment. During his strike he wrote about the incident in a *New Yorker* self-profile:

For years he had complained with some reason of an inability to work up a satisfactory amount of hate. And now he had it. The first piece which he wrote against Lowell and Fuller was by all odds, to his mind, the best he had ever done for his paper. Nor had his momentum quite subsided when editorial censorship set in. It was a little as if somebody shouted to a pole vaulter in mid-career, "Please go no further."

He was allowed one column in the *World* in which to explain his reason for the strike, and he found a metaphor in baseball:

Once there was a pitcher on the Giants who was sued for breach of promise, and fortunately this suit resulted in his love letters being made public. The memory of one of these I have always treasured. He wrote, "Sweetheart, they knocked me out of the box in the third inning, but it wasn't my fault. The day was cold and I couldn't sweat. Unless I sweat I can't pitch."

Broun's radicalism was at bottom sentimental. The stories his newspaper colleagues cherish most are those in which Broun displayed, so to speak, the gilded tattoo under his black arm band. James Thomas Flexner still delights in the memory of one night when he followed Broun to the Bowery, an excursion Broun hoped would publicize the terrible conditions in New York's public houses. Broun went with the intention of spending the night, but he left after dinner, just after they showed him the corner of the cold floor on which he was supposed to bed down. In 1927, Oswald Garrison Villard of the *Nation* offered him weekly space for a column that would be completely free of censorship. After carefully checking out whether he would be breaching his contract with the *World* by doing so, Broun accepted—and used the space, for example, to urge Villard to broaden his mind by going to a few "leg shows." His irreparable break with the *World* resulted from another article he wrote for Villard criticizing his old paper for being vacillating, insecure, weak under pressure and basically illiberal. But when Roy Howard of the Scripps-Howard chain offered him $30,000 a year to work on the rock-ribbed Republican *Telegram,* figuring Broun to be worth 50,000 in circulation in his battle with Hearst's *Journal,* Broun agreed. He also kept his friendship and social ties with Swope and Ralph Pulitzer, as well as his membership in the Racquet and Tennis and in the Algonquin group.

(Top) Benchley in a snooze. (Bottom) Benchley discoursing on *The Romance of Digestion*. By the mid-1930s, after the Academy Award-winning *How to Sleep,* appearing in shorts would become Benchley's chief means of livelihood, in part because of the expenses and debts he had incurred.

(Top) Benchley with his *New Yorker*. (Bottom) Benchley trying to explain government spending in *How to Figure Income Tax*. He finally found justification for his spendthrift ways in 1930: "I might point out that of a possible $5,000 which I have made since I left school, I have had $3,000 worth of good food (all of which has gone into making bone and muscle and some nice fat), $1,500 worth of theater tickets, and $500 worth of candy; whereas many of my business friends have simply had $5,000 worth of whatever that stock was which got so yellow along about last November."

Robert Benchley, as his son Nathaniel tells the story, was sitting in his room one night grappling with a piece he had not yet begun to write. After considerable shifting in his chair, lighting a pipe and setting it down, he typed the word "The." That done, he got up and went downstairs and out for the night. Hours later, he returned, looked at the page in his typewriter and finished the sentence: ". . . hell with it." Not long after that he decided that this sort of life would never do; his work was simply not getting done. So he moved out of his Algonquin room and moved into the less popular Royalton across the street. "You can keep my friends from coming up," he explained to Frank Case on the way out, "but you can't keep me from coming down." The Royalton seemed to him Victorian, with its mahogany woodwork and diamond-shaped window panes, and Benchley decided to take that style the full distance, installing thick red drapes to cut off all light, a dark red carpet, a tassled cover of red velvet on a living-room table and green library lamps. He even hung three pictures of Queen Victoria around the place. Actually, his intellectual interest at that time was in the Queen Anne period; "as a salve to his conscience and as proof that he could do some serious writing," Nathaniel Benchley wrote, he decided "to write a history of the humorists in the time of Queen Anne." That plan changed; the "serious" book later became a general history, then a play—but not a word was ever set to paper. His room at the Royalton quickly became as raucous and renowned a gathering place as his room at the Algonquin had been, and Queen Anne and Queen Victoria gathered dust. Late in 1927, Thomas Chalmers of Fox Films asked him to do *The Treasurer's Report* as the first all-talking movie. Benchley agreed. It was only to be an experiment. In December of 1927, Stewart was smarting from a failure on Broadway called *Los Angeles,* which he later acknowledged having hacked out for the money, so Benchley dropped by with what he hoped would be encouragement—the chance that both of them could have bright futures in the emergent talkies. Given Benchley's resentment in later years of what he felt Hollywood had done to him, what better work it prevented him from doing, his declaration to the Stewarts that day must be one of his life's most poignant ironies. "Kids," he said, "our troubles are over."

NO
GOOD-BYES

In early 1928, most of the writers of the Round Table were in full professional ascendance, and so, commensurately, was the public stature of the privately splintering group. Even Broun's chancy stand against the *World* had advanced him professionally. Dorothy Parker's first book was a best-seller in its eighth printing, and her second, *Sunset Gun,* was in production. FPA's collection of "Conning Tower" columns was a success, and another was to be published later in the year. Kaufman and Ferber had struck gold in their collaboration after a moderate hit, with *Minick,* in 1924; *The Royal Family* ran through 1928. Ferber also had *Show Boat* on Broadway that year, and Kaufman had *Animal Crackers,* which he had written with Morrie Ryskind. Ross and *The New Yorker* were a success. Woollcott brought out his fifth book of collected articles, *Two Gentlemen and a Lady.* Sherwood's *The Love Nest* was on Broadway and *The Queen's Husband* was in his typewriter. Connelly and Mankiewicz, though to no one's particular credit, staged *The Wild Man of Borneo.* Benchley published a popular collection, *The Early Worm.* Broun's biography of Anthony Comstock, written with Margaret Leech (soon to be Mrs. Ralph Pulitzer), was one of the Literary Guild's first selections and enjoyed a fine sale. The group's renown had become so great, and so many other celebrities were welcome now to lunch with them, that every lunch hour brought a log jam of tourists to the Algonquin lobby, and Frank Case soon decided to move the Round Table to a less visible spot in the Pergola Room, where the group had begun.

It was just at this point when the Algonquin group began to fall apart. Simple geography had something to do with it; like Broun, Murdock Pemberton, Deems Taylor, and Adams by now had homes in Connecticut to which they retreated with increasing frequency on weekends and even during the week. At the same time, the Thanatopsis game was becoming less attractive in proportion to its higher stakes and increased danger. Before the decade was out, Swope and Kaufman would begin bringing rich friends into the game who would finally outprice the original members. The incursion of economic realities with the Crash probably did more to dampen their group spirit than any other single factor, and to the extent that they were drawn together by ties of mutual insecurity and the hope for success by association, their very successes rendered the

THE ALGONQUIN, BY ONE WHO HAS HEARD ALL ABOUT IT

Ellison Hoover's "The Algonquin, By One Who Has Heard All About It," which appeared in *Judge*. Lois Long took the opposite tack in *The New Yorker*: "Upon entering a lobby that looks exactly like any other lobby to be found in the West Forties, you will see before you an entrance to a dining room. . . . In the center of this room, which is done in pink, is a large round table, surrounded by one or two woeful-looking gentlemen munching. At about one-thirty, others come in and sit down beside them. These, my children, are the Celebrities. . . . The great luncheon dish among them now seems to be stuffed date, pecan, and cream cheese salad, and this is the high point of a menu that is otherwise a lot like other menus. . . ."

Benchley with Mac-Arthur and Beatrice Stewart engaged in the consuming practice of conversation. By 1928 Benchley had begun to make a virtue and a joke of his disconnected-ness, wiring Charles Brackett the year before in Paris, for example: ANY TIDINGS OF LINDBERGH? LEFT HERE WEEK AGO. AM WORRIED.

group obsolete. But there were more proximate causes in rifts in the Round Table of 1928 as well: the delicate balance of certain marriages was thrown off by their gathering fortunes, and Woollcott's dark side was becoming an increasingly insistent force in the group.

The domestic arrangements destined to fail did so now. Robert and Gertrude Benchley continued to play out their householding roles together in Scarsdale and to deal with his public affairs in private. George and Beatrice Kaufman's relationship had devolved into the sort of mother-son relationship so prevalent in his early plays between husbands and wives—the wives who get their bumbling husbands out of business corners, who are wise where their husbands are foolish and generous when they fail. But Beatrice drew social recognition from the arrangement and the perquisites of wealth; George drew some measure of emotional security in a world that for him was mined everywhere with the possibility of failure. "I couldn't get through the day without Beatrice," he said that year. Their adopted daughter Anne, who lived with her governess in an adjoining but separate apartment, came to find the situation confusing at best. "Daddy must have had *something* to turn the ladies on," she told a reporter later, "because throughout his life he had dozens of mistresses—almost as many mistresses as Mummy had lovers. It was a very complicated household, with 'his' and 'hers' phones being installed wherever we lived, and a lot of unexplained comings and goings, arrivals and departures."

But for Broun and Ruth Hale, there was no question of making such accommodations to personal insecurity. Their disaffection was a long and painful process for both of them; it did not culminate legally until 1933, but it began just after Broun's battle with the *World*. There were some who said it was only Ruth Hale's passionate advocacy of the two accused anarchists that prodded Broun to their defense—that, indeed, Hale was the social conscience behind his best work from 1920 on. It is a fact that she wrote many of his columns, as he wrote some of her film and book reviews for *Judge* and other magazines. Nor was Broun the active partner in their separation. It was Hale from the beginning who had insisted that they have affairs at will during the marriage and that each of them should be free to leave the other at any time. Broun took most advantage

Broun in Palm Beach in 1928 with his former boss's wife, Margaret Swope. "The trouble with me," Broun wrote, "is that I inherited an insufficient amount of vengeful feeling. Kings, princes, dukes, and even local squires rode their horses so that they stepped upon the toes of my ancestors, who did nothing about it except to apologize. I would then have joined most eagerly in pulling down the Bastille, but if anybody had caught me at it and given me a sharp look, I'm afraid I would have put it back again."

of their libertarian agreement, but it was Ruth Hale, resentful of her increasing submergence in his career, who finally insisted on a separation. Broun had heard and rebuffed her arguments before, but now he reluctantly agreed.

Harold Ross and Jane Grant also separated in 1928. His career was their mutual obsession, but his success and the magazine's seemed to overwhelm the marriage. Woollcott's rising animus helped matters not at all; his attempts to drive a wedge between them after Grant gave him notice to move was, she said later, "the final straw. . . . I felt he played a big part in making our marriage impossible." At first, Ross and Grant used the vacated space to make separate bedrooms, but Ross continued to stay away from 412 West Forty-seventh Street for days at a stretch, while she continued presiding over the house's full social calendar. Just after Christmas of 1927, Ross returned early from a boys' weekend with MacArthur in Atlantic City to tell her, as she recalled his words: "We can't go on this way. . . . Must have more breathing space. You don't seem to want me around. Why don't you take a trip—go to China, around the world, anyplace—so I can have this house with some privacy." She took a sick leave from the *Times* and went to Palm Beach. When she returned, she set up housekeeping for herself at the Barclay Hotel. "They must patch up their differences," Charles Brackett said to his *New Yorker* colleague Alison Smith. "They owe it to all of us to carry on. What would we do without 412?" They did live together once more, on advice of her lawyer that she fortify her legal position by occupying the house until Ross moved out—as finally, after they reached financial agreement, he did. As Broun and Hale did, but at somewhat more distance, they remained affectionate friends.

It was a watershed time for Woollcott as well. In the early months of 1928, one fact filled his life: his sister Julie was languishing in a New York hospital with a progressive brain disease. She was his only sister, he had lived with her in his first days in New York, and she was the one member of his family with whom he had always been close. As he sat now at her bedside almost daily reading aloud, he felt his whole past to be dissolving with her. In a letter to her best friend from their childhood days in Kansas City, Mrs. Lucy Christie Drage, Woollcott mused at length on the decline of the New Jersey commune where he was born. "The

Phalanx is ghostly now," he wrote. "There are strangers in the little cottage, so that what Aunt Anne used to call the Julie light can once more be seen through the trees. But the big house is mostly dark. . . . The last to go was Uncle Will. . . . That was only a month ago. So one by one the lights go out." He wrote Julie's friend about the day he was born unwanted, as Julie had told him about it on her sickbed, and he contemplated his continuing feeling of unworthiness: "I am sick at the thought of what swinishness and poltroonery and malice the spectators would find if ever my guards were dismissed and I could no longer edit myself for my neighbors' inspection. But the Julie that was turned toward you and toward me was the same all the way through—a gentle and gracious and gallant person in the very core of her. There was nothing base in her."

When Julie died, Woollcott seemed to some of his friends to change: in place of his viciousness came an uncharacteristic self-effacement. For the first time in his life, he decided to seek psychiatric help. The problem, he told Dr. Barach, was his weight, but in their few hours together the dominant subject was Julie's death, and Barach told him he was turning his animus on himself. After three weeks, Woollcott quit analysis and went to see a "fat doctor," who prescribed drugs to no lasting good. In March he told Swope that he was not going to renew his contract with the *World* for another season. Swope tried to change his mind with a $1,000 annual raise and a two-year contract, but Woollcott was firm. Drama criticism, he wrote at the time, was "hardly a career which a decent man would map out for himself," and he was "incurably disposed" to quit doing it. But if the evidence is that Woollcott intended to make a break with his "swinish" self and conduct his life and his work in a more serious manner, the result was quite the opposite.

When the Broadway season ended in May, he persuaded Alice Miller, Harpo Marx and Beatrice Kaufman to spend the summer with him in a villa on the Riviera instead of Neshobe, and on May 19 they all boarded the S.S. *Roma*. Until the Villa Galanon was ready for them, they stayed in a small hotel in Antibes, where Harpo noticed that Woollcott was "oddly—for him—placid. He would stand for long moments of silence gazing from the top of the cliff at the deep, cold-blue sea and the shallow hot-blue sky." It was the first opportunity

Ruth Gordon (far left) and Beatrice Kaufman were Woollcott's solaces on the Riviera in the summer of 1928—until he recovered and surpassed his old public affect.

for reflection he had allowed himself since Julie's death, he wrote his sister's friend. "I think I invented things to preoccupy me, made a great pother about work to be done, ran round and round in busy little circles, anything rather than sit down and face the fact that there was no Julie any more and never would be again." The letter was written in June at the hotel in Antibes.

His interlude of quiet self-reckoning did not last. It was swallowed up in the social clamor that had been building in Antibes for several summers past, as Woollcott perhaps knew it would be, and in the whirl of parties among people Woollcott liked to think were his superiors, all his outward self-effacement disappeared. "I did not like the particular kind of dog Aleck put on on the Riviera," Harpo wrote later.

The party-giving along the Riviera in that summer of 1928 was extreme. The Woollcott entourage entertained and was entertained by Peggy Hopkins Joyce, Otis and Cornelia Skinner, Mary Garden, Grace Moore, Irene Castle, Lady Mendl and Frank Harris, among others. Elsa Maxwell gave a party on the beach whose main event was the arrival of Sidney Lejon and Gertie Sanford riding surfboards under spotlights in formal attire as the orchestra on top of the cliff played "Over the Waves." There was a canning heiress's masquerade. There was the hostess with two pools—"one for anybody," Harpo remembered, "and one stocked with live salmon for her pansy friends to swim in." The best hostess of all by Harpo's recollection was Daisy Fellowes, who was equipped with a sewing machine fortune and two yachts, the larger of which served for week-long after-dinner parties. Harpo stayed on the ship for ten days, and while withholding details, he called their time at anchor "a very interesting voyage." Fellowes once told Woollcott and Harpo after a party, "You are all so talented. You write or dance or sing or act. But I do *nossing*." Woollcott replied, "My dear, I have heard different."

Despite Woollcott's more methodical approach to social life, Harpo outdistanced him socially all summer, usually in a tuxedo made of pool-table felt with large brass buttons and on at least two occasions in nothing at all. The first of these was at Somerset Maugham's villa, where Harpo interrupted Maugham's guided tour of the house by stripping and diving into the fountain-fed pool

WIT'S END

Parker told Edmund Wilson that Woollcott was in love with Harpo—or, at least, that a Jungian psychiatrist told him he was. It was probably nothing more than Parker's imagination, since there is no record of Woollcott's ever having seen a Jungian. But Woollcott clearly cherished Harpo—for his lack of inhibition, his unselfconsciously playful personality, the very lack of *politesse* that made Woollcott nervous.

through the master bedroom window. Woollcott was appalled, but Maugham was delighted; he unsuited and dove in himself. Later in the summer, on the day Woollcott had finally got Bernard Shaw to come to lunch and busied himself frantically to make sure everything was just so, Harpo went swimming nude. When the Shaws drove up, Harpo managed to throw on a towel as Shaw bellowed, "Who the hell are you?" After they exchanged introductions, Shaw snatched off Harpo's towel and said, "This is Mrs. Shaw." To Woollcott's great chagrin, Harpo became the Shaws' companion-cum-chauffeur for the rest of the summer. "Harpo Marx and George Bernard Shaw," Woollcott sniffed. "Corned beef and roses."

In mid-summer Beatrice was called back to New York by George, who wanted hand-holding while he directed *The Front Page* for a fall opening. Alice Miller left to visit a friend in Egypt. ("I think you should know I'm living with a sheik," the friend wrote her tantalizingly.) Shortly after they left, Ruth Gordon arrived. One day, Woollcott put his arms around Gordon and Harpo and told them, "You two are the world, you know that? Every man as pretentious as old Alexander should have at least one Louisa [his nickname for Gordon] and one Harpo beside him always, to remind him of what really makes the world go around, and that everything else is pretending." But that summer and later, pretense won out.

The season's most exclusive party was held at the Eden Roc in August, and only Woollcott was invited from Villa Galanon. Gordon and Marx decided to gate-crash and thus sparked one of their only rifts of the summer. Marx led Gordon into the party through the kitchen, and they took up a table adjacent to Woollcott's on the terrace. When the main course—a whole salmon—was served to their table, Marx grabbed it off the platter and flipped it off the terrace and onto the beach. "Don't think I care for the fish," he told the astonished waiter. "What's on the Blue Plate tonight?" Everyone laughed but Woollcott, who glared. Harpo heard him tell the woman to his left, "I don't know. I've never seen that vulgar person before in my life." Next day, Marx and Gordon were mentioned on the Antibes newspaper's society page; Woollcott was not. After some ribbing from his friends to that effect, Woollcott left the villa in a huff,

leaving his poodle, Cocaud, behind in Harpo's care. The day after that, Harpo took Cocaud to Nice with him, and the dog began leading him, apparently with some destination in mind. Harpo followed to an inconspicuous town house where a Frenchwoman seemed to know the dog and invited Harpo in. There in the parlor of a luxurious brothel, Woollcott was reclining on a couch between two lovely prostitutes and being fed grapes.

At summer's end, Harpo and Ruth Gordon returned to full calendars in New York. Woollcott returned to very little: no deadlines to meet, no regular freelance commitments, indeed no visible means of support except for a trickle of royalties and a contract for book reviews with *McCall's*. Nevertheless, he bought a cooperative apartment on the East River at 450 East Fifty-second Street, where Alice Miller and Ralph Pulitzer lived and, if anything, stepped up his style of living in extravagance and outrageousness. He had the bathroom tiled with pictures of himself sitting on the toilet. He ordered a daily visit from the St. Regis barber to trim his hair and whiskers (he was trying to grow a goatee). He bought a Minerva automobile and a full-length fur coat. He rebuilt his kitchen to suit his houseman and to increase his capacity for entertaining. Frank Adams called the new apartment Ocowoica, an Ojibway term, he said, that meant "Little-Three-Room-Apartment-on-the-East-River-That-It-Is-Difficult-to-Find-a-Taxicab-Near." But it was Dorothy Parker's characterization that stuck. She called it Wit's End.

There Woollcott encamped, adding yet another adjunct to the Round Table. At Wit's End, the main event was Sunday breakfast, a convocation of whatever friends and acquaintances he could bring together, over which he would preside in baggy pajamas and bathrobe at his bad-mannered worst. "It was as though he brought people together just to exhibit their weaknesses to each other," one communicant at Wit's End rituals told Samuel Hopkins Adams. Russell Crouse said that "most people were flattered at being insulted by Woollcott. [It] placed you a few rungs up the ladder to social success." But his old *Stars and Stripes* comrade, John Winterich, was not among the flattered. He was so taken aback by Woollcott's comments to and about him one Sunday morning that he pulled Woollcott aside and asked, "Look, Aleck, do you hate me?"

The Hayes-MacArthur bathroom. Placing Woollcott's portrait above the throne apparently was not meant (although Woollcott may have taken it that way) as a sign of endearment. "He was always either bedazzled or contemptuous," Hayes wrote of Woollcott. "There was nothing in between. He believed he was the center of the universe and that, since he was the sun, everything and everybody revolved around him. . . . A cosmic sport, Alex had somehow managed to create this universe by employing his superiors as satellites."

Woollcott at Wit's End, which was decorated with, among other things, all his favorite caricatures of himself. He also installed a steam cabinet, the front wall of which was a window—and he showed no reti- cence to take steam when the apartment was full of guests. "I don't know why there always came a time when you'd had enough of Aleck," Jane Grant wrote. For her and several Round Tablers, that time had come.

Woollcott tried to explain his behavior to an old friend, Alice Root Nichols, who thought him sunk low indeed. "Look," he protested, "you don't know New York. If you're going to do any good in New York, you have to be noticed. You don't know the game. Look at so-and-so, or so-and-so. They're as good as I am, or better. Who ever heard of them? What paper ever mentions them? They've soft-pedaled themselves into obscurity. That sort of thing isn't going to happen to me." It was his first recorded justification of what his first New York *Times* editor, Carl Van Anda, finally, regretfully concluded was the "sacrifice of his brilliant gifts and varied acquirements to the dramatization of himself as a personality."

That fall, Swope quit the *World* himself. "It is bad to be a hired man too long," he said in a terse statement. The tributes flowed from colleagues and co-workers, and among his farewell dinners was one at the Hardware Club, at which Woollcott delivered his testimonial. James M. Cain, one of the writers on Swope's *World,* was there that evening and saw a Woollcott he had not seen before.

> *In the several seconds he took before speaking . . . various things crossed my mind, like the transformation in him, from the reasonably lean sergeant I had talked to, at the* Stars and Stripes *office in Paris a bare ten ten years before, to this fat, puffy personage, with eyes so dismayingly venomous, who briefly smirked his acknowledgment of the applause.*
> *It crossed my mind what terrible things money, success and adulation, plus gnawing secret bitterness, can do to human appearance.*

There was no obvious sign at the beginning of 1929, except for a two-year bulge in unemployment, of the economic debacle then so close at hand. The Round Tablers' new year began with an extravagant bash at the Swopes' new estate in Sands Point, this one even more commodious than their Great Neck place had been. The winter was busy for most of them: Kaufman was collaborating with Ring Lardner on *June Moon,* Connelly was working on a new play, Stewart was working on a novel, Parker was writing short stories and her *New Yorker* columns, Benchley was commuting to the film studios of New Jersey while writing his drama criticism and other magazine articles. Woollcott the free lance was re-

peating his several subjects—murder cases, war stories, backstage vignettes—for *McCall's,* the *Saturday Evening Post* and *Vanity Fair,* where he became a consulting editor; he also began his "Shouts and Murmurs" column in *The New Yorker,* although to decidedly mixed reception among the magazine's editors. For all that, however, it was a winter of play. Harpo wrote of those months as "one long party" extendng back to the Swopes' New Year's Eve, as each night everyone—including Kaufman, Parker, Woollcott, Alice Miller, Bea Kaufman, Neysa, Ruth Gordon and a floating cast of a dozen more—met backstage at the Forty-fourth Street theater, where the Marx Brothers were doing *Animal Crackers,* then set off together to one of their houses for an all or most-of-the-night party. And met again next day for lunch at the Algonquin.

The summer, too, was undarkened and high-spirited. At various times, nearly everyone in the group visited Neshobe, along with the celebrated Skinners, Ethel Barrymore, the Lunts and Noël Coward (several of whom soon became *New Yorker* Profile subjects for Woollcott). Benchley went to Europe with his family and visited the Murphys. Sherwood went to Europe and saw *The Road to Rome* in Vienna, where he also began thinking about the setting for a new play. Stewart partied with the Paysons and Whitneys and Hamiltons and Lovetts on Long Island and worked on a novel about "the loss of the play-spirit in the obsession with the making of dollars." Parker and Connelly saw a good deal of each other in early summer, as she helped him type out the final version of *The Green Pastures,* and she became a drinking partner of Broun's at Tony Soma's when Connelly accepted an invitation from John Garrett, grandson of the B & O Railroad's founder, for a month's cruise in the Mediterranean. FPA and Broun also spent a good deal of time with Swope, whose neighbors and croquet-playing partners tended now away from culture and toward the world of money, among them, Chryslers, Fieldses, Guggenheims, Harrimans, Morgans, Pratts, Schiffs, Tiffanys, Vanderbilts and Woolworths. "Herbert thinks he's going social," Woollcott said, "but he's only going financial."

FPA spent most of the summer in Connecticut, where his neighbors were Groucho Marx, the Gershwin brothers and Newman Levy. On a joint outing one Saturday it was like a reprise of early Round Table days: they found a lake

The Marx Brothers in *Animal Crackers* at the Forty-fourth Street Theater. Backstage after the show, which was one of the biggest hits of the 1928–29 season, all the Algonquinites would meet and then head for a party at Ruth Gordon's apartment, or Alice Duer Miller's, or Woollcott's, or Neysa's—and, as Harpo wrote, "the fun and games would go on until morning."

Although Harpo was the most involved of all the Marx brothers in Round Table play, the wit Kaufman wrote for them was in the same genre as that attributed to the Algonquin group generally—brittle, quick, thrown out almost too fast to catch, like Groucho's line in the show: "One day I shot an elephant in my pajamas. How he got into my pajamas I'll never know."

In the fall of 1929,
Harpo wrote: "There
were grave responsibili-
ties to face . . . plants to
be watered, poodles to
be walked, and the deci-
sion on whether or not
to take the Cubs over the
Athletics at six-to-one
in the Series."

property for sale near Bridgeport and began arrangements—subsequently deferred—to form a private club on it. Groucho said he wanted the deli concession.
The Thanatopsis group narrowed somewhat for the summer—to Adams, Swope,
assorted Wall Street executives and Broun, who had repented that particular reform of his character—and they met on Tuesday nights so as not to interfere
with country weekends. The game continued even after Swope left for the August
racing season in Saratoga.

In late summer, FPA wrote in his newspaper diary mock-plaintively:

> *In the country, I am frantick to get my work done that I may play . . .
> and in the city I am hard put to get it done at all what with the interrup-
> tions that come; and what frets me is that I have such trouble doing it
> because I like too many other things better, such as family, friends,
> books, musique, plays and all manner of games.*

Harpo wrote that as he left Neshobe that summer he felt he could hardly face
"another grueling nine months of all-night poker and all-day croquet, Round
Table lunches and Long Island weekends. Back to the grind of cooking up puns
and practical jokes."

The American of 1929 generally was, as Leo Gurko well described him, "an
admirable fellow, with a large capacity for enjoying life. . . . Belief in the idea
of progress and the good life was never stronger. If the Arabs were slaughter-
ing Jews in Palestine, if there was labor trouble in Gastonia, if William B.
Shearer was suing certain ship-building firms for back pay incident to his services as a propagandist against naval disarmament at the Geneva Disarmament
Conference in 1927, if one had to flout the law by frequenting speakeasies and
patronizing bootleggers—well, these were minor irritations in a world that was
essentially on the right track. . . . His materialism was benevolent and forward-
looking, previsioning a future that would engulf everyone in a tide of lasting
prosperity." There were, of course, millions of people for whom the boom aspect of the Twenties was just so much newspaper lineage; in the last golden
year of 1929, according to a later Brookings Institution study, only 2.3 percent of American families had incomes of over $10,000 and 60 percent fell
below the $2,000 income minimal for "basic necessities." Unemployment had

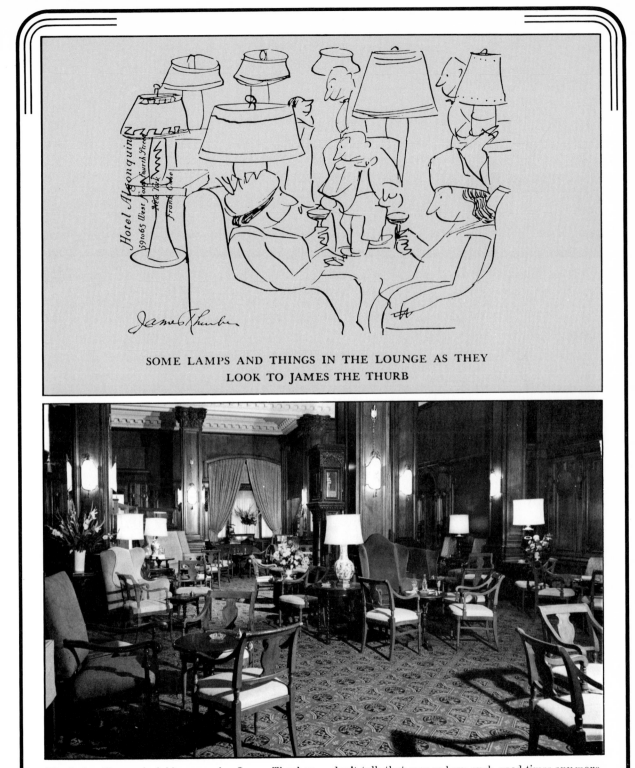

SOME LAMPS AND THINGS IN THE LOUNGE AS THEY
LOOK TO JAMES THE THURB

(Top) An Algonquin lobby scene by James Thurber, who came to the hotel full-fledged (a writer for *The New Yorker*) when the Twenties were almost over. (Bottom) A photograph of the remodeled lobby. Echoes of the Round Table seem to persist there, and conversation often turns to the group—how people don't talk that way or have such good times any more. But the Algonquin group could have happened in no other decade, and, as FPA once wrote, "Nothing is more responsible for the good old days than a bad memory."

From a quarter of a million dollars on paper, Harpo's fortune dropped to zero. "Martial law had been declared against us Croquetmaniacs and Thanatopsians and Sitters of the Round Table, and all the other overage children of our world. We were under house arrest. The sentence was the abolition of the 1920s."

been rising for twenty months. The idea of prosperity, promoted by the greatest public hard-sell spree in history, weathered such developments in the decade as mushrooming crime rates, urban overcrowding and inner-city ghettoes. The U.S. Public Health Service estimated that by 1931, the smoke from coal-burning furnaces had cut off one-fifth of New York City's sunlight.

But after the Crash, the boom consciousness persisted, as the feeling of an amputated limb does. Harpo, who lost a great deal, wrote of realizing at last that "the bam-sock-and-pow part was over. Our million-dollar playground was condemned." But at the time, most of the Round Tablers found it an event of merely practical annoyance. FPA sat watching the ticker that black day and wrote in his diary that he found it "much more fascinating to gaze at when things were going badly than when they were going well, just as poker and craps hold my interest more when I am losing than when I am winning." At year's end he noted that he was better off than he had been the previous year. Dorothy Parker hadn't thought to invest her large and incoming royalties, and Viking had contracted with her for another book of poetry. Broun had never got enough money together at one time to do much investing except at poker and the race track. Kaufman lost only $10,000 on the one stock he ever bought. He took the loss gracefully. "Anyone who buys a stock because the Marx Brothers recommmend it *deserves* to lose," he said. Harpo and Woollcott lost all the savings they had, but they were soon able to replenish their losses.

The Crash struck hardest at the monied culture that nurtured the Algonquin crowd. In September of 1929, Swope was worth $14 million on paper, thanks to tips from Bernard Baruch and others; owing to his belief in the market's continuing strength, despite Baruch's contrary advice, he found himself $2 million in debt on November first and would not see black ink in his personal finances for seven years. He kept the Sands Point estate, selling only his racing stable, and kept up his accustomed style of living, but he did so on money loaned him by friends like Baruch, Joshua Hertz and Albert Lasker, and entertainment at the Swopes' would never be quite as carefree again. John Baragwanath was playing rummy with the Harold Talbotts, Edward, the Prince of Wales, and Prince George in Sunningdale, England, the night before the Crash. Next day, Talbott

John Held, Jr. (above, in 1930), had made himself famous with his caricatured flapper in the 1920s— he actually gave flappers and their raccoon-coated escorts a model of how they should look to be authentically in type. But he was also one of the first ruefully to note the precipitous sobering of spirit that followed the Crash of 1929. The champagne Twenties had gone flat.

and Baragwanath boarded a ship for home and spent the trip in the ship's brokerage office watching each other's investments being wiped out. Even the Murphys finally moved back to New York after the Crash to take personal control of the family business.

As it had been part of the public manifestation of the Twenties—the speakeasy and high-life cultures, the theatrical boom, the fads of entertainment that came and went—so the Algonquin group remained more a creature than a creator of the times that confronted it now, reflecting the dazed belief in quick recovery that characterized most of the nation at that time. For half of 1930, the main preoccupation of the public mind seemed to be miniature golf; for the other half it was the New Humanism of Irving Babbitt and Paul Elmer More, which called on Americans to tighten their morals and listen to the "inner check" on excess of all kinds—in part a reaction to the extravagances of the Twenties which, after years of batting about in intellectual magazines, got its first real hearing only as faith in prosperity began to flag. There was another flurry of hope in "technocrats"—a new word for a breed that promised an economy efficiently managed with the simplicity of a chart by unnamed specialists in that sort of thing who never quite materialized. In various ways, all these à la mode fixes seemed to serve as psychological locks between the high-water Twenties and the low-tide Thirties.

Thus the Round Table ended, as it had begun, in the daze following a cataclysm, a public fixture whose fashion flowed and ebbed with public events that made little immediate impact on most of them as individuals. After the Crash, the cultural medium in which the group was nurtured grew slowly sour, and one can almost gauge the importance of their later work by the speed with which they came to realize it and to excuse themselves for other things.

Sherwood had been the first and remained most decisive about it. Having breached his association with the Round Table in 1926, he began increasingly to turn his back on the entire decade, which he called "the most sordid of periods." Perhaps as a function of his greater involvement in the war, Sherwood had been more deeply affected than his Round Table companions seemed to be with the Treaty of Versailles, a disillusion that struck everyone, it seemed, but members

of the Round Table. From the fixing of the 1919 World Series onward, Sherwood saw everywhere grim resonances of that famous phrase, "Say it ain't so, Joe." *The Road to Rome* in 1926 had been, as even Woollcott wrote, dramatic proof that "every sacrifice made in the name of war is wasted," and it drew what Sherwood considered a "deadly and disturbing" parallel between the Philistinism of ancient Rome and that of the American Twenties. And if Sherwood had "started out with a big message and ended up with a good evening's entertainment," as he ruefully said of the play, he was not content with that. In his preface to *The Queen's Husband* in 1928, he implicitly distanced himself from Kaufman's dictum about calling Western Union if you have a message, and denounced "the muse who wears a green eye-shade [and] wields a blue pencil." The playwright, he wrote, should be "just a great, big overgrown boy, reaching for the moon. . . . The moon is never more beautiful than when it is seen shining down on an insecure balcony, in a painted Verona."

They were, as his biographer noted, "green words," but they signified the tug of events on him and his struggle to find dramatic expression of his times. He was clearly finished with sophistic wit. While abroad in 1932, he met Shaw for the first time, and his reaction is notable if only in contrast to the idolatry Woollcott showered on him just four years before in Antibes. In Shaw was the measure of Round Table wit; he "taught us the art as undergraduates," as Cowley put it. But where Woollcott saw a sage and master, Sherwood saw an outdated trickster. "I believe," he wrote in his journal, "that Shaw is an unconscionable poseur—that he says a great deal, emphatically and of course effectively—that he doesn't really mean. He affects to approve wholeheartedly of the Russian system. Telling how they dispose of all recalcitrant nonconformists by simply blowing their heads off from behind, he said he thought that an excellent idea—but it goes without saying that under such a system Shaw himself would be the first to suffer decapitation. [He is] just going through the motions of being a radical, a hurler of monkey-wrenches."

Sherwood's painted moons and clay-footed idols were naïvely fashioned but apparently crucial elements in his further development as a playwright. He credited much of his thinking and writing after 1930 to a reading of Joseph Wood

A Mack Sennett girl in the mid-Twenties, Madeleine Hurlock came to New York in 1928. Howard Dietz introduced her to Connelly, who found her "a beautiful and storm-tossed girl."

Krutch's *The Modern Temper,* a bleak depiction of intellectual self-alienation in the Twenties. In retrospect, then, it is not surprising that his most successful comedy, *Reunion in Vienna* (1931), was prefaced darkly. The playwright said he had "the ill luck to occupy the limbo-like interlude between one age and another," a period when "Democracy—liberty, equality, fraternity and the pursuit of happiness . . . all the distillations of man's maturing intelligence [had] gone sour." Sherwood called *Reunion* "another demonstration of the escape mechanism in operation," but it was clearly more than that as well. Brooks Atkinson wrote of Sherwood after seeing the play: "He is not one of the wits, of whom we have several, but he is one of the humorists, of which we have few."

That Sherwood saw the pernicious nature of the Twenties as clearly as he did was no doubt partly due to Mary Brandon Sherwood, who provided a living symbol of the wrong turn the Twenties had taken him on. Beginning in 1932, his fate—and the fate of his marriage—intersected with the fate and marriage of Marc Connelly in a way that said a good deal about them both.

Connelly's career also came to a crescendo as the country was falling. *The Green Pastures* won the Pulitzer for 1930, the same year Connelly won the O'Henry Prize for a short story called "The Coroner's Inquest." On October 4 of that year, in full flush of his celebrity, he married Madeleine Hurlock, a former Mack Sennett beauty he had met through Howard Dietz two years before, and for the four years their marriage lasted, *The Green Pastures* was on continuous tour, allowing Connelly to live comfortably without working. He did take directing assignments in theater and some writing jobs in Hollywood (he bought a house in Bel Air in 1931), but he never remotely met the challenge of bettering the play that is thus considered his masterwork. Among the Algonquinites who kept to their former schedule of play in the early 1930s, Connelly was prominent.

The Sherwoods and the Connellys became close friends, finding as a foursome an elation of spirit they had lost as couples. Madeleine came quickly to tire of Connelly's waggery and constant performance, as Sherwood was growing weary with Mary Brandon's petulant demand for center stage. They toured Europe together in 1932, and were back in Europe together the following year for Connelly to direct the London opening of Sherwood's new play, *Acropolis.*

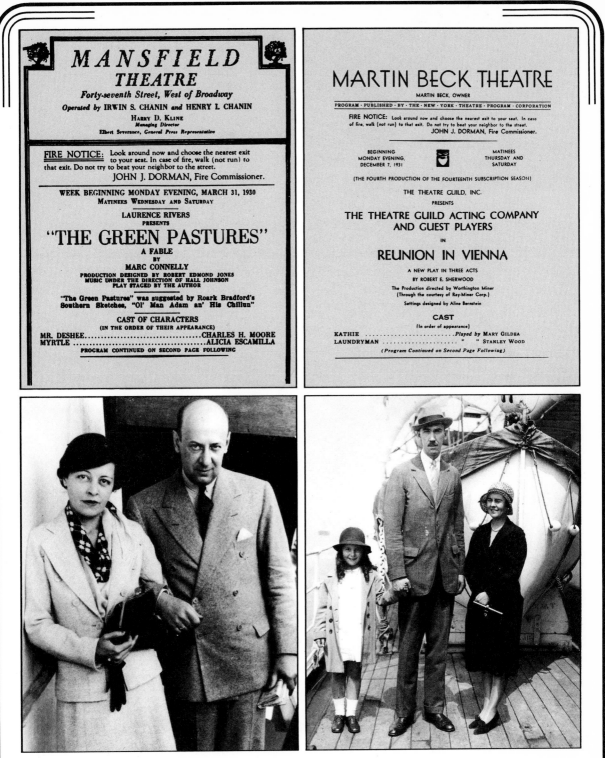

In the full flush of fame brought to them by such plays as *Green Pastures* and *Reunion in Vienna*, Connelly and Sherwood went to Europe with their wives and "little Mary" Sherwood. They left just before Prohibition was repealed, thus leaving behind them the remnants of speakeasy life and the Twenties. The trip would completely change the relationship of the two old Rose Room tablemates. Almost as soon as the two couples returned to New York, they began divorce proceedings.

Just before his marriage to Madeleine in 1935 (left), Sherwood wrote Woollcott: "There is no disguising the fact that this business has hurt Marc sorely, or that from certain points of view I must appear a prime shit. But the only answer to everything is that I love her very much and want to make her happy."

As John Mason Brown noted, the play was, if not his greatest work, a pivotal one: S. N. Behrman wrote that in *Acropolis,* Sherwood had for the first time written a play that seemed not to be at odds with his preface—and Sherwood himself considered *The Petrified Forest, Idiot's Delight* and *Abe Lincoln in Illinois* to have sprung in some measure from the play. He also used one of the speeches in it for *There Shall Be No Night.* The work that thus nourished Sherwood's three Pulitzer-winning plays, that bespoke the playwright's self-integration, also occasioned his admitting the inevitable as regarded both Mary Brandon and Madeleine Connelly. "Let me tell you one thing," Alan Squier says in *The Petrified Forest.* "Any woman is worth everything that any man has to give—anguish, ecstasy, faith, jealousy, hatred, life or death." However torn Sherwood patently was—about divorce, about hurting Connelly—he was no longer capable of defying gravity, in his life or work. He and Madeleine Connelly were married in 1935.

Kaufman proved to be always the constructionist of plays that others wrote. In 1929, he suffered a failure with Woollcott on *The Channel Road,* a comedic retelling of Maupassant's *Boule de Suif* that most critics panned for its logorrhea; they surmised that the blame, like the idea for the play, was Woollcott's. Then came his more successful collaboration with Lardner on the dramatization of Lardner's story "Some Like Them Cold." As in Kaufman's other works, the plot only provided a skeleton on which a spoof, this time of the songwriting industry, could be draped, which was enough for a very profitable run on Broadway. As George Jean Nathan said, "The theater that aims at amusement alone, which isn't such a bad aim after all, is represented in Ring Lardner's and George S. Kaufman's *June Moon.*" (A hit play was what Lardner had always dreamed of, along with writing music for the stage. But his life was at bottom before the year was out. He and Kaufman talked about writing another play together, this one serious and about alcoholism, about which no one could write more authoritatively than Lardner, but depression overtook him. At one point he called Kaufman to ask if his committing suicide would have a detrimental effect on *June Moon* at the box office. From 1930 on, Lardner steadily declined, in health, spirits and work. He died in 1933.)

In the speeches of Alan Squier, delivered onstage and in the film by Leslie Howard (above, with leading lady Peggy Conklin in the Broadway production), Sherwood poured out all his Krutchian views of the lost Twenties: "For eight years I reclined there, on the Riviera, on my background—and I waited for the major artist to step forth and say something of en- during importance. He preferred to remain inarticulate. . . . I'm one of the intellectuals . . . brains without purpose. Noise without sound. Shape without substance." He says he is headed for the Petrified Forest. "Perhaps that's what I'm destined for—to make an interesting fossil for future study. Homo Semi-Americanus—a specimen of the in-between age."

Kaufman eventually gained some measure of security in his talent, but Lardner died with the feeling that his success was unearned, his work insubstantial, and he never allowed himself to enjoy the acclaim that greeted *June Moon.*

To say what Kaufman was doing in the last years of the Round Table is simply to list his credits: *Strike Up the Band* with Ryskind and *Once in a Lifetime* with Moss Hart both opened in 1930; *The Band Wagon* with Howard Dietz and *Of Thee I Sing* with Ryskind and the Gershwins opened within six months of each other in 1931. Kaufman was not only opening plays as fast as ever but was spending an increasing amount of time doctoring them on the road, and he had also begun to direct. *Of Thee I Sing* was the biggest and best received hit that Kaufman ever had; in the year of *Mourning Becomes Electra, The Animal Kingdom, Reunion in Vienna* and *Counsellor-at-Law,* it won the Pulitzer Prize. Benchley panned it in *The New Yorker*—"The whole thing, during great stretches, was reminiscent of an old Hasty Pudding 'scoop' in which lese majesty was considered funny enough in itself without straining for any more mature elements of comedy"—but he stood alone among the critics. Even before that, *Variety* estimated that Kaufman was making $7,000 a week, equivalent to an annual income today of about $2 million. It was enough security for him finally to quit his editing job at the *Times* and make upward adjustments in his style of living. He bought a new town house on East Sixty-third Street, hired several more maids and a better governess for Anne and began going around town in a chauffeur-driven limousine. The principal change in Kaufman's view during the Depression was the more luxurious scenery of his own life.

Dorothy Parker, the first to sense a false, hypnotizing glare in the spotlight thrown on the Round Table, was, at decade's end, still decrying its effects from within and denying to her closest friends that she liked going to the Round Table at all. In 1929, she wrote an adoring article on Hemingway for *The New Yorker.* In it, she credited him for "avoiding New York, for he has the most valuable asset an artist can possess—the fear of what he knows is bad for him." She quoted commendingly something he had told her—"Scratch a writer and find a social climber"—and she contrasted him favorably with those writers whose deepest ambitions were "beckoned toward the North Shore of Long Island." Stewart knew the remarks were aimed at him; at Tony's not long before, she had charged him with "trading in his pen for an alpenstock." In early 1930, they met at the Murphys' house, and Stewart asked her what the hell she had meant by her re-

BEGINNING WEDNESDAY EVENING, OCTOBER 9, 1929

MATINEES WEDNESDAY AND SATURDAY

SAM H. HARRIS
PRESENTS

"JUNE MOON"

A PLAY BY RING LARDNER AND GEORGE S. KAUFMAN
MUSIC AND LYRICS BY MR. LARDNER
STAGED BY MR. KAUFMAN

CHARACTERS

FRED STEVENS.....................................NORMAN FOSTER
EDNA BAKER..LINDA WATKINS
PAUL SEARS..FRANK OTTO

PROGRAM CONTINUED ON SECOND PAGE FOLLOWING

Kaufman had a great deal to feel secure about. Between the fall of 1929 and the end of 1931, he had four smash hits on Broadway with four different collaborators. (Top, right) Fred and Adele Astaire in *The Band Wagon* (260 performances). (Bottom, left) Victor Moore and William Gaxton in *Of Thee I Sing* (441 performances). (Bottom, right) Spring Byington as Helen Hobart in *Once in a Lifetime* (305 performances).

Party girl to the end, Parker (fourth from left) posed in 1930 for an antic-in-the-tropics photograph with, from left, Madeleine Connelly, Margaret Case Morgan (Harriman), Neysa McMein, Clare Booth Brokaw (Luce), Alison Smith and Laurie Jacques.

marks in the Hemingway piece. She replied that of course she hadn't really meant *him,* and "it was all love and cognac," Stewart wrote. But, for the nascent leftists Parker and Stewart, the years immediately following would soon seem regressive in the extreme.

Nineteen-thirty was Stewart's best year. His play *Rebound* was produced on Broadway to enthusiastic reviews and great profit. He had worked on a screenplay of *Dulcy* called *Not So Dumb,* which opened in a Broadway theater that year, and his first and only musical comedy, *Fine and Dandy,* opened there in the fall as well. He was under contract to MGM to write a film called *Laughter,* an assignment he undertook in part because it allowed him to stay in his house on the Whitney estate and work in a studio he had made for himself there. His justification for "going Whitney"—"an enjoyable life for Bea and the baby" —was outdated now, but he had come to value the friendship of the Whitneys for itself. The last memorable events of his year were the Harvard-Yale game, to which he and Whitney went in Whitney's private railroad car, and a drunken night of Christmas Eve shopping with Charles Payson, as the Payson limousine followed them from store to store down Fifth Avenue. He could afford to be generous that year. Paramount was beckoning, and Stewart, at the top of his writing form, was willing. "Harry Kurnitz once described movie writing as a horrible ordeal in which sadistic producers torture you almost beyond endurance by holding your jaws open while they drop a monotonously maddening succession of gold dollars into your helpless mouth," Stewart wrote. "I opened wide—and I didn't close it for many years."

Clearly, Stewart's high living impinged on his productivity not at all. Similarly, the behavior Parker came so impassionedly to denounce in herself was the seedbed for some of her best short stories. Nineteen-thirty and 1931 were among the most personally difficult and professionally productive years in her life. It was almost as if there were two Dorothy Parkers, one living on drink and parties and gossip, the other writing it all down with bitter precision. Her writing was so autobiographical as to be almost confessional: stories about abortion, of which she had a few, about older women going dotty over younger men, about empty love affairs and gossip and social pretense and the void of

WIT'S END

MacArthur, Harpo, Parker, and Woollcott at the Garden of Allah, where they and other Round Tablers tried with mixed results to form an enclave of the Twenties in the Thirties.

cocktail parties and mornings-after—all the most grimly salient characteristics of her own life. Masterfully and mercilessly, she wrote what she perceived as dire truths about herself and those around her and continued playing out her fiction in her life.

If there was a time when self-denigration was only the best pose she knew how to strike for her audience, that time was now past. She came out of an affair with a businessman in whom no one, including Parker, saw much of anything, to take up with a brokerage clerk ten years her junior whose declared intention was to sleep with all the rich and important women he could. Eventually, he refused to see her any more and countered her advances by relating seamy stories about her to her friends. The blackouts were beginning, and Benchley told her she might try going to Alcoholics Anonymous, which she did. When she saw Benchley later at Tony's, he asked how it had been. "It was lovely," she told him. Was she going to join AA? "Certainly not. They want me to stop *now!*"

Some of her friends thought it was the pain of rejection that led her to begin dating homosexuals, others that their inaccessibility attracted her. Parker said only that she needed "good fairies to protect me." And in her "Diary of a New York Lady," subtitled "During Days of Horror, Despair and World Change," she wrote:

> *Called up and found I could get two tickets for the opening of* Run Like a Rabbit *tonight for forty-eight dollars. Told them they had the nerve of the world, but what can you do? Think Joe said he was dining out, so telephoned some divine numbers to get someone to go to the theater with me, but they were all tied up. Finally got Ollie Martin. He couldn't have more poise, and what do I care if he is one?*

One of her most frequent escorts was a young actor named Alan Campbell, and soon they were living together—he the household administrator, cook, launderer, dog walker, bartender, schedule arranger; she the talent in need of nurturing and, even he admitted it, the meal ticket. In 1931, her last book of poetry, *Death and Taxes,* was a commercial and critical triumph. FPA raved: "More certain than either death or taxes is the high and shining art of Dorothy Parker." *The New Yorker* said she deserved a Pulitzer. But her private life had become a

She would later cruelly ridicule him as she had Eddie Parker, but many of their closest friends agreed with Donald Ogden Stewart that Campbell "wasn't a villain. He kept her living and working."

haunted midway. She went to a ball for male homosexuals and took a place on the balcony shouting, "Come on, everybody, I'm a man." She and Campbell went down to the Lower East Side one night and had themselves tattooed.

In 1933, Campbell asked her to marry him, in part as a business arrangement. His small acting career had shrunk to nothing, but he felt they would make a successful screenwriting team. Parker had proved herself to Hollywood in 1931, when she worked three months for MGM. "After some weeks I ran away," she told a reporter. "I could not stand it more. I just sat in a cell-like office and did nothing. . . . I would imagine the Klondike like that—a place where people rush for gold." Nevertheless, in 1933, she and Campbell did marry and move to California. They set up housekeeping first in the Garden of Allah, where Benchley was already living and Stewart was a frequent visitor, as were Sherwood, Kaufman, Connelly and the Round Tablers who had moved out in the Twenties. A schism would soon separate some of the old friends from others along ideological lines, but in the early 1930s their salaries of $5,000 a week and more bought a temporary injunction against the Depression. The day of Roosevelt's inauguration, Stewart was visiting the Paysons. After Roosevelt delivered his famous line, "We have nothing to fear but fear itself," Stewart wrote in his autobiography, "we descended to the waiting limousine and drove through the wintry slush past several closed banks to the pier where we embarked without fear on a sunny pleasure cruise to Haiti and Santo Domingo."

———

In New York, the change was not so easy to ignore, however diligently some of them tried. Between the end of the *World* in 1931 and of the "noble experiment" in 1933, the New York the Algonquinites had known collapsed at their feet.

The end of the *World* marked the beginning of a steady decline for the group's paternal figure, FPA, whose stock had been falling in any case. One of his earliest contributors, Newman Levy, had opened the attack on him in the *Nation* as early as 1929:

> *FPA has ever allowed himself to be concerned with minutiae and to tilt against toy windmills. Great moral issues have come and gone, social injustices have passed by unnoticed while he directed the sharp barbs of*

Parker and Alan Campbell were credited on fifteen films between 1933 and 1938, including *A Star Is Born,* but Parker soon found the money small consolation for what she considered enervating, degrading work. "Hollywood money isn't money," she told an interviewer years later. "It's congealed snow, melts in your hand, and there you are. I can't talk about Hollywood....When I got away from it I couldn't even refer to the place by name. 'Out there,' I called it. You want to know what 'out there' means to me? Once I was coming down a street in Beverly Hills, and I saw a Cadillac about a block long, and out of the side window was a wonderfully slinky mink, and an arm, and at the end of the arm a hand in a white suede glove wrinkled around the wrist, and in the hand was a bagel with a bite out of it."

With the demise of the *World*, many of its writers and readers saw the end of an era. But Broun, who wrote for the merged *World-Telegram*, and FPA, who went to work for the *Herald Tribune*, took the change well— some old colleagues thought all too well.

his wit against such evils as the misuse of the objective case, dry-sweeping and invisible house numbers. A brilliancy that might have been a potent social force has been expended to express the irritation of a petulant proofreader. . . . The Conning Tower, from which he might have surveyed the seven seas, is but a tower of ivory after all.

FPA did not disagree; that was not his purpose. That which was his purpose, however, was a declining fashion. Levy remembered in his unpublished biography of Adams that by 1930 the Contribunion dinner was a lifeless vestige.

What had originally been an impromptu gathering of youthful enthusiasts had become a formalized institution. But, more important, the boys and girls had grown up. They still retained their sentimental affection for The Colyum, but they were now writing plays and novels, winning Pulitzer Prizes.

Adams was visiting Swope when word reached them by telephone that the last hope of preventing the *World*'s merger with the *Telegram* was gone. Hearing the news, Adams said to his host, "Where are you buying your apples these days, Mr. Swope?" It was, of course, a facetious question; Adams was not retained by the *World-Telegram,* but he was picked up by his old paper, the *Tribune,* as a featured columnist. Still, his light was dimming and would soon go out. What finally saved him was the emergence of the radio panel show *Information Please,* a forum uniquely appropriate to his compulsive grasp of trivia.

Woollcott's literary persona was also wearing thin. At *The New Yorker,* Ross was put off equally by the quality of Woollcott's columns and the affectations of his old friend. Neither his bell ringing for his friends in Profiles, nor his column of theater items, satisfied the magazine's refining tastes. His style was becoming self-parodic, a condition aggravated even more than before by his selling the same piece, or nearly so, to several magazines at once. "Aleck only knows about nine words," Ross complained to James Thurber, "and he uses them all the time. He writes about putting on his tippet and going buckety-buckety to the theater . . . and he uses 'these old eyes' and 'at long last' in every third sentence." It was only a part, Thurber wrote, of a stock lecture Ross delivered

(Top, left) The *World*'s own story of the merger. (Top, right) FPA in the role he found for himself in the late Thirties on *Information Please*. (Bottom) FPA with fellow panelists, from left, Marcus Duffield, Paul de Kruif and Lewis Hacker. FPA took the downfall of the *World* blithely. In his first "Samuel Pepys" column on the *Herald Tribune*, he wrote that his week had been full of "heartbreak and elation, the former over my old associates and their journal, and the latter over my new ones and theirs." He made the transition from print to radio with similar equanimity.

Woollcott in a macabre vest embroidered for him by Mrs. Theodore Roosevelt II. "It was intended for home wear," Samuel Adams wrote, but it "became a beacon light of theater and hotel lobbies, of Broadway and Fifth Avenue sidewalks. . . . He could not bear to shut it away from public view even in the harshest weather."

on "the sins of Woollcottism," another installment of which went more to the man himself:

> *He has the emotions of a fish. He'll do anything for two hundred dollars—I get tired of seeing his face in testimonial ads. Goddamn it, the magazine once printed a photo of him lounging in the back seat of some make of automobile. I didn't catch it in time. Nobody ever tells me anything. Have you been to one of his famous Sunday breakfasts? . . . You're lucky. He sits there like a fat duchess holding out her dirty rings to be kissed.*

Wolcott Gibbs's position on the Woollcott question was less complicated: "I guess he was one of the most dreadful writers who ever existed."

The timing of his radio debut was fortuitous: it was the month before the failures of *The Channel Road* and the stock market—September of 1929. Officials of the Mutual Broadcasting Network station WOR in Newark approached him because they rightly believed he would use all his famous friends on the show; he enthusiastically agreed, in part because he could get no more mileage from them in any other medium. The debut had its problems. Woollcott lost his sense of timing and let his voice betray his nerves. Ross wired him: "You were wonderful. I lost my dinner." But by the end of his first thirteen weeks, he had attracted a small following and a sponsor, the Gruen Watch Company.

How he capitalized on his air time was not to everyone's notion of good taste or good ethics, but it was entirely in keeping with the public role he fashioned for himself. As he had been a salesman for Broadway as a drama critic —not on anyone's payroll but still to the industry's benefit—he now became a seller of books as *The Early Bookworm*. According to Harry Hansen, his $500 fee for the show was raised by passing the hat among publishers. No one claimed that his opinions were bought, but bad reviews on the program were few indeed. Not only did Woollcott take money for commercials he read himself, he had, as well, an inflated notion of their worth. In his third month as a broadcaster, a prominent woman in Utica, New York, disappeared, and her friends tried to enlist Woollcott, who had been a friend of her family's, to help on the air with a nationwide search for her. Woollcott said he would be glad to help, on condition

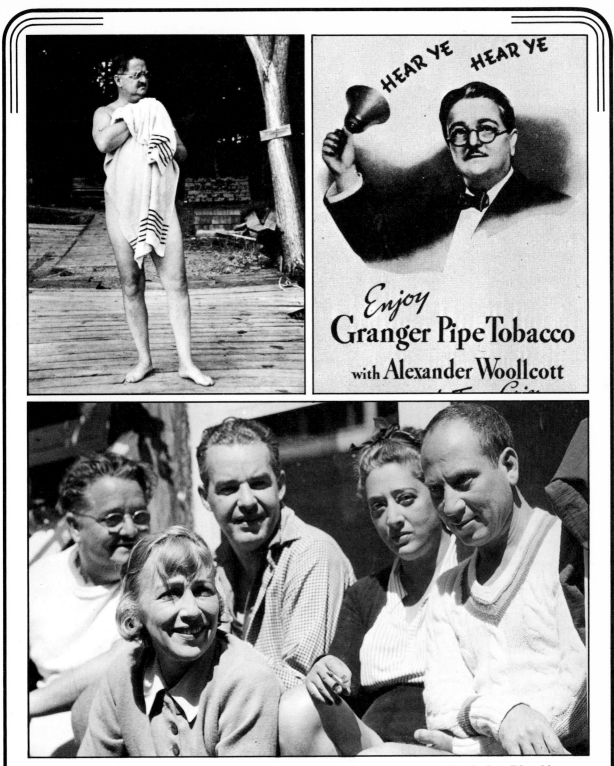

(Top, left) Woollcott unadorned at Neshobe. (Top, right) A poster for *The Town Crier*. (Bottom) Woollcott with, from left, Neysa, Alfred Lunt, Beatrice Kaufman and Harpo, at Lake Bomoseen. Woollcott became increasingly a caricature of himself. In the late 1930s he told one Canadian reporter that "I love to be libeled," and then he wrote a letter of congratulations when the story was published, describing him as a "moonpuss" whose "jowls would shame a bulldog with the mumps . . . his head is as wide as a broodmare's rump." He would soon complain that Gibbs's portrait in *The New Yorker* was "nastier than any of the other articles published about me"—and then delight in dramatic caricatures more damning by far.

Of all the compliments he received on his *Town Crier* performances, the one that Woollcott cherished above all others was sent to him by a wealthy woman whose cook had said: "Dere's voodoo in dat voice an' glory in dem tales."

that they give him $2,500, five times what he was getting to do commercials. They refused. (The woman had drowned in a canal near her home.)

In his greater celebrity, Woollcott began making even greater demands of his friends, and those who stood their ground against his insistences did so at the friendship's peril. His feud with Swope dates from this period. It began with one of their legendary and bitter bouts of croquet—a grudge match, $1,000 to the winner, in which each man accused the other of making up rules to serve himself. No grudge match after that could console either of them, and Woollcott sealed their disaffection by preventing Swope's friend, Joshua Hertz, from buying an apartment in his building. Swope thought Woollcott's only reason for doing it was that Hertz was Jewish. He wrote Woollcott: "There is a price you must pay when you translate unkind thoughts into venomous action, and that price is my friendship." They continued to snipe at each other throughout the Thirties, Woollcott suggesting that Swope was responsible for the fall of the *World* and that he had become a leech on his monied friends, and Swope denigrating Woollcott whenever the opportunity arose. "He has had a profound influence on writers," Swope wrote Dudley Nichols, "all to the bad." When Swope received the Christmas letter Seagrams sent out over Woollcott's signature, he wrote the company: "As he never drinks whisky . . . I have canceled my order for your product, and I shall advise my friends to follow the same course." They didn't see each other until the end of 1940 and were never friendly again.

The Woollcott-Ross relationship also deteriorated, more gradually but eventually to the same conclusion. Their old mentor-to-boob relationship had lost something when *The New Yorker* proved so successful, and Woollcott did nothing to pull in the slack with his continual resignations over minor editorial changes. Ross used to dread those days when Woollcott would come into the office ("like a butterfly in heat," as Rea Irvin put it) to lodge his protests. "All the time Aleck wrote for us he was a trial," Ross told Samuel Adams, "something of a nuisance and an embarrassment." Woollcott's taking money for plugs on his drama page drove Ross wild, and finally he decided that Woollcott would have to go. "That was just at the time he was getting drunk with power," Ross said later. "I figured he was too big for us, was becoming a big, national personality,

Woollcott with Moss Hart at the Boston tryout of *The Man Who Came to Dinner*. According to legend, Hart got the idea for the play from a visit Woollcott had made to his Bucks County estate, during which he, Woollcott, ordered the servants about, disdained the food, had a group of his own friends over and finally wrote in the guest book, "This is to certify that on my first visit to Moss Hart's house, I had one of the most unpleasant times I ever spent." Wouldn't it be horrible, Hart later asked George Kaufman, if Woollcott had had an accident there and had to stay for a prolonged period of time? Thus was the premise conceived. Asked by indignant friends what he thought of the play, Woollcott's most thoughtful reply was, "I didn't know I had friends who cared that much about me."

Woollcott as Harold Sigrist in S. N. Behrman's *Brief Moment*, which ran for 129 performances in the 1931–32 season. "Sigrist is very fat," Behrman wrote, "about thirty years old, and lies down whenever pos- sible. He somewhat resembles Alexander Woollcott, who conceivably might play him." So he did—and then he played Behrman's similar character, Binkie, in *Wine of Choice* seven years later.

and the magazine couldn't hold him." It was a Profile of Woollcott written by Wolcott Gibbs that made the breach irreparable. "Ross was very odd about the Profile," Gibbs recalled for Thurber. "He supplied most of the really damaging stories." After their argument over the Profile, the old comrades from the *Stars and Stripes* never saw each other again.

One of the last in-character sessions of the Round Table featured Heywood Broun as the Socialist Party candidate for Congress from Manhattan's silk-stocking district in 1930, with his Rose Room friends in various supporting roles. If the very idea is absurd—the Racquet Club Socialist and his libertine comrades playing out their tricksterish sensibility on the larger field of party politics—the result was equally so.

Prefiguring those marvelous scenes in Hollywood in the 1930s in which bejeweled ladies and gentlemen in dinner clothes toasted the revolution with fine champagne in palatial homes, Broun decided to tell his father he was joining the Socialist Party only after he'd had a rubdown at the club. His father played backgammon as he heard the news. As it happened, Broun *père* was less taken aback by his son's candidacy than the Socialists were. Broun admitted his credentials were a little thin; his reading on the subject was limited to two books, *Looking Backward* by Edward Bellamy and Shaw's *An Intelligent Woman's Guide to Socialism*. Then there was his drinking, tolerable to younger moderates but anathema to the old guard. Even some members of his own party turned out during the campaign to jeer him, and communists tagged him at every opportunity as a "petty-bourgeois clown." But it was Broun's unshakable belief that anything worth doing was worth doing "wet," and when he opened campaign headquarters at the Algonquin, among the first and most prominent installations was a closetful of bathtub gin.

Broun's father died during the campaign, and Broun wrote in his column in the *Telegram*:

> *The most important thing to mention is that Mr. Broun was just about the most charming man anybody had ever known. . . . I take pride in the fact that my father was a gay man. That he liked to give and receive*

parties. For many years after he was well past seventy he kept, with all
the ardor of a religious rite, a cocktail hour.

I have always felt that truly kindly people, like my father, must
be men who have themselves a flair for fun. Only from the exuberant is it
possible to get an enlivening return in the execution of the commandment,
"Love thy neighbor as thyself." Nor would his tombstone have a better
inscription than this: "He took and gave much joy in life."

Perhaps, as Broun's campaign treasurer, Morris Ernst, mused more than forty
years later, the campaign would have been stronger and more orthodox had his
father lived, had his paternal model of patrician charm not been brought back to
him so forcefully.

The campaign was based on the issue of rising unemployment and the need
for federal intervention to ease it, but Broun was a Socialist with whom the elite
of New York could feel safely at home. The Algonquinites on his staff, particularly Woollcott as head of the arts committee, collected endorsements from
such diverse figures as George Gershwin ("He'd be grand"), Don Marquis, John
Dewey, Fannie Hurst, Edna Ferber, Minnie Maddern Fiske and scores of others.
Benchley ran intereference for Broun with the press on occasion. Parker used the
headquarters as a favorite watering hole and pitched in where she could. Ruth
Hale ran the campaign despite her separation from Broun.

Broun trebled the previous Socialist vote in the district, but his party was
unimpressed, and when he demonstrated for Al Smith at the Democratic National Convention of 1932, his Socialist Party colleagues brought him up for
censure. Before the process could be completed, Broun resigned.

Despite Broun's campaign and the evidence of social and economic failure
all about them, the political activity of the other Algonquinites retained for the
time the quality of an after-dinner game. In 1931, Broun ran in his column a
"Give-a-Job-til-June" campaign, which found make-work jobs for about 1,000
people. In the same year he spent a good deal of his own money to produce
a show called *Shoot the Works,* whose purpose was to provide work for unem-
ployed actors, stagehands and anyone else with an act, an effort for which several
of the Round Tablers provided dialogue and moral support. But in that limbo
between the psychologies of prosperity and Depression, politics became a source

Broun's mother, a conservative, said her son's problem was that he had never been an employer. Broun wrote of her: "When the revolution comes, it's going to be a tough problem what to do with her. We will either have to shoot her or make her a commissar. In the meantime we still dine together."

of increasing friction among them—particularly so as the pressures of economic realities (other people's, to be sure) began to demand the taking of sides.

Quite naturally, the Algonquinites' first demonstrations of support of workers over management came during waiters' strikes. One reporter for the *World-Telegram* clearly relished the assignment of covering a strike at the Waldorf the night "strike missionaries" came to ask diners to walk out in sympathy and Benchley, Parker and Woollcott turned up to give their support. Two editors of *Common Sense* were bloodied in a melee with house detectives, the reporter wrote, while the Round Tablers

> gibed at the detectives with a running fire of extemporaneous bon mots and "wisecracks." . . .
> Beaming as the six-foot [Norman P.] Burstine went flying down the marble alley under heavy escort, Woollcott shrugged himself into his coat, adjusted his scarf and summed up the spectacle in a single phrase.
> "Just a swirl of ugly passion," he said, and left with Miss Parker.
> Benchley got back into his fur-lined coat.
> "Here I've been in bed all day with a cold," he remarked, "and Woollcott called me ten or twelve times to get to this thing. I come and do this thing for the waiters, and I suppose when I come out with this fur coat some striking waiter will sock me."

The reporter did not neglect to note that the Round Tablers had made sure to have eaten their dinner before the "strike missionaries" began to do their work.

Their blithe attitude came to seem less and less appropriate as the symptoms of the Depression became vivid, and the last scenes of the Round Table were marked by sniping over political consciousness or lack of it, sniping from which even Broun was not immune. He was, after all, still a frequent guest at the houses of some of New Yorker's premier capitalists—even if now, during a game of Murder, he could credibly give Averell Harriman the alibi that he was in the kitchen trying to organize the help. (And it was true.) The same evening as the Waldorf strike, Broun met Parker for a drink at Jack and Charlie's, ignoring the picket line of waiters outside that establishment. Benchley arrived shortly after they did, and they tried to hide but he spotted them, righteously berated Broun and chided Parker: "Don't you bat those ingenue eyes at me." The fact,

In the changed, more somber spirit of the 1930s, the wit of the Round Table came to strike Broun, as it would Parker and some others, as a symptom of the politically innocent—and therefore regressive—Twenties. "Humor is the coward's livery," Broun wrote, "and there is great wisdom in the popular challenge 'Laugh that off.'...'Does it matter' is the underlying mood in almost every expression of humor. And of course it does matter."

"These things do not last forever," was Frank Case's remark on why the Round Table ended. In 1933, he tried to start an Algonquin Supper Club, whose opening (left) was attended by, from left, Betty Starbuck, Richard Halliday, Tallulah Bankhead and John Bryan. It did not catch on.

of course, was that Benchley had also crossed the picket line in search of a drink, but for some reason his misstep was overlooked, perhaps only because he'd caught them first.

Finally what had seemed cute turned serious. Margaret Case Harriman speculated that the final rift in the Round Table came when the Algonquin waiters went on strike in 1931. Word reached Broun, who was in Philadelphia, that all his old friends—Kaufman, Benchley, Parker and the rest—had donned waiters' uniforms and made a lovely mess of trying to serve dinner for Frank Case. Broun was outraged and wrote a column seriously accusing his old friends of being scabs and scoundrels. Woollcott replied testily in a letter Broun printed whole in his column: "I should be sorry," he wrote, "to have my many old friends among the striking waiters believe me guilty of such repulsive didoes, and I am surprised that you yourself believed it, even for the few minutes it took you to write that column of rebuke." Woollcott and Broun were not on good terms for a long while after that and never reestablished the camaraderie they had enjoyed before the incident. But the astounding reaction came from Benchley, who seemed downright cranky. He said that secondhand accounts "may sound the way you want them to sound for your column, but they aren't always true. And you know damned well that they aren't, but does that matter? I will go as far as you will for the waiters of the Algonquin, and I'll thank you not to make a column out of a story which you know had no foundation in fact." He even accused Broun of professional cross carrying. That the waiters' strike incident did indeed mark the end of the Round Table is dubious speculation, but when Benchley was aroused to public anger against an old friend, the bloom was clearly off.

No one remembers when the Round Table actually ended. Marc Connelly tried years later and said it was "like remembering falling asleep." If any one thing stilled the twelve-year marathon of talk and play, no one took notice of it. Peggy Wood remembered only that she was playing in England for over a year, came back in mid-1932 and found no familiar faces in the Rose Room. Edna Ferber told Margaret Case Harriman how she discovered the fact in 1932: "One day, having finished a long job of work and wishing to celebrate, I flounced into the

With a stroke, the speakeasy subculture was brought above ground and dispersed. *The New Yorker* suggested in "Comment" that the Waldorf should set up a fake speak for old time's sake, and Ogden Nash wrote disconsolately: "After all those years of intimate and secluded sipping I find that to order and drink a drink in a hotel gives me the naked feeling of a scallop torn from its shell...."

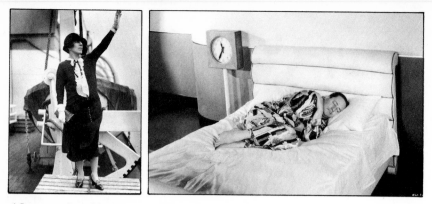

Ferber quarreled with Woollcott in the 1930s and never saw him again, but Benchley could not sustain such animosities. In the early 1940s he had what he called a *"retour d'age flirtation"* with Woollcott and wrote to assure him: "I really am very fond of you personally."

Algonquin dining room, sat down at an empty place at the Round Table—and found myself looking into the astonished and resentful faces of a family from Newton, Kansas, who were occupying the table on their New York stay. I mumbled an apology and left."

It was years before any of them mentioned the Round Table in print, and then the first remarks were Parker's vicious comments in a piece she wrote about the Spanish Civil War for the *New Masses* in 1937. "The only group I have ever been affiliated with is that not particularly brave little band that hid its nakedness of heart and mind under the out-of-date garment of a sense of humor," she wrote. "I heard someone say, and so I said it too, that ridicule is the most effective weapon. Well, now I know. I know that there are things that never have been funny and never will be. And I know that ridicule may be a shield, but it is not a weapon."

None of them ever bid a genuine good-by to the Round Table—one, that is to say, which neither excoriated it for its foolishness nor pretended that the group had been fabricated by the press for its own delight, the line to which Kaufman resorted in later years. Perhaps, as they avoided with humor the vulnerability of a fixed position, they were unwilling to identify themselves too much in public with a group whose stature in the Thirties was undecided. Woollcott, the one with most to gain from the association and the one whose extremes of sentiment would be most likely to produce roseate hindsight, also deferred writing about the subject, except to say in a letter to John Peter Toohey shortly before he died, "I should enjoy seeing just once more those old chums that I still dislike with a waning intensity."

But perhaps Woollcott did provide the curtain scene after all. On an outing with Harpo to Plymouth, Vermont, on a warm summer day in 1934, Woollcott asked the chauffeur to stop beside a local cemetery. Taking Harpo by the arm, he got out and walked through the gate to a spot he seemed to have visited before: the grave of Calvin Coolidge, distinguished only by a little American flag and a bunch of flowers someone had left not long before. Silent Cal—somnolent symbol of the decade when America tripped over itself for capital and crazes and the best liquor gangsters could provide; custodian of an era whose symptoms

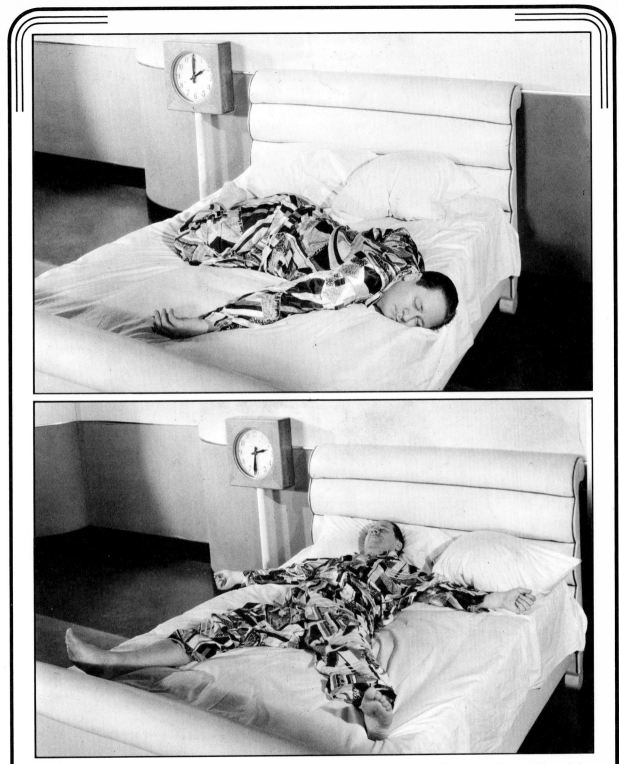

Benchley in his 1935 short *How to Sleep*. He made forty-six such shorts before his death in 1945, but he could never feel comfortable with his life or work in Hollywood. For all that he made millions laugh, and made a great deal of money doing it, he fell into a regimen of sleeping pills at night and Benzedrine during the day, and finally, he gave up the Benzedrine, as Nathaniel Benchley wrote, "because he could think of no particular reason for wanting to stay awake anyway."

Calvin Coolidge's world was, and was not, Alexander Woollcott's; the latter could not have thrived without the former. The stolid President (third from right) was perfect counterpoint to Woollcott and his friends; what they represented was nothing less than the conscious antithesis of "Silent Cal."

ranged wildly from unchecked materialism to bottomless disillusion, from multiplying profits to misplaced values; a humorless grinch in a high-spirited decade of whom Dorothy Parker had wondered when he died, "How do they know?" "I can think of nobody who ever lived who was more unlike Woollcott than Calvin Coolidge," Harpo remembered, "yet Aleck had a half-secret, perverse fondness for the tight-lipped Yankee President." Woollcott stood there for several minutes, studying the marker in silence. Finally he raised his eyes to his friend. Harpo thought Woollcott might have been embarrassed by the devotion he had betrayed for Coolidge; but perhaps also by way of a nostalgic sigh and farewell, he looked back at the marker, went up on his toes and did a cheerless little jig on Coolidge's grave.

AFTER: AN EPILOGUE

Social and literary ambitions do not seem peaceably to co-exist in many writers. The light of most such double-burning candles is dim and fleeting. The Algonquinites were urged to nourish both by novel social and historical circumstances: they were among the first writing celebrities of a new mass culture, an accredited "smart set," just the thing for a changing high society. That they were swept up by such currents in their time is no wonder; giving in to glamour is easy, and easier yet when one can do it with one's friends. But it is both a wonder and a tragedy of sorts that, when this particular group was finished, its most perceptive and promising members seemed to have lost the means of resolving that abiding conflict of their lives in the Twenties.

The happy warriors of *Stars and Stripes* showed no desire or need to change in the years that followed. Ross's intentions for his magazine were never more evident than during the 1930s, by which time his famously compulsive attention to word usage, grammar and clarity—at whatever expense to vision—had given the magazine its lapidary finish. Elsewhere in the Depression, precious gems were, if not out of fashion, kept discreetly out of sight, but as late as 1937, Dwight MacDonald could rightly accuse the magazine of "upper-class display," of "ruling class" bias, of toothless humor and of outdated fictions. Ross's most touted writing recruitment in those awful years was Clarence Day, and E. B. White's cries of indignation at the plight of ordinary people in "Notes and Comment" were distinctly at odds with the predominant elements of the magazine's editorial decor.

For the obsessive, custodial approach to language and literature that he shared with Ross, FPA paid the extreme price in his forgotten poetry and in his patent coolness toward many of the most original writers of his time. As the phrase "most unique" had stopped his reading of Fitzgerald's *The Beautiful and the Damned,* so, a decade later, all he could see in Dreiser's *Dawn* were facts got wrong:

> *He always speaks of Halstead Street in Chicago instead of Halsted Street. Of Samuel Smile instead of Samuel Smiles; Oconomowac insead of Oconomowoc; Ann Harbor instead of Ann Arbor; of Laura Jean Libby instead of Libbey; of William Seabrooke instead of Thomas Q. Seabrooke; of Mc-*

Vickar's Theater instead of McVicker's; of Jenkins Lloyd Jones instead
of Jenkin Lloyd Jones; and he says Vae Victus instead of Vae Victis. . . .

The "Comma Hunter of Park Row," as his *Evening Mail* colleagues had called him, found no market for that singular faculty in his last years, and Ross sustained him financially by hiring him to scan the *Congressional Record* for *New Yorker* column fillers.

Nor was Woollcott ever reconstructed, as socialite in private or as self-promoter in public. During the Depression, he tried to form a new group locus in the Berkshire Hotel in a private club he named the "Elbow Room." Little is recalled of it except that its prices were too high, especially for the times, and that Gerald Murphy suggested its motif of blue-tinted mirrors might have made for an excellent swimming pool. Woollcott did keep Bomoseen abustle to the end of his life, and Sunday breakfasts at Wit's End continued well into the 1930s, and Woollcott became more and more a caricature. Other men might have taken great umbrage at such portraits of themselves as are drawn of Woollcott in Brackett's novel *Entirely Surrounded* or in *The Man Who Came to Dinner,* but Woollcott—as P. T. Barnum would have done—reveled in the fact that he was written of at all. He even toured in the Kaufman and Hart play, and he played himself twice on Broadway in 1930s in plays by S. N. Behrman. The end of the approval he had sought among the warriors of World War I was the egregious taste he showed as the Town Crier of CBS Radio. A letter he wrote to Walt Disney near the end of his life, about the animated film *Dumbo,* shows almost more than one wants to see of Woollcott. "I suspect that if we could get far enough to see it in its place," he wrote in June of 1942, "we would recognize it as the highest achievement yet reached in the Seven Arts since the first white man landed on this continent."

For Parker and some others in the group, the 1930s were spent on politics. She and Stewart showed the most dramatic change. "They dropped us like hot potatoes," Adele Lovett remembered in 1977. "I've never been treated so badly in all my life by people who had been good friends." Other Long Island patrons and Manhattan drinking companions felt the same way. Stewart's turnabout, despite his great success as a Hollywood screenwriter, was unstinting, including eventually a divorce from Beatrice Ames, the rupture of his friendship with Benchley and self-exile to England, where he has lived ever since. "The trouble with us was that we stayed young too long," Parker wrote for Stewart's *Fighting Words:*

> *We remained in the smarty-pants stage—and that is not one of the most attractive ages. We were little individuals; and when we finally came to and got out it was quite a surprise to find a whole world full of human beings all around us. "How long," we asked, "has this been going on? And why didn't somebody tell us about it before?"*
>
> *I think the best thing about writers now is that they grow up sooner. They know you cannot find yourself until you find your fellow-men—they know there is no longer "I"; there is "we"—. They know that a hurt heart or a curiosity about death or an admiration for the crescent moon is purely a personal matter—thank God! Now the poet speaks not just for himself but for all of us—and so his voice is heard, and so his song goes on.*

But, of course, Parker's song did not go on. Her last book, except for the Viking Portable, was published in 1939, and, except for his autobiography, *Fighting Words* was Stewart's last. It was published in 1940.

That Parker wrote at all (she kept writing reviews, occasional short stories and even one play, *The Ladies of the Corridor,* before her death in 1967) is perhaps explained by her inability to give herself wholly to social-causism. Her taste in fiction was not, after all, as suited to the mass palate as her doctrinaire statement for Stewart seemed to demand. Nor was her attitude toward her old smart-cracking self as consistent as she may have wished it. In interview after interview, she despaired of her reputation as a Round Table wit (she later told Andrew Anspach of the Algonquin that that was why she deprecated the group —because her fame was based on such a trivial and frivolous aspect of her life), but each interviewer was also supplied with a new bright remark. And despite her unequivocal renunciations of Woollcott and the Round Table, her actions betrayed an abiding attachment to them both. She kept going to Bomoseen in the 1930s, and Woollcott's collection of papers at Harvard includes two long, affectionate letters from Parker dated 1941. In 1975, Beatrice Ames, who was one of Parker's best friends at the end of her life, remembered going with

Parker to a gathering for Woollcott the night he died in 1942: "Dotty and I were sitting in a corner with Woollcott's secretary, Joe Hennessey, when in swept George Kaufman and Beatrice and some others of the old crowd, and Dotty said, 'We have the Round Table with us. Let's get out of here.'" But the day after Woollcott's funeral, Parker joined the Kaufmans, Neysa, Harpo and other Round Table alumni for one last drink in the Rose Room.

Broun's final predicament was similar. When Parker went to Spain in 1937 and came back to deliver her jibe at the Round Table in the *New Masses*, Broun wrote a column tacitly agreeing with her:

> *It probably is true that the prevailing rule in her* [sic] *group used to be, "When in doubt, make a wisecrack." Doubts are always disturbing dinner guests, and it is easier to snub them than resolve them. . . . There is no fury like that of a convert. Those who come at the eleventh hour have more steam in their punches for rounds twelve to fifteen inclusive . . . and at that stage of a fight, I think the regulation has to be, "Quit your kidding."*

In the same column, however, he wrote, "I do not know more than a handful of old liberals who haven't become very tired in recent years," and he could have been thinking of himself. Broun had never been more politically involved than in the years after the Round Table ended. In the summer of 1933, he wrote his most famous column, a plea for a newspaper guild, the cause that consumed him to the end of his life and that earned him acclaim at the time and in history. He wrote impassioned and effective columns about the Scottsboro Boys, he denounced Red-baiting tactics, he sang the praises of FDR. But as he had once felt he was betraying his gifts as a "performing seal" among the high life, he came increasingly to feel that his political and social commitment had also betrayed him. In May of 1939, Broun became one of Monsignor Fulton Sheen's famous converts to Roman Catholicism. When Roy Howard fired him in October of the same year, the indifference of some Newspaper Guild colleagues took him to a depth of depression that one friend, Morris Ernst, could not forget almost forty years later. A few weeks after that, Broun contracted a disease he had always feared—pneumonia—and he told Dr. Barach in the hospital: "If I pull through, I will remember that Ring Lardner would have lived ten years longer if

he had only written what he really wanted to write. And I will write only about horse-racing, night clubs, gambling and life." He died a few hours later.

Despite deeply felt regrets about the work he was doing and the life he was leading, Benchley was unable to change at all. He became one of the best and best-loved film comedians of his time, turning out several shorts each year until his death and several more books in the same comedic vein. But as he lived out the Twenties in the Thirties, he despaired of it, as if the young man of his pre-1917 diary, the believer in Prohibition and social service and Serious Writing, were lording over him all his vain successes and too-late nights—his "mixing up in circles which must consist of the country's most frothy and inconsequential citizens." He said he despised the young man who wrote that diary when he re-read it toward the end of his life, but clearly the young man was very much with him, a reminder of his prophecy to Parker: "Each of us becomes the thing he most despises." In the late 1930s, Benchley attended a Hollywood party with, among others, Parker, Fitzgerald and Sherwood, and many years later, Sherwood told Nathaniel Benchley about a scene his father made that night that had haunted Sherwood ever since. Nathaniel wrote:

> At one point, late in the evening, Benchley was heard to say, "Those eyes—I can't stand those eyes looking at me!" Everybody stopped and turned, and saw that Benchley was backing away from Sherwood. They waited, already smiling and set to laugh at the joke that was about to come. But Benchley was serious. He pointed at Sherwood and said, "He's looking at me and thinking of how he knew me when I was going to be a great writer. . . . And he's thinking now look at what I am!"

It could be argued (and no doubt will be) that the writers of the Round Table did precisely what they were capable of doing—no more, no less. Still, it is hard to think that the group had no effect on their capabilities, and easy to see how the group's will helped some of its members succumb to currents in the time that they might successfully have resisted as individuals. Certainly without the Round Table they would have had more time for work—and it seems likely that had they kept more distance between their lives and their works, had the group not helped so effectively to smudge the boundary, their vision might have been

PARKER

BENCHLEY

WOOLLCOTT

ROSS

ADAMS

KAUFMAN

CONNELLY

STEWART

BROUN

SHERWOOD

The lobby of the Algonquin as it was in the late 1960s. The hotel management has refused in recent years several lucrative offers to capitalize on the Round Table's having been there—television and radio shows "emanating from the historic Algonquin Round Table." But even without such sons of the Round Table, the legend persists as strongly there as the legend of Paris in the Twenties persists at Sylvia Beach's bookshop.

clearer and longer and encompassed more. Perhaps Woollcott, Ross and Adams were no less for having been Algonquinites; perhaps, indeed, they were more for the group association. But the same cannot be said of Benchley and Parker, who left just enough writing behind to prompt the vain wish that they had written more. Fame came quickly to the Algonquin group, a fame that even now out-shines their accomplishment.

They had all promised so much when they met in that spring of 1919. John Peale Bishop hailed "the first literary generation in America," and they had been in perfect shape to show him right: full of talent, will and youth. George Kaufman might say, in his only recorded reminiscence of the group, that it was "just a motley, nondescript bunch of people who wanted to eat lunch and that's about all," but it was hindsight twenty years, a dozen commercial triumphs and a thousand self-justifications removed from the grim vision of his *The Butter and Egg Man.* Similarly, Marc Connelly could recall forty-five years later that "we were dynamic and full of energy and fun, a complete microcosmic sanctuary and full of love for one another" without wondering when or how he lost his youthful vision in the sanguine good times the Twenties and the Round Table taught them all to have. That they had good times worth remembering and retelling now is a certain, happy fact, but it is hard, on close retrospect, not to feel that all their high-pitched antics and wonderful talk were pyrrhic triumphs, that the end of wit was a resounding silence.

INDEX AND PHOTO CREDITS

WIT'S END

P. 4, Culver Pictures, Inc. (3). P. 5, Culver Pictures, Inc. P. 6, Brown Brothers. P. 7t, United Press International Photo. P. 7b, Culver Pictures, Inc. P. 8, Photo by Brassai. P. 9, Culver Pictures, Inc. P. 13, Brown Brothers. P. 16tl, United Press International Photo. P. 17tl, Culver Pictures, Inc. P. 17tr, Brown Brothers, Pp. 18–19, Brown Brothers, P. 23, Brown Brothers. P. 24, Culver Pictures, Inc. P. 25, The Conde Nast Publications, Inc. P. 26, Culver Pictures, Inc. (4). P. 27, Culver Pictures, Inc. P. 30, The Conde Nast Publications, Inc. P. 31tl, Robert Downing Collection, Humanities Research Center, The University of Texas. P. 31tr, Vielor Young, Chicago. P. 31b, Wisconsin Center for Film and Theater Research. P. 32, Culver Pictures, Inc. P. 33t, The Conde Nast Publications, Inc. P. 33b, Brown Brothers. P. 36tl, Photograph by Steichen, Courtesy of The Conde Nast Publications, Inc. P. 36tr, Robert Downing Collection, Humanities Research Center, The University of Texas. P. 37, Brown Brothers. P. 40, Photograph by Florence Vandamm, Courtesy of The Conde Nast Publications, Inc. P. 41, Culver Pictures, Inc. P. 42, Theatre Collection, New York Public Library (3). P. 42br, Photograph by Nickolas Muray, Courtesy of The Conde Nast Publications, Inc. P. 43, Photograph by James Abbe, Courtesy of The Viking Press. P. 44, Theatre Collection, New York Public Library. P. 45, Theatre Collection, New York Public Library. P. 48, Culver Pictures, Inc. P. 49, Culver Pictures, Inc. (2). P. 50, Courtesy of The Players. P. 52, Culver Pictures, Inc. P. 53tl, Photograph by James Abbe, Courtesy of Kathryn Abbe. P. 53tr, Culver Pictures, Inc. P. 53bl, Photograph by James Abbe, Courtesy of The Conde Nast Publications, Inc. P. 53br, Photograph by Nickolas Muray, Courtesy of The Conde Nast Publications, Inc. P. 54, Underwood & Underwood. P. 55, Woodcut by John Held, Jr., from The Stephen Greene Press, Brattleboro, Vermont. P. 56, Brown Brothers. P. 57, Brown Brothers (2). P. 57b, United Press International Photo. P. 60, Brown Brothers. P. 61, Photograph by James Abbe, Courtesy of The Viking Press. P. 62tl, Brown Brothers. P. 62tr, Culver Pictures, Inc. P. 63, Theatre Collection, New York Public Library. Pp. 64–65, Photograph by James Abbe, Courtesy of Kathryn Abbe. P. 68tl, United Press International Photo P. 68tr, Photograph by James Abbe, Courtesy of Kathryn Abbe. P. 70, Museum of The City of New York. P. 71, Theatre Collection, New York Public Library. P. 73, Courtesy of The Algonquin Hotel. P. 77, Courtesy of Robert and Adele Lovett. P. 78, Photograph by Florence Vandamm, Courtesy of The Conde Nast Publications, Inc. P. 79, Brown Brothers. P. 83, Courtesy of Hamilton College (3). P. 83br, Courtesy of William Harris. P. 84, Culver Pictures, Inc. P. 85, Photograph by Nickolas Muray, Courtesy of William Harris. P. 88, Culver Pictures, Inc. P. 89, Drawing by Hirschfeld. P. 90, Culver Pictures, Inc. P. 91t, Painting by Will Cotton. P. 91b, Richard Carver Wood. P. 92, Richard Carver Wood. P. 93, Richard Carver Wood (2). P. 94, Richard Carver Wood. P. 95, Richard Carver Wood. P. 96, Richard Carver Wood. P. 97, Richard Carver Wood. P. 98, Courtesy of Marc Connelly. P. 99, United Press International Photo. P. 104, Culver Pictures, Inc. P. 105, Culver Pictures, Inc. P. 108tl, Culver Pictures, Inc. P. 108tr, Maurice Goldberg. P. 109, Culver Pictures, Inc. P. 110, Caricature by Sam Berman, Courtesy of The Conde Nast Publications, Inc. P. 119, Culver Pictures, Inc. P. 123tl, Culver Pictures, Inc. P. 123, Richard Carver Wood (3). P. 124, Richard Carver Wood. P. 125b, United Press International Photo. P. 127, Culver Pictures, Inc. P. 128. The Bettmann Archive. P. 129t, Courtesy of Charles Scribner's Sons. P. 129b, Theatre Collection, New York Public Library. P. 130, Culver Pictures, Inc. P. 131, Schomburg Collection, New York Public Library. P. 132, Photograph by Florence Vandamm, Courtesy of The Conde Nast Publications, Inc. P. 133, Culver Pictures, Inc. P. 134, Caricature by Ralph Barton, Courtesy of The New Yorker. P. 135tl, Courtesy of The Players. P. 135b, Photograph by Florence Vandamm, Courtesy of The Conde Nast Publications, Inc. P. 138, Courtesy of The Players. P. 139tl, Theatre Collection, New York Public Library. P. 139tr, Theatre Collection, New York Public Library. P. 139bl, Photograph by Florence Vandamm, Courtesy of The Conde Nast Publications, Inc. P. 139br, Photograph by Maurice Goldberg, Courtesy of The Conde Nast Publications, Inc. P. 140, Courtesy of The Players. P. 141, Culver Pictures, Inc. P. 144, Caricature by Hirschfeld. P. 145, Culver Pictures, Inc. P. 148, United Press International Photo. P. 149, Keystone Press Agency, Inc. P. 157tl, United Press International Photo. P. 157, Courtesy of Honoria Donnelly (2). P. 160, Wide World Photos, Inc. P. 161, Courtesy of Honoria Donnelly. P. 162, The Bettmann Archive. P. 163, Culver Pictures, Inc. P. 164, Caricature by Hirschfeld. P. 165, Photograph by Nickolas Muray, Courtesy of The Conde Nast Publications, Inc. P. 168t, Courtesy of The Algonquin Hotel. P. 168b, United Press International Photo. P. 169, Caricature by Hirschfeld. P. 170, Drawing by Rea Irvin, Courtesy of The New Yorker. P. 171, Caricature by Ralph Barton, Courtesy of The New Yorker. P. 174, Culver Pictures, Inc. P. 175, Culver Pictures, Inc. P. 178, Culver Pictures, Inc. (2). P. 179, Culver Pictures, Inc. (2). P. 183, Courtesy of The Players. P. 184, Culver Pictures, Inc. P. 185, United Press International Photo. P. 188, Richard Carver Wood (2). P. 189, Richard Carver Wood. P. 192, Herb Gehr, Life Magazine © Time Inc. P. 193, Culver Pictures, Inc. Pp. 196–197, Culver Pictures, Inc. P. 198, Culver Pictures, Inc. P. 199, Courtesy of The Algonquin Hotel (2). P. 200, Culver Pictures, Inc. P. 201, Courtesy of The Conde Nast Publications, Inc. P. 204, Wisconsin Center for Film and Theater Research. P. 205. Harris Lewine Collection (2). P. 205bl, Wide World Photos, Inc. P. 205br, United Press International Photo. P. 206, Wide World Photos, Inc. P. 207, Culver Pictures, Inc. P. 208tl, United Press International Photo. P. 208tr, Culver Pictures, Inc. P. 209tl, Theatre. Collection, New York Public Library. P. 209tr, Harris Lewine Collection. P. 209bl, Culver Pictures, Inc. P. 209br, Theatre Collection, New York Public Library. P. 210, Courtesy of Robert and Adele Lovett. P. 212, Wisconsin Center for Film and Theater Research. P. 213, Photograph by George Platt Lynes, Courtesy of The Viking Press. P. 215, Culver Pictures, Inc. (2). P. 217tl, Richard Carver Wood. P. 217b, Richard Carver Wood. P. 218, Culver Pictures, Inc. P. 219, Courtesy of The Algonquin Hotel. Pp. 220–221, Courtesy of The Conde Nast Publications, Inc. P. 224, Underwood & Underwood. P. 225, Culver Pictures, Inc. P. 226, United Press International Photo. P. 227, Underwood & Underwood. P. 228tl, United Press International Photo. P. 228tr, Culver Pictures, Inc. P. 229, Culver Pictures, Inc. (2). Pp. 230–231, Underwood & Underwood. Pp. 240–241, Courtesy of The Algonquin Hotel.

The text type for this book was set on the Linotype in DeVinne, an American type face that is actually a recutting by Gustav Schroeder of French Elzevir. It was introduced by the Central Type Foundry of St. Louis in 1889. Named in honor of Theodore Low DeVinne, whose nine-story plant called "The Fortress" was the first building in New York City erected especially for printery, the type has a delicate quality obtained by the contrast between thick and thin parts of the letters. An enormously popular type during the early part of this century, DeVinne combines easy readability with a nostalgically atmospheric feeling. The display type, Broadway, was designed by Morris Fuller Benton for American Type Founders in 1929.

This book was composed by American Book—Stratford Press, Inc. Printing and binding was done by Halliday Lithograph.

Graphics were directed by Harris Lewine. Book design was styled by Stephanie Tevonian. Production and manufacturing coordination was directed by Raymond Ferguson. Manuscript and proof coordination was handled by Sam Rudovsky.

WIT'S END